POLITICAL PHILOSO

Chief Editor of the Series:
Howard Williams, University of Wales, Aberystwyth

Associate Editors:
Wolfgang Kersting, University of Kiel, Germany
Steven B. Smith, Yale University, USA
Peter Nicholson, University of York, England
Renato Cristi, Wilfrid Laurier University, Waterloo, Canada

Political Philosophy Now is a series which deals with authors, topics and periods in political philosophy from the perspective of their relevance to current debates. The series presents a spread of subjects and points of views from various traditions which include European and New World debates in political philosophy.

For other titles in this series, please see the University of Wales Press website: www.wales.ac.uk/press.

POLITICAL PHILOSOPHY NOW

Lyotard and the End of Grand Narratives

Gary K. Browning

UNIVERSITY OF WALES PRESS • CARDIFF • 2000

© Gary K. Browning, 2000

British Library Cataloguing-in-Publication Data
A catalogue record for this book is available from the British Library.

ISBN 0–7083–1479–1 (pb)
ISBN 0–7083–1507–0 (hb)

All rights reserved. No part of this book may be reproduced, stored in a retrieval system, or transmitted, in any form or by any means, electronic, mechanical, photocopying, recording or otherwise, without clearance from the University of Wales Press, 6 Gwennyth Street, Cardiff, CF24 4YD.
www.wales.ac.uk/press

The right of Gary K. Browning to be identified as author of this work has been asserted by him in accordance with the Copyright, Designs and Patents Act 1988.

Typeset by Action Publishing Technology Ltd, Gloucester
Printed in Great Britain by Dinefwr Press, Llandybïe

Contents

Acknowledgements		vii
1	Introduction	1
2	Postmodernity and the Delegitimation of Modernity	21
3	The Development of Lyotard's Thought: From Phenomenology to the Game of Justice	40
4	Beyond the Postmodern Condition: *The Differend* and After	62
5	Lyotard and the Political	86
6	Hegel and The Critique of Closure	108
7	Marx and the End of Emancipation	128
8	Conclusion	148
Notes		172
Select Bibliography		193
Index		198

Acknowledgements

While writing this book I became acutely conscious of Lyotard's notion of the sublime, a feeling of something overreaching our capacities of imagination, understanding and expression. This project conjured up the exquisite mix of pleasure and pain that is a sign of the sublime. Lyotard is a demanding thinker, complex and a strain to live with. He takes paths that are the other side of where most of us are going. In writing about a thinker, there is a tendency to want to get inside the person and see things from their perspective. Whether this is ever done is debatable, but I am not sure I wanted to do this completely with Lyotard. His work, though, is important, and offers flashes of inspiration as well as sustained hard thinking that challenge much in what we are and how we operate. I have found living with his thought over the past four or five years a valuable if demanding exercise. It has been my experience that his works assume greater significance and value the more they are worked over.

Lyotard's radical scepticism over schemes of reason and grand narratives that are designed to provide order for the social world challenges most current ways of thinking about politics. I am critical of Lyotard's conceptions of Hegel and Marx. Nonetheless, I regard Lyotard as maintaining a thoughtful engagement with Hegel and Marx that shows how they continue to exert an impact even, or perhaps most emphatically, when they are rejected.

I am happy to acknowledge a number of debts that have been incurred in the writing of this book. First, I would like to acknowledge the help of the British Academy who furnished me with a grant to help prepare this book for publication. I was given money to visit the Bibliothèque Nationale and to use the Oxford Brookes Translation Service for a second opinion on passages of Lyotard's translated and untranslated work that I wanted to be sure I had worked out. I also tried out my developing ideas on Lyotard at a number of conferences, including a lively affair at Oxford Brookes University entitled, 'Modernity–Postmodernity: From the Personal to the Global'. In particular I remember enjoying talking things over with Richard Brown, Peter Case, Andy Kilmister, Matthew Pateman and Susan Stephenson. Colleagues in the Politics Department at Oxford Brookes University have helped in ways of which they might not be aware. I have had a sense that what I am doing fits in with a scheme of things that is not unduly coercive. Undergraduates and postgraduates at Oxford Brookes University have shown an interest in Lyotard and have reminded me that researching, learning and teaching are not the entirely separate activities they are sometimes taken to be. Howard Williams has been a very helpful, patient and encouraging series editor for this book and I am grateful for his general support over the years.

What is very challenging is to take on a project that extends you while carrying on with a round of duties, diversions and simple and less simple pleasures and activities that make up a life. I would like to thank my family, Raia, Eleanor and Conal, for helping me feel that following the trail of abstract thought is not a blind alley from which there is no escape. I have felt the warmth of a family that has reminded me of enduring values, a sense of roots and a context of responsibilities and love.

Abbreviations of Titles

In the text the following works are referred to without their subtitles.

The Differend: Phrases in Dispute
The Inhuman: Reflections on Time
The Postmodern Condition: A Report on Knowledge
The Postmodern Explained to Children: Correspondence 1982–1985

1 • Introduction

Introduction

The aim of this book is to elaborate and assess Lyotard's repudiation of grand narratives. Lyotard's *The Postmodern Condition* is a defining moment in the transmission of his ideas and in promoting the popularity of a postmodern alternative to modern notions bound up with generalizing theories that Lyotard deprecates as grand narratives.[1] This Introduction rehearses the themes that underpin this disavowal of grand narratives, and which are evident throughout Lyotard's career.

The meaning of Lyotard's phrase 'the end of grand narratives' is analysed, and then his conceptions of reason and reality, identity and difference and politics are examined. These themes are shown to inform the subsequent treatment of Lyotard in chapters on *The Postmodern Condition* and its critique of grand narratives, the development of Lyotard's philosophy and then assessments of Lyotard's politics and his critiques of Hegel and Marx. The Conclusion emerges out of this exploration and is a summative evaluation of Lyotard's notion of the end of grand narratives. The overall verdict combines respect for aspects of Lyotard's critique of grand narratives with a recognition of the tensions involved in his radical and general critique of theory.

Grand narratives

Lyotard's obituary for grand narratives is delivered in *The Postmodern Condition*. Lyotard sees their role in legitimating knowledge in the modern world as redundant in the light of the advent of postmodernity, a condition in which synoptic perspectives give way to heterogeneity and invention. A critical preoccupation with *The Postmodern Condition*, however, is manifestly unable to encapsulate the breadth and complexity of Lyotard's philosophical and political perspectives that exemplify the spirit of inventive heterogeneity endorsed in *The Postmodern Condition*.[2] Lyotard himself directed critical attention away from *The Postmodern Condition* by criticizing aspects of its argument, notably its tendency to cast the postmodern as a historical successor to modernism, and its inflationary reading of the narrative form.[3]

While a preoccupation with *The Postmodern Condition* that neglects the diversity and depth of Lyotard's theorizing is to be condemned, its critique of grand narratives condenses into an economical formula a number of recurring themes of Lyotard's philosophical career. The formula serves as a credo for a philosopher whose political career traces a loosening and abandoning of Marxist commitment and whose philosophical career is defined in terms of its rejection of theoretical systems such as Hegelianism and structuralism.

Throughout his career, Lyotard continually revises his theoretical vocabulary and style. He remains, however, a constant critic of rationalism. Lyotard is unremittingly sceptical over the claims of reason to explain reality. For Lyotard, the gap between the real and its rational representation is not to be effaced, even by incremental progress. Rather, novel disruptive vocabularies are continually invoked to register the manifestation of *events* that dislocate the very idea of representational schemes. In *The Postmodern Condition* Lyotard deprecates grand narratives that aspire to provide meta-perspectives by which all other narratives are to be explained. Lyotard takes the universalizing impetus of grand narratives to be insensitive to the heterogeneity and incommensurability exhibited in language games that compose the social bond.

Fraser and Nicholson recognize that Lyotard's critique of grand narratives is directed primarily against their *meta* aspect. It is their aspiration to operate at a level of detachment, permitting a universal perspective, that renders grand narratives palpable but redundant threats to the variety of social interaction. Fraser and Nicholson remark:

> In his (Lyotard's) conception of legitimating metanarrative, the stress properly belongs on the 'meta' and not the 'narrative'. It purports to be a privileged discourse capable of situating, characterizing and evaluating all other discourses, but not itself infected by the historicity and contingency which render first-order discourses potentially distorted and in need of legitimation.[4]

A grand or 'meta' narrative in *The Postmodern Condition* is seen as specifically legitimating narratives of scientific knowledge. The significance of the meta aspect of grand narratives, though, is exhibited in its retention as a formula for Lyotard's opposition to general theoretical schemes subsequent to Lyotard's recognition that he had exaggerated the claims of traditional narratives and overstated the role of the narrative in scientific thought.[5] A grand narrative, for Lyotard, serves as a metaphor for the theoretical *other* to which he is resolutely opposed throughout his writings.[6] A grand narrative insofar as it purports to subsume a multiplicity of events and perspectives into the orbit of its own theory is to be resisted so as to register the unassimilability of processes and heterogeneous standpoints. In his revisionist account of postmodernism Lyotard identifies it with the resistance of modernist avant-garde artists and recalcitrant theorists to essentialism and rationalism.[7] These latter features of modernity are captured in Lyotard's image of a grand narrative.

Lyotard's opposition to grand narratives is framed by his distinctive philosophical conceptualization of the relations between reason and reality, and identity and difference, and inspires a radical political antagonism to the centralized organization of society and cultural conformity. In his writings Lyotard intimates the fundamental opacity of reality to reason, privileges difference over unificatory forms of identity, and opposes state communism and the development of Western capitalism. His work, though, is a continuous process of inventing new terms and relations to explore these conceptions.

Aspects of Lyotard's deprecation of grand narratives harmonize with wider intellectual and political currents. Disillusionment with absolutist schemes of rationalist political renewal, engendered by the failure of totalitarianism and the erosion of credibility for radical socialism, lend support to Lyotard's standpoint. His critique of the feasibility of shaping society so as to fit with a rationalist scheme also fits with a prevailing consensus on the circumspection with which social theory must operate. Anglo-Saxon analytical philosophy in its various guises tends to inform and limit the theoretical ambition of contemporary liberalism.[8] Liberal theorists tend to accept an identification of philosophy as a second-order discipline that responds rather than dictates to empirical developments and value preferences. Likewise contemporary critical theory, as represented by Habermas, presents itself as avowedly post-metaphysical.[9]

If Lyotard's critique of reason matches a prevailing mood, then his positive valorization of difference reflects a contemporary turn towards the recognition of the politics of cultural diversity. This form of politics presents itself in uncompromisingly aggressive strains of nationalism that continue to disturb Central Europe, the Middle East and Africa as well as impacting upon apparently more firmly established states in, for example, the UK and Canada. Contemporary feminism, insofar as it aims at deconstructing a hegemonic male discourse so as to allow the flourishing of dissident forms of feminism, also attests to the current significance of the politics of difference.[10] Lyotard's sensitivity to incommensurable difference is also reflected in the apparently chronic conflicts over ends that inform persisting disputes over the nature of society, gender and culture.

Lyotard's philosophical commitment to the significance of difference and the defeasibility of theory aligns him to wider cultural and intellectual currents, but his philosophical and political standpoints remain distinctive. His individuality arises out of his radicalism. Lyotard presses his critiques of rationalism and homogenizing identity to the point where the prospects of achieving foundations for knowledge and social unity are undermined. His political radicalism arises out of the severity of his critique of reason and the extremism of his valorization of difference. Social connections and conditions of practical life are expressly politicized by Lyotard's recognition of the contingency of social arrangements and the lack of extra-political means of establishing incontestable forms of practice.

Lyotard's philosophizing generates tensions that, in part, he embraces himself as the price of his scepticism. His own philosophy is frankly accepted as devoid of foundations; its rule is declared to be the performative invention of its own rule. Philosophical awareness of the *différends* that are intimated in his later writing as fracturing the possibilities of holistic explanation is conceived to be inscrutably sublime. Lyotard takes the incommensurability of perspectives to be so pronounced that they preclude social consensus or any rule-bound practice of justice.[11]

The self-disclosed tensions within Lyotard's thought do not exhaust its internal problems. While his profoundly critical perspective would seem to prohibit definitively synoptic sociological and historical accounts of the present, he frequently resorts to highly general depictions of society. Again, his critique of unifying identities is the reverse side of his active promotion of difference and differentiating inventiveness. The promotion of these latter qualities trades upon but cannot be supported by his recognition of difference as a feature of the world. Moreover, the rhetorical appeal of his valorization of difference cannot be conceived as appealing straightforwardly to selves for his critique of identity extends to unificatory notions of personal identity that might underpin such an appeal.

Another only semi-disclosed tension involved in Lyotard's critique of essentialist theories is that his criticisms of classic modern social theories, such as Hegelianism and Marxism, impute absolutist essentialist identities to them. This identification of their theories is as questionable as the allegedly essentialist doctrines themselves. Likewise Lyotard's valorization of the political heightens the possibilities of disputatious political conflict, while failing to supply argumentative resources for handling political conflict. Lyotard assumes that the recognition of difference is either sufficient or all that can be accomplished.

Reason and reality

Lyotard's repudiation of grand narratives, announced in *The Postmodern Condition*, epitomizes his persistent scepticism over the claims of theory. This scepticism deepens what is at stake in Lyotard's critique of classic modern social theory. In *The Postmodern Condition* Lyotard counterposes a Wittgensteinian conception of an indeterminate plurality of language games to the rationalist presumptions of grand narratives that affect to explain the totality of social and intellectual practices in terms of their conformity to a universal pattern. Reality, for Lyotard, cannot be specified by an overarching theory. A general theory of language is redundant. What is real is as indeterminate as the character and number of language games.

This reading of language and reality embraces what Williams designates the materiality of Lyotard's thought.[12] Lyotard abrogates a Hegelian sense of reason glimmering within and thereby superseding refractory spheres of nature and practice. Theory, for Lyotard, must respect the contingency and tensions within the processes with which it deals. The actual practices or games in which practical and psychical life is conducted are taken by him to determine their own terms and development. Language games, in *The Postmodern Condition*, are not susceptible to the requirements of a meta-game for they neither observe necessary, logical conditions nor conform to essentialist, common criteria.

Lyotard's disavowal of the power of reason to supervise indeterminate practices in *The Postmodern Condition* is matched by preceding and succeeding philosophical studies that similarly conceive of reality as eluding the representational schemes of reason. In his semi-autobiographical lectures on his philosophical development, *Peregrinations*, Lyotard refers to thought and the drift of his own thinking as the passing of clouds. Clouds are invoked as a metaphor for thoughts so as to highlight the insubstantiality of thinking in relation to the reality that is to be conceived.[13] Throughout his philosophical career, Lyotard experiments with terms to depict the fragility of reason and its indeterminate grasp of the real. From his early investigation of figural disruption of discursive structures to his late invocation of the *différend* as a testimony to the unresolvable tension whereby a contrary perspective is excluded by a prevailing linguistic regime, Lyotard highlights the gap between the real and the rational.

In a late essay, 'Mainmise', Lyotard offers a succinct and paradoxically clear expression of the elusive, non-rational character of the real.

> I have to say here. Nothing of this love of knowledge and wisdom that the Greeks instilled in us under the name of philosophy. For it seems to me that I, like many others, have only ever loved what would not let itself be known or mastered. And perhaps what we are talking about is not even a place. In any case, not a locale. And not a utopia either. I would rather grant it the privilege of the real. Let us suspend for the moment the question of its name or label.[14]

Lyotard's specification of a sceptical critique of the powers of reason serves as an antidote to general, absolutist theories that explain nothing by reducing everything to the terms of their theory. But his meta-explanation of the range and validity of his sceptical standpoint paradoxically excludes consideration of the insights generated by absolutist theoretical standpoints.

Identity and difference

Just as Lyotard's notion of the end of grand narratives reflects a profound sense of the intractability of reality, so it reflects his perception and valorization of incommensurable difference. Difference is taken to be irreducible, for reality itself, in its recalcitrance to rational schemes of thought, harbours the disruptively contingent and different. This irreducibility of difference is a persisting feature of Lyotard's thought and is highlighted in *The Differend*, whose title testifies to incommensurable difference.

In *The Postmodern Condition*, Lyotard's valorizes difference by adverting to an incommensurability between language games, by opposing general consensus as a goal and by envisaging only provisional, local agreements between players in the variety of language games. Lyotard's respect for difference, however, begs questions over how differing units, such as language games, are to be individuated. Lyotard does not specify precisely in any of his works how elements valorized on account of their difference are to be identified as maintaining their identity over time and in relation to other elements. For instance, Lyotard is disinclined to see individual human beings as possessing a unified identity, though he never provides a comprehensive account of agency and individuality. Moreover, the limiting point of pure difference paradoxically slips into pure unity. The *différend* maintains its identity despite its heterogeneous exemplifications. The upshot is that Lyotard's account of difference is partial and problematic.

Lyotard, in *The Postmodern Condition*, and notably in *The Differend*, urges that the gap between the operation of prescriptives and descriptives exemplifies an irreducible difference. The 'is' and the 'ought' are taken as operating according to different rules, and Marxism, for example, is condemned for running the two together. Notwithstanding this recognition, however, Lyotard's positive promotion of heterogeneity appears to derive from the actual evidence of difference in the world. Likewise, his promotion of inventiveness is linked to his perception of the actual evidence of the restrictiveness of theoretical schemes and merely conventional behaviour. For Lyotard, inventiveness is of a piece with the very disruptiveness of reality itself.

Lyotard's valorization of difference and inventiveness, then, is in express tension with his recognition of the independence of prescriptions from descriptions of the world. Lyotard acknowledges the tension between his critique of theory, and his theoretical promotion of the values of difference and experimentation. Lyotard accepts the tensions consequent upon a philosophical style that admits an incommensurability between values, a lack of secure foundations for theorizing and yet promotes a particular perspective on the social world.[15] The tension between Lyotard's confident promotion of the values of inventiveness and difference and his critique of theory is complicated by the generality of his conception of social and historical development in *The Postmodern Condition* and succeeding works. The promotion of difference and inventiveness in *The Postmodern Condition* arises out of a questionable identification of science as progressing through a paradigmatic paralogical creativity and an equally contestable general characterization of society as showing an increasingly monochromatic performativity in the organization of its activities.[16] The measure of all activities, for Lyotard, is the constant reduction of the time taken to perform them. The prevalence of performativity is seen as overriding difference and spontaneity, notwithstanding the effectiveness of unprogrammed creativity in science. Lyotard's highly general reading of the contemporary sociological condition underpins his espousal of difference and inventiveness. It is at odds, however, with his critique of social theory. Rojek observes the irony involved in Lyotard's perception of 'his own work as a break with totality. Yet it cannot have escaped the reader that Lyotard's application of "performativity" assumes that it operates as a totalizing concept.'[17] Lyotard's late work operates with the totalizing concept that the contemporary social world exhibits a neototalitarian uniformity imposed by an inhuman logic of appraising all social phenomena in terms of their contribution to processes of complexification.

Political radicalism

Commentators are united in their recognition of the significance of the political dimension of Lyotard's work.[18] His radicalism extends the range of what counts as political and intensifies its operations. He identifies a multiplicity of sites for resisting the hegemony of universalizing political schemes and repressive social conformity. The notion of politics is intensified by his insistence on the contestability of procedures and practices which arises out of an incommensurability of perspectives. The intractability of this contestability signals the potential ubiquity and intensity of politics. Bennington observes, 'Lyotard is fundamentally a political thinker, to the precise extent that he contests the totalisations fundamental to most ideas of politics.'[19] What is underplayed by Bennington and other commentators sympathetic to Lyotard, however, is that Lyotard's political standpoint is essentially deconstructive of other totalizing political ideas. The radicalism of Lyotard's sensitivity to difference and to the injustice involved in denying the expression of different standpoints renders his perspective devoid of resources to engage in the construction of political procedures that might unify discordant elements and secure peaceful discussion of disputed questions.

Lyotard's politics emerge out of his emphatic rejection of grand narratives that purport to provide universal criteria for ordering society. His career as a Marxist member of the group *Socialisme ou barbarie* is marked by his stretching of Marxist categories to cover features of his contemporary political situation. Lyotard's drift from Marxism coincides with his involvement in the events of May 1968 and a commitment to valorize the revolutionary processes of breaking with conformity. Subsequently, Lyotard advocates a pagan subversive style of agonistic politics in which justice is to be determined by indeterminate means. In *The Differend* the aim is to testify to exclusion of perspectives by dominant modes of discourse. In essays subsequent to *The Differend*, Lyotard eschews any traces of a revolutionary politics in presenting a melancholic reverence for and recognition of an openness towards the indeterminacy of existence.[20]

The variety of styles and modes in which Lyotard's politics are expressed converge upon a valorization of difference and an opposition to a politics of unity and social conformism. Notwithstanding the trajectory of his political thought that sees an emigration from revolutionary politics and the adoption of a sharply critical perspective that condemns Marxist totalitarian politics and the neo-totalitarianism of Western society, Lyotard remains a political radical. His thought is radical because his critique is directed against all manifestations of conformity and unificatory political projects. Contemporary political theory generally accepts that reason is unable to provide objective foundations for politics. Habermas, for instance, self-consciously terms his approach post-metaphysical, and in his study *Between Facts and Norms* he urges that his concept of communicative reason recasts received notions of practical reason so that 'it no longer provides a direct blueprint for a normative theory of law and morality'.[21] Habermas, however, aims to identify norms of procedural reason that will shape a consensus. Many post-metaphysical political theorists follow Habermas in aiming to frame non-metaphysical bases of political unity and consensus.[22] Lyotard rejects consensus as a goal. He is radically opposed to all post-metaphysical manœuvres of reason to achieve unity and consensus. He aims to testify to radical difference.

The strength of Lyotard's commitment to a politics of difference is a serious challenge to unificatory political projects that abstract from the intensity of differences. Lyotard may be seen as contributing to a wider radical challenge to the orientation of political theory whereby the deconstruction of repressive forms of unity is seen as more pressing than the construction of political unity. Martin, in *Contemporary Social and Political Theory*, observes:

> The social theories and concepts which have oriented political theory since modernity are increasingly open to question as society itself changes. Exactly how we should conceive ourselves as subjects, our relations with each other and our common needs is now more than ever a matter of open dispute. This has led to a concern to rethink the political in the face of expanding social differences.[23]

Lyotard's political perspective, like his overall philosophy, appears most plausible in serving as a critique of other perspectives. In itself, it suffers from valorizing difference while failing to address questions of how a reasonable political order, permitting difference, might be constructed or maintained. Lyotard fails to develop constructive accounts of how questions of social justice, or the discrimination of legitimate from illegitimate activities within a polity, might be developed. Iris Marion Young is right to note how Lyotard's sense of justice highlights the role of listening to others, but the achievement of justice also requires a commitment to work out and establish just conditions applying to all within a community.[24] Anne Phillips, in a recent book, has emphasized that feminism cannot afford to situate itself in favour of difference and against universality, because it is a political movement that aims at uniting standpoints as well as appreciating diversity.[25]

Drifting towards the end of grand narratives

The core elements of Lyotard's philosophy that shape his repudiation of grand narratives derive from the relations he posits between reason and reality, and between identity and difference. Lyotard maintains that reason can never fully capture and articulate reality. Real differences are taken to thwart the unificatory schemes of thought and undermine the possibility of establishing commensurating identities. In line with a restless resistance to theoretical explanation, Lyotard's philosophy assumes the aspect of a discontinuous exploration of reality and difference. These explorations are traced in subsequent chapters of this book.

Chapter 2 focuses upon the argument of *The Postmodern Condition*, in which Lyotard introduces the phrase 'the end of grand narratives' and diagnoses the condition of postmodernity. The three models of grand narrative that Lyotard identifies with modernity are inspected and evaluated. Lyotard's analysis of the problematic character of claims to comprehensive knowledge assimilating multiple perspectives is seen to be insightful. The tension between the sociological and logical dimensions of Lyotard's treatment of postmodernity and grand narratives, however, is diagnosed as being equally problematic. Likewise the affiliated strains evident in Lyotard's simultaneous derogation of social theory and his easy, optimistic espousal of an agonistic politics of difference are diagnosed as raising unanswered questions.

This chapter on *The Postmodern Condition* highlights several dimensions of Lyotard's critique of grand narratives, and shows how the critique and its embrace of postmodernism involves acknowledged and unacknowledged tensions. Chapters 3 and 4 revisit the philosophical standpoint underlying the repudiation of grand narratives and interrogates Lyotard's preceding and succeeding philosophical work. Chapter 3 looks at key philosophical texts of Lyotard from his *Phenomenology* (1954) to his paradoxical project of establishing justice without criteria in *Just Gaming*, published in 1979, the same year as *The Postmodern Condition*. Four major texts – *Phenomenology, Discours, figure, Libidinal Economy* and *Just Gaming* – are reviewed, and other texts are invoked insofar as they relate to points raised in the analysis of these texts.

In *Phenomenology* Lyotard exhibits a close interest in the project of phenomenology and some sympathy for Husserl's eidetic identification of the givenness of essences in experience and Merleau-Ponty's subtle evocation of the implication of the body in perception. Ultimately, however, Lyotard is critical of phenomenology because of its privileging of intentionality. Lyotard counterposes a commitment to Marxist materialism to what he sees as the disguised idealism of phenomenology. His unequivocal defence of Marxism expresses a committed allegiance to a grand narrative that is subsequently registered in the force of his denunciation of both Marxism and grand narratives. His materialist critique of phenomenology also advances his commitment to the primacy of the material to be explained over the form of rational comprehension.

In *Discours, figure*, Lyotard opposes the privileging of discursive structures over contingency and difference by evoking the figural disturbance of secondary processes of discourse and reason. The figural refers to a series of ways in which physicality and transformative action interweave with and disrupt discourse. Perception, writing, metaphor, poetry and unconscious movements of desire interrupt and transgress against the order of discourse. The negative side of Lyotard's project is persuasive in its critique, for example, of a structuralist conception of language, but his elaboration of the interweaving of discourse and figure appears to valorize primary forces of unconscious desire over reflective patterns of social interaction without convincing evidential corroboration.

Libidinal Economy is a wild and important work in its register of a definitive break with Lyotard's Marxist past. Lyotard opposes the very notion of rationalist representations of reality with a fury that testifies to the energy of desire. The point, for Lyotard, is not to engage in laborious essentialist critiques of the system, but to contrive to release the flow of desire in new ways. *Libidinal Economy* is a work pulsating with energy that highlights the gap between the reality of things and the scheme of reason that affects to represent them, and forces a recognition of the distortion of theory and reality that can attend affirmative and critical theories. On the other hand, Lyotard's image of the ubiquity and potency of forces which reduce everything to the libidinal fails to discriminate the distinctive aspects of, for instance, ethical obligations and political commitments.

Lyotard himself is subsequently critical of the provocative reductionism of *Libidinal Economy*. In *Just Gaming* he restores an independence and significance to ethical judgement that had been compromised in *Libidinal Economy*. He maintains that determinate criteria for ethical questions cannot be furnished and denies the possibility of establishing general criteria governing the particularities of practice. His aim, instead, is declared to be the achievement of justice without established criteria. The paradigm for this exercise is taken to be the notion of a regulative indeterminate judgement that is invoked by Kant in his aesthetics. Lyotard's reliance upon Kant and the notion of indeterminate judgement prefigures a subsequent preoccupation with a Kantian aestheticized conception of politics and philosophy. Lyotard's notion of the practice of justice without criteria highlights the contestability of politics, and the irreducibility of decision-making. Its vagueness in privileging heterogeneity, however, rehearses, without resolving, tensions involved in the espousal of a form of heterogeneous politics in *The Postmodern Condition*. Lyotard valorizes a subversive, particularist pagan standpoint against approaches to political philosophy, like Plato's, that aim to found political order on supposed metaphysical truths. This break with a metaphysical politics is a plausible move, given the disputability of notions about human nature. Lyotard's embrace of a particularist, pluralist standpoint, however, alongside a commitment to universal regulative judgements, raises questions over how pluralism can be united with a Kantian ethical universalism that are not explored in any detail in the text.

In Chapter 4, the later philosophical works of Lyotard are reviewed. *The Differend* is an elegant philosophical text that reflects a self-conscious response by Lyotard to what he takes to be defects within the argument of *The Postmodern Condition*. Lyotard jettisons much of his preceding theoretical vocabulary, abandoning the rhetoric of language games due to their anthropocentric connotations, and instead takes phrases, rather than games, to be the bedrock constituents of language. Phrases are held to be radically contingent, their sense being developed by their fit with those that precede and succeed them, contingently linked together by phrase regimens within genres of discourse. Characteristically, Lyotard disclaims the possibility of universal rules of linkage, so reality is conceived as being shaped by incommensurable, differing patterns of language. The incommensurability entails that a standpoint can be excluded by a prevailing pattern of discourse. This exclusion is termed a *différend*, and Lyotard sees his task as testifying to *différends*, a notion that highlights his commitment to recognize difference.

The Differend is an economical, persuasive work, but, like its predecessors, entertains tensions. It specifies a general conception of a *différend* that rests upon the paradoxical denial of a general formula for the actual operation of phrases. The specification of incommensurability rehearsed in *The Differend* is an evocative expression of the limits of language. The evocation of radical difference, however, is only to be appreciated by an undemonstrable feeling of disquiet at an exclusion of something that presses to be articulated. The notion of a *différend* remains enigmatic.[26] It is presented as being self-justifying and self-sufficient. The argument of *The Differend* bears upon politics in that the evocation of a *différend* is presented as being the way of responding to injustice. Recognizing an injustice, however, might be taken to be a promise that needs to be redeemed by remedial action rather than the conclusion of an ethical dilemma.

In subsequent texts, Lyotard retains the standpoint of *The Differend* but elaborates upon how philosophy is engaged in identifying and registering an extra-discursive sense of being and difference that is signalled by a *différend* and he expands upon the forces at work within and the significance of current social development. In his *Lessons on the Analytic of the Sublime*, Lyotard draws upon Kant's aesthetic to highlight the tension involved in a sublime judgement that is taken to be the model for recognizing a *différend*. A feeling of the sublime is conceived by Lyotard as registering the tension within and between the faculties of imagination and understanding on encountering something that is in excess of what can be presented or comprehended. This excess is the sense of disturbance that Lyotard consistently attributes to a reality that overpowers the framework of human thought. His express invocation of non-demonstrable feeling to convey the conflicts to which human thought and imagination are subject relieves his standpoint from having to supply a considered rationale of its judgements, at the cost of admitting its manifest lack of demonstrability.

In *The Inhuman* and in a number of essays in the latter part of his career, Lyotard revisits the sociological analysis of performativity in *The Postmodern Condition* and the correlative discussion in *The Differend* of the contemporary tendency to reduce all questions to that of economizing on time. The mentality of performativity and the reduction of the multifarious aspects of reality to the measure of the time taken in their production are seen by Lyotard as constituting the motive force of contemporary sociological and technological development. A technical mentality and vocabulary renders emancipatory humanistic projects anachronistic and also threatens to extinguish the uncanny sense of an inhuman world of unknown and unmastered possibilities that is linked by Lyotard to a childhood that human beings, hitherto, have never entirely vanquished by their elaborate rituals and processes of socialization.

Lyotard fears that the current drive of social development towards achieving ever greater forms of complexification may abolish human access to the otherness of experience, the allusiveness to the sense of 'something happening' that his entire philosophical project aims to evoke without ever encapsulating. This uncanny allusiveness seems a world away from sober academic analysis. Of course, it is. Lyotard is concerned to show how the onward course of social development threatens to override what appears superfluous or unprogrammable to the achievement of ever greater degrees of complexification. Lyotard's standpoint in his later writings encapsulates the tensions of his general philosophizing. It aims to testify to the *other* of discourse and reason through discourse. At the same time, he articulates a notion of sociological development that expresses a theoretical reading of the present that relies upon a form of rational discourse that he impugns. Lyotard never satisfactorily resolves these tensions.

Chapter 5 is devoted to Lyotard's political writings. A consequence of his critique of grand theory is that he denies the 'necessary' or 'universal' character of any order of rules that co-ordinates human activities. The upshot is to sensitize Lyotard to the possibilities of political repression. He valorizes difference and what is dissonant to the course of instrumentalist social development. Lyotard extends and intensifies the domain of politics to incorporate resistance at many points. The radicalism of this conception of the political is distinctive and its elucidation and appraisal are vital elements in an appreciation of Lyotard's standpoint. His general valorization of political action runs counter to dominant traditions of Western political ideology that tend to dismiss political action as being relatively insignificant. Liberals tend to valorize private activity that is seen as non-political, conservatives often see politics as a practice that should be reserved for traditional élites and Marxists envisage communist society as dispensing with politics.[27]

The emergence of Lyotard's political standpoint out of a Marxist perspective is traced through commentary upon his essays dealing with significant public events, notably the Algerian War and the events of 1968. Lyotard was an active member of *Socialisme ou barbarie* until 1964. His critical engagement with the practice of this group drew him into disturbing and controversial confrontation with the force of the grand narrative that is Marxism. The political demand for commitment to a cause conflicted with Lyotard's increasingly open review of messy practical situations. Lyotard's political reporting on Algeria for its journal is instructive in showing how a political activist subscribing to a grand narrative strains to make (non)sense of a particular situation. The tensions detectable in Lyotard's account of the war anticipate his later repudiation of classical Marxist theory while raising questions about the possibilities of writing politically outside an informing theoretical perspective.

Lyotard's essays on the events of May 1968 express his political standpoint in drifting from Marxism. Lyotard endorses and enacts the revolutionary, playful and disruptive events of May 1968, breaking with cultural conformity and a unidimensional Marxism. Lyotard's embrace of a disruptive politics, disengaging from general theory, signals his movement away from conventional notions of what is to count as politics. His later writings on political questions of public concern, such as human rights and the Gulf War, confirm a radical political standpoint that is dedicated to the disruptive deconstruction of rationalist, conventional perspectives that block creativity.

Lyotard's break with grand narratives is not to be understood as presenting a conventional form of politics. Keane, for instance, is mistaken in taking Lyotard's perspective to be deliverable by the organization of participative democracy.[28] Far from aiming for an aggregation of interests or perspectives, Lyotard favours intensifying differences. The women's movement is celebrated by Lyotard for deconstructing forms of male essentialism, but he is aware of its potential incubation of a feminist form of essentialism.[29] Lyotard's political thought challenges both the left and the right. The ideologies of Western liberalism and leftist collectivism are rejected due to their constriction of the play of political imagination.

Ultimately, the value of Lyotard's radical notion of politics turns upon its critique of prevailing normalizing perspectives. Lyotard takes the possibilities of incommensurability seriously. He recognizes that unity always entails the prospect of submerging dissident standpoints. He valorizes dissensus in his sensitive reaction to contemporary social and technological currents that threaten dissident standpoints. This radical critique of unity and promotion of dissensus is a valuable counter to paradigmatic notions of the political that privilege unity and consensus. On the other hand, Lyotard's conception of the political begs a number of questions, notably whether it is essentially reactive and incapable of generating a sustainable account of how a just, peaceful and socially co-ordinated sphere of politics can be organized. Lyotard's account of politics also trades upon a general conception of the directionality of society that smacks of the kind of large-scale theorizing that he himself repudiates. Above all, his insistence upon the impossibility of commensurability and the premium he places upon disruptive inventiveness deprive politics of resources to tackle injustice and repression. My study of Lyotard's politics echoes the doubts that are raised by Boyne, who designates their problematic character a 'Pascalian wager that the current basis of calculating the odds will be entirely overturned by the very act of placing the stake, and its apparent lack of self-investment'.[30]

Chapters 6 and 7 examine and assess Lyotard's critique of classic grand narratives by focusing upon Lyotard's engagement with the classic authors of grand narratives, namely Hegel and Marx. The most significant philosophical *other* for Lyotard is undoubtedly Hegel. Carroll observes accurately that his initial philosophical text, *Phenomenology*, directs its most pointed criticisms against Hegel's supposed subsumption of all forms of consciousness within the embrace of a totalizing philosophy of consciousness that denies genuine resistance and difference to the object.[31] Throughout his writings, Lyotard stigmatizes Hegel as a powerful but mystifying antagonist. He takes Hegel to be the archetypal grand theorist of modernity. In a letter commenting on *The Postmodern Condition*, Lyotard observes, 'Hegel's philosophy totalizes all of these narratives (metanarratives), and, in this sense, is itself a distillation of speculative modernity.'[32]

Lyotard's critique of Hegel is instructive, but partial. He is perceptive in recognizing that Hegel's absolutism does not allow sufficiently for historical contingency and the contestability of perspectives. On the other hand, Hegel's philosophy provides insights into modern social and political circumstances that are ignored in Lyotard's perspectives. Hegel's philosophy is more open and susceptible to diverse interpretations than is acknowledged by Lyotard. The upshot of Lyotard's closed interpretation of Hegel is that it casts doubt upon a core element of Lyotard's critique of preceding theory, its professed mould-breaking openness. If Hegel's philosophy can be interpreted in a revisionary spirit that emphasizes its critical and insightful perspective on modernity then it is not to be rejected in the paradoxically totalizing way that is enjoined by the anti-totalizing postmodernism of Lyotard.

If Hegel represents the philosophical *other* for Lyotard, then Marx is the political *other*. Chapter 7 undertakes a review of Lyotard's relation to Marx. Lyotard turned away from philosophy to concentrate on political work for the Marxist group *Socialisme ou barbarie* for a number of years. In his 'Memorial to Marxism', he confesses that his commitment drifted until he had to admit that he no longer could see the world through Marxist eyes.[33] There was a *différend* between him and Marxism. The chapter explores the nature of this *différend*.

Lyotard's observations on the Algerian War show him to be opening to a perspective that distances him from classic Marxist concepts. His participation in the events of 1968 confirm a drift in his revolutionary perspective whereby revolution is not to be worked out in terms of a reflected comprehensive alternative scheme but rather is to promote and enact disruptive events that expose an underlying contingency in the social world. *Libidinal Economy* is a dramatic break from Marx that infuses Marxist concepts with libidinal desire and takes capitalism to provide opportunities for libidinal investment. Lyotard turns decisively against the project of theoretical critique because he diagnoses it as implicated in the structures that are represented in its critical discourse. He aims at subverting political and repressive structures by infusing them with libidinal energy.

Lyotard's recognition of Marxism's tendency to reduce reality to the terms of a critical perspective that is entangled with the criticized discursive and institutional structures is perceptive. It explains, for instance, how nationalism, the absorption of the working class into the system and the homogenizing tendency of a cultural cult of performativity, are underplayed or misrecognized by conventional Marxist categories. Lyotard, however, notes differing schools of Marxism while dismissing Marxism as a closed system of thought that contrives to assimilate rather than recognize difference. His closed reading of Marx is not open to the possibilities engendered by the variety of readings of Marx. The closure of Lyotard's reading of Marx signals a lack of openness in his own postmodern perspective.

This tension is heightened by Lyotard's sociological reading of the present.

Lyotard's diagnosis of contemporary society as operating according to a formula of economizing on time, as he himself recognizes, rehearses aspects of what is conveyed in Marx's analysis of the logic of capital.[34] Lyotard's sociological vision, though, is highly abstract, eschewing the close analysis of political economy developed in Marx's elaboration of the operation of capital. As it stands, Lyotard's sociological analysis does not press its analysis of the means by which the logic of performativity is promoted and the modalities of its operation. A critical development of Lyotard's notion of performativity demands an open engagement with rather than a closed dismissal of Marx's conception of the intensification and extension of capital's domination of society and the wealth of critical commentaries on Marx that explore questions relating to the economic domination of national economies and global society.

Chapter 8, the final chapter of this book offers a summative assessment of Lyotard's interconnected philosophy and politics. It is tempting to succumb to Lyotard's disruptive style and accept his postmodern critique of grand narratives and to have done with the false trails of absolutist theories that have dominated modern social theory and political practice. It is also easy to sit on the critical sidelines and dismiss Lyotard as offering an irrationalist escape from the sober business of reasonable theoretical and political construction. What this book attempts to do throughout is to provide a more balanced assessment of Lyotard, and to present a nuanced examination of the various expressions of his thought, giving special attention to his distinctive treatment of the political and his critiques of the classic grand narrators, Hegel and Marx.

Lyotard is seen as being especially compelling in negating aspects of classic modern thought, such as its easy adoption of a universalist perspective, and in serving as a counterpoint to mainstream trends in contemporary political theory that limit the scope of political imagination. His philosophical and political standpoint in itself, however, is too contrary and beset with internal tensions to elicit support. The worth of Lyotard's thought resides primarily in its critical resistance to contrary constructive discursive standpoints.

Lyotard's late study of Malraux epitomizes the drift of his thought. Lyotard is attracted to Malraux due to his appreciation of what he takes to be Malraux's determination to recognize the transitoriness and lack of foundations of life itself. Malraux's *Anti-Memoirs* are taken to disavow the conventionalities of biography for the deconstructive but creative signing or recognition of the evanescence of what is in any life. Lyotard observes,

> Rather than Malraux's life its matter would consist of the 'Malraux life'. Not the biography of a 'guy who has this name' but, rather, the singular name of that which signs life-writing itself as the immanent enigma of all life, as that which slips away from life and disregards it.[35]

This appreciation of Malraux's aesthetic evocation of the immanent enigma of a reality that resists discursive elucidation does not lend itself to constructive thinking about practical possibilities.

Ultimately, Lyotard's work offers a suggestive reading of the limits of human awareness and an aestheticized invocation to press against and beyond these limits. In the late set of essays *Postmodern Fables*, Lyotard emphasizes the difference between his evocation of a sensibility that is alive to what exceeds conventional discourses and a contemporary aestheticized cultural mood that allows for the consumption of conventional, undemanding images and standpoints.[36] His perspective strains to perceive and criticize the possibilities of repression and social conformism masquerading as justice and social emancipation. Lyotard, though, tends to valorize an individualized, extra-discursive resistance to cultural conformity and oppression rather than considering deliberative modes of political construction. Lyotard ignores the complex if contestable possibilities that are offered by social practices for enabling individuals to develop and negotiate the world.

2 • Postmodernity and the Delegitimation of Modernity

Introduction

This chapter analyses the arguments of Lyotard's *The Postmodern Condition*, with its related notions of plurality and unity, modernity, postmodernity and grand narratives. It focuses in particular upon the notion of grand narratives, and considers whether or not Lyotard's arguments are a conclusive testimony to their redundancy. The variety of arguments and standpoints that Lyotard develops in *The Postmodern Condition* are lightly sketched. These invite a number of questions, and are not to be seen as ephemeral reflections. They express persisting aspects of Lyotard's philosophical and political perspective.

Whatever problems may be detected in the argument of *The Postmodern Condition*, its cultural significance should not be underestimated. In the immediate aftermath of its publication, it served as a cultural signpost pointing towards the postmodern and away from modernity. General texts of sociological and political theory were quick to acknowledge its authoritative identification of postmodernity as a feature of the cultural landscape.[1] A case can be made for saying that *The Postmodern Condition* actually achieved what Fukuyama's *The End of History and the Last Man* set out to do, namely it indicated and offered a plausible account of the directionality of history.[2] Its exposure of the bankruptcy of emancipatory political rhetoric accorded with a prevailing mood. Similarly, its critique of large-scale social theory harmonized with a contemporary unease over the gap between the expectations and practical viability of speculative social theory and radical ideology, and accorded with a fashionable street-level relativism and a modish aestheticism.[3] Its valorization of difference also resonated with a developing concern for the fate of cultural minorities and feminist resistance to repressive cultural and political forces.

The current verdict of events and critical commentary on *The Postmodern Condition* is more ambiguous. The collapse of communism in Eastern Europe and the consequent disillusionment of leftist intellectuals have combined to reinforce the scepticism of *The Postmodern Condition* over large-scale social theorizing. The concomitant tendency for political theory to advocate a procedural neutrality between members of a political association has also served to legitimate its scepticism over theorizing substantively about the public good.[4] Conversely, *The Postmodern Condition* itself has been subjected to substantial criticism, not least by Lyotard himself. He disparaged the work in later writings, confessing to skimming the literature on science that he invoked to distinguish the character of postmodernism.[5] Moreover, Lyotard deprecated the awkwardness of its sociological and temporal reading of postmodernity, and criticized what he termed its overly generalized account of narratives for underplaying the differences distinguishing the operation of styles of narratives such as those in history and science.[6]

Lyotard's retrospective criticisms of *The Postmodern Condition* identify weaknesses of the text. Its accounts of narrative, science and society are sketchy and insufficiently supported by argument and evidence. Equally disturbing, however, and not fully acknowledged by Lyotard, are the tensions generated by its adventurous presentation of the development of a new mentality and culture and its radical scepticism over large-scale theorizing. Notwithstanding the indictment of grand narratives maintained in *The Postmodern Condition*, the text sets out a generalized, contestable sociological reading of the present and an elliptical and adventurous historical account of modernity, premodernity and postmodernity. Moreover, its designation of the social bond as consisting in an indeterminate number of distinct, incommensurable language games and its unequivocal endorsement of an agonistic mentality within and between games raise unanswered questions about how subjects and social practices are to be sustained.[7] The problems associated with Lyotard's conceptions of a dispersed society and an agonistic mentality on the part of game players are compounded by the image of a fragmented self that Lyotard proffers, but neither examines nor explains in any detail.

Readings, a sympathetic commentator on Lyotard, concludes his review of *The Postmodern Condition* that is developed in his book, *Introducing Lyotard: Art and Politics*, by posing two questions. What is the status of the narrative (in *The Postmodern Condition*) of classical, modernist and postmodernist art; positivist, verificationist and postmodern epistemology; capitalist, communist and minoritarian politics? Is there a metanarrative of the failure of metanarratives?[8] While he concedes that the answer to the latter question might be yes, he concludes that the answer is no if Lyotard is to be taken as disrupting and deconstructing discourse rather than providing an alternative, oppositional theory to a dominant discursive order.[9] This verdict of Readings, inclining towards a vindication of the coherence of Lyotard's enterprise, is problematic because Lyotard predicates the project of deconstruction on a generalized reading of social development. Bernstein is perceptive in observing that Lyotard's deconstructive turn invokes something like a grand narrative itself: 'Of course, even the deracinated social world of capital, governed, tendentially, by temporary contracts, is still a world, social and historical in its roots; and so inevitably legitimates itself through grand narratives repeatingly telling the story of the end of grand narratives...'[10]

The problematic character of *The Postmodern Condition*, however, should not obscure its critical insights that disturb the assumptions within conventional social theory and politics. Lyotard's elliptical explorations of history, science and society disengage the material and practical world from any absolute conceptual specification of its character. This disengagement is underpinned by Lyotard's evocative depiction of the social bond as consisting in the provisionality and indeterminacy of disparate language games that resist subordination to the rule of a grand metalanguage. Lyotard's critique of grand narratives highlights the lack of uncontestable criteria for determining social and political practice.

Lyotard's positive endorsement of an agonistic mentality amidst practitioners of diverse language games lacks convincing argumentative support. It challenges, however, a prevailing consensus on the value of consensus in mainstream contemporary political theory and responds to the oppressiveness that is felt by minority and subordinate cultural groups towards the established social order. Coole, in an article that expresses a feminist sympathy for Lyotard's postmodernism, concludes: 'In subverting narratives of mastery, feminists might render obsolete their own grand narrative. But it is nevertheless their postmodern strategy of deconstructing gendered oppositions, that lies at the heart of radical assaults on modernity.'[11] Again, Lyotard's commendation of a political practice consisting in local and provisional agreements may seem insubstantial and unconvincing, but it serves as a useful rhetorical counterpoint to the credible image of contemporary society as incubating a pervasive one-dimensional functionalism.

Plurality and unity

The express purpose of *The Postmodern Condition* is contained in its subtitle, *A Report on Knowledge*. It rehearses a relatively conventional sociological notion of the displacement of industrial society by an information society, highlighting the expanding role assumed by knowledge, as transmittable information, in all sectors of contemporary economic and social life. Lyon underlines Lyotard's recognition of the contemporary significance of information by remarking, 'power and its legitimation have everything to do with data storage and accessibility'.[12]

Lyotard identifies the consonance of a functionalist 'closed' systems theory with the contemporary trend for performativity to serve as the criterion determining the operation of social and intellectual practices. Performativity commensurates thought and action by appraising actions in terms of their capacity to increase operational efficiency. A prevalent managerialism in political and intellectual practice complements the instrumentalism of the economic sector. The introduction of performance indicators to sectors traditionally taken to be outside the remit of a purely instrumental mentality, such as education and health, serves to corroborate Lyotard's sociological analysis.[13] His conception of the pervasiveness of the logic of performativity allows him to explain the commodification of intellectual and ethical transactions that were previously assumed to be beyond the scope of the market.[14] This understanding of commodification exhibits the continuity of Lyotard's social theory with his former Marxist conception of alienation.[15]

Lyotard perceives the menace implicit in the prospective closure of a social system governed by performance optimization as being impervious to a countervailing critical theory. The performance of Western capitalism in the late twentieth century, notably in its delivery of consumer abundance and in the deradicalization of the working class, is taken as precluding its wholesale supersession. Lyotard sees the dichotomous standpoint of critical theory in opposing the irrationality of capitalist society and in supporting what it takes to be the polar opposite, rational emancipation, as being vitiated by the implication of holistic opposition in the internal dynamics of the system. A critique of the system that assumes a revolutionary and universal character operates with the same bogus universalism that is maintained by the system.[16]

Lyotard, though, is not thereby ready to sacrifice a commitment to radical deconstructive difference by acquiescing in the systemic functionalism of the contemporary instrumentalist culture. In *Modern Conditions, Postmodern Controversies*, Smart highlights Lyotard's critical standpoint. He observes: 'The prospect of technocratic context control, the arrogance of decision makers, threats to the imaginative development of knowledge and the possibility that "the computerisation of society" will only enhance efficiency of control and regulation are each subjected to criticism ...'[17] Instead of framing a general alternative form of society to the closure and uniformity maintained by one-dimensional, technocratic managerialism, Lyotard deconstructs its essentialism and embraces a radical pluralism that demands a multiplicity of differing forms of activity.

Lyotard conceives of language as necessarily involving an indeterminate plurality of language games. He follows Wittgenstein in recognizing language as being inexorably social in that addressors and addressees are implied in any linguistic operation.[18] Language games are taken to be shaped by the moves undertaken by their several players. These moves, in turn, presume and modify the rules constituting language games. Hence, the rules of language games, the communicative arteries of the social bond, are perceived as being internal and dynamic aspects of a variety of interactions. Structures in modern social theory, either in the structural functionalism of Talcott Parsons or the critical structuralism of Marx, tend to be seen as relatively fixed, dominating features of the social landscape. Lyotard, however, sees institutions as inherently provisional in their reflection of the contingency of the rules they are designed to protect. Institutions, from this perspective, are crystallizations of linguistic rules; they embody the rules of the game, but rules and games themselves are subject to change.

For Lyotard the character of the social bond is of a piece with the indeterminacy and controvertibility of the rules by which games are played. The social world is plural and contingent; it is to be deduced neither from alleged incontrovertible features of human nature nor by the express, universal agreement of the total number of game players.[19] The self itself is seen as being provisional and malleable, lacking a fixed or continuous identity. It is composed, decomposed and recomposed by the variety of linguistic moves it makes and to which it reacts.[20] The image of language games enables Lyotard to depict the inescapability and contingency of the social context within which individuals operate. He draws upon the contingency of social arrangements and rules to endorse an agonistic, pluralistic mentality. The constant possibilities for inventiveness and conflict within and between games are taken by Lyotard as favouring a contestual style amongst practitioners. An agonistic perspective harmonizes with the pragmatics of language. If the world admits of no fixed reference points, then the point of being in the world involves its contestability. Reality for Lyotard does not follow the logic of an unfolding general plan for humanity. Any move to block the development of moves in and between games is stigmatized by Lyotard as terroristic.[21]

Lyotard's promotion of a playful, agonistic mentality amongst the practitioners of language games composing the social bond is intelligible in the light of his recognition of the contingency and contestability of the rules shaping language games. This support for a particular mentality, however, betrays an evaluative form of discourse that is itself inherently contestable. The espousal of an agonistic mentality is necessitated neither by Lyotard's account of the pragmatics of language nor by the facts arising out of a denotative discourse, such as history or science. The contingent, dispersed character of the social bond depicted in the imagery of language games is compatible with an indeterminate set of attitudes. Mentalities fostering co-operation, loyalty, connoisseurship and intelligence and the conservation of institutions are rival attitudes that may be favoured. The privileging of agonistics is intelligible but contestable. Indeed, the irony of promoting an agonistic mentality is that the very success of this project would intensify contestability. If society is conceived as a contest amongst a plurality of attitudes, then the process is liable to evoke mentalities that challenge and supersede agonistics. Moreover, Lyotard's valorization of radical pluralism and an inventive agonism would seem to underrate the level of social trust and co-operation required for the flourishing of social practices and to ignore the reciprocity of social action that links the operation of individualism with the maintenance of social norms and conventions.[22]

Modernity

Lyotard's conceptualization of the social bond as being constituted by a multiplicity of language games runs counter to dominant self-images of modernity. Lyotard picks out science and the justification of scientific knowledge as emblematic of a legitimating absolutist *modern* self-image. He takes modernity as being essentially bound up with the development of scientific knowledge and the nation state. The modern nation state promotes the conditions for scientific development and in turn is dependent upon technological expertise. Lyotard identifies modernity by contrasting its legitimation of science with the transmission of social knowledge in traditional societies. He sees modern science as being legitimated by allegedly absolute rational criteria, whereas skills and knowledge are passed on in traditional societies by narratives that identify members of the society and important forms of knowledge without having recourse to criteria and theories that are external to the processes of narration.[23]

Traditional narratives are recognized as interweaving the various strands of established social life in their discourse. Lyotard sees a diversity of language games as being acknowledged and justified by features and characters that are immanent to the process of narration. Narrators and audience are identified in the stories. Their social roles are inscribed in the telling and retelling of stories. Drawing upon anthropological accounts of the Cashinahua Indians of South America, Lyotard observes how the authority of the narrator is established at the outset of primitive narratives, just as the prospective authority of the auditor to retail the story is also established immanently in the narration. Generalizing freely and, as Connor suggests, somewhat wildly, Lyotard maintains that traditional narratives enable practices and information to be passed on without the need for contestable supra-contextual schemes of justification.[24]

Lyotard contrasts modernity with the practice of primitive society, as it has broken the defining links between the present and inherited narratives by valorizing universalistic procedures of verification that privilege scientific discourse over its rivals. The modern focus upon the need to legitimate science, and to ensure the application of scientific knowledge to economic activity in a modern society, is taken as engendering the emergence and exaltation of the modern nation state. The centralized nation state is seen as performing a significant dual role in relation to the emergence of science. It promotes and legitimates science and technology, by organizing a system of education and by mediating between economic and scientific organizations.

Lyotard's examination of modernity, then, highlights the interdependence of the nation state and science in playing key roles in the establishment and development of modernity. His identification of the nation state and science as contributing significantly to the identity of modernity is uncontroversial and his specification of their linkage is supported by historians and sociologists embracing a variety of theoretical perspectives.[25] The contrast that Lyotard draws between modernity and primitive society is also unexceptionable in its stress upon the delegitimation of merely traditional knowledge. What is more debatable about Lyotard's characterization of modernity, however, is what is left out of his account. He tends to ignore the development of individualism and the growth of markets. While Lyotard self-consciously focuses upon knowledge, restricting the scope of his account of modernity, he nonetheless defines modernity in terms of its mode of legitimation and in so doing does not explore the role individualism and market operations play in shaping modern cultural standpoints and forms of knowledge. Consequently, Lyotard's highly generalized account of modernity appears partial and undeveloped.[26]

Postmodernity

For Lyotard, the modern preoccupation with the legitimation of science turns upon the simple but disturbing axis that science and the justification of science are different enterprises. The emergence of the scientific mentality, dramatized in the dialogues of Plato, shows that the quest for epistemological knowledge is distinct from scientific knowledge.[27] The justification of science must rely on what is not science. Lyotard conceives of grand narratives as arising out of the requirement to justify science in the modern world. Grand narratives are seen as being motivated by the quest for legitimate and totalizing knowledge.

The core of *The Postmodern Condition* consists in its explanation of the key role played by grand narratives in legitimating science and thereby defining the terms of a specifically modern form of knowledge. The reverse side of this coin is that Lyotard's diagnosis of the failure of grand narratives to operate as foundational schemes of legitimation serves notice on modernity and signals the onset of postmodernity. Lyotard defines postmodernity as the condition post-dating the quest for epistemological legitimation. Postmodernity is a condition that abandons the project of legitimating knowledge by means of a set of extra-contextual criteria.

Lyotard's general characterization of postmodernity is elaborated by his reading of the sociology of the present and by an idiosyncratic conception of science. The liquidation of grand narratives is seen to be reflected in the ubiquity of performativity as an operative principle within society. The prevalent tendency to measure objects and activities according to their capacity to maximize performance is taken as exemplified in their commodification and in the obsolescence of the nation state. The state's obsolescence is seen to be a token of its disposability as a mechanism for facilitating processes of maximizing performativity. A developing global system is deploying mechanisms other than the state to maximize performance.

Lyotard's sociological reading of the present offers what Connor has referred to as 'bad news and good news'.[28] The bad news is the tendency for cultural instrumentalism to operate terroristically so as to obliterate the multiplicity of discourses in society. The power exercised by capital and organizational bureaucracies in their drive to maximize returns overrides the pragmatics of diverse language games. This tendency is viewed as running counter to the more positive potential of performativity exhibited in its avoidance of external measures of assessing activities.

Performativity has the potential to operate as an internal mode of legitimation for an activity. It thereby breaks with the modern, unsustainable mode of legitimation via a universal grand narrative. The justification of a practice or discourse in terms of effectiveness is seen as avoiding a supervening form of narrative imperialism. The process of justifying a practice by the efficiency of its performance allows for a process of legitimation whereby evaluation is not conducted by external criteria but by examination of the internal efficiency of a language game or social practice.

This positive side of performativity is exhibited in Lyotard's focus upon contemporary higher education and scientific research. He sees contemporary higher education as breaking with a preceding ideological self-image of being dedicated to the pursuit of disinterested truth and being driven by the goal of maximizing economic performance.

Scott, a contemporary sociologist of education, confirms Lyotard's characterization of a specifically postmodern university. He observes, 'Today it (the university) is expected to create not only cultural capital but also economic wealth, and as global competitiveness has superseded military rivalry as the measure of national success, higher education has become a key arena.'[29] For Lyotard, the postmodern university equips economic agents with the informational skills to function in a post-industrial society. The increasing alignment of the university with the economy poses the threat of the subordination of knowledge to the requirements of capital, but Lyotard observes that the advancement of information-processing skills will put a premium on the imaginative deployment of data that will enhance the general performativity of students. He envisages that the further development of techniques such as group brainstorming will concentrate on maximizing the capacities of students to manipulate knowledge and so undertake new moves in information-based games.

Lyotard, then, sees as positive higher education's substitution of a new self-image, namely serving as a vehicle for enhancing social and economic performance, for its former self-conception of promoting the pursuit of pure, disinterested knowledge. Likewise, he sees contemporary science as representing positive features of postmodernity. In what Lyotard himself subsequently admitted to being a sketchy review, he construes scientific research and progress as depending upon imaginative, paradoxical leaps that defy orderly, methodical, rational methods.[30] Lyotard draws upon the paradoxes of fracta, undecidables and catastrophe theory to present an image of *postmodern* science as being inherently paralogical in progressing without rules and consensual criteria of legitimation.

The construal of higher education and science as intimating a cultural break with imperialistic discourses in their promotion of an imaginative form of performativity is problematic. On the one hand, there is no evidence to suggest that higher education is preparing students for practices in which they will have access to perfect information, and in which they will be free to indulge in skills calling for the unconstrained manipulation of data. Again, Lyotard does not demonstrate that contemporary science depends upon and promotes divergent thinking. His references to contemporary scientific paralogy are superficial and skewed towards mathematics. His account takes insufficient account of the impact of government and capital on research programmes, particularly in those areas like experimental physics where huge capital investment is a prerequisite of a viable research programme. Lyotard emphasizes what Kuhn, the sociologist of science, has identified as the impact of innovative theory and serendipity on paradigm shifts in science.[31] Kuhn recognizes the role of imagination and unregulated virtuosity in developing science, but he also highlights the role of sociologically normalizing paradigms in directing the course of science outside revolutionary situations.[32]

Lyotard's dualistic account of postmodernity is suggestive but far from convincing. Aspects of the narrative positively embrace paradox without convincingly demonstrating an underlying truth. The depiction of science as paralogical is questionable and insufficiently supported by evidence. Paralogy itself would seem to be a fragile mode of thinking upon which to rely, and yet its paradoxical, undemonstrable style of reasoning accords with the aesthetic model of judgement that Lyotard draws from Kant and valorizes in his later writings. The analysis of the changing role of higher education is elliptical. The depiction of the homogenizing effect of performativity is consonant with the affinities between social activities and cultures observed in contemporary literature on globalism and the post-industrial society, but it provides little in the way of convincing evidence of its thesis. Above all, the narrative of contemporary social development in terms of its positive and negative aspects jars with the disavowal of grand narratives. The truth of Lyotard's highly general account of the present is profoundly contestable, and no doubt would be contested by the inventive, agonistic individuals he commends to his readers.

Grand narratives

The notion of the end of grand narratives is at the core of Lyotard's account of modernity and postmodernity. Grand narratives are the legitimating forces that identify modernity and the critical notice of the redundancy of grand narratives establishes a postmodern condition. Grand narratives of modernity, for Lyotard, characteristically impose a general, supervening pattern of meaning, explanation and direction upon the variety of ways men and women think and act. Lyotard conceives of a grand narrative as a term 'to designate any science which legitimises itself with reference to a discourse making an explicit appeal to some grand narrative, such as the dialectics of

Spirit, the hermeneutics of meaning, the emancipation of the rational or working subject, or the creation of wealth'.[33] Conversely, he envisages postmodernity as abandoning the project of legitimating knowledge, and hence it relinquishes the quest for epistemological foundations. Postmodernism, for Lyotard, is relaxed about difference; it does not dictate universal standards to which the variety of social actors must subscribe. It accepts an incommensurability of standpoints.

Lyotard focuses upon the logic of two ideal types of grand narrative. One of these aims to legitimize science by depicting it as contributing to the progressive political emancipation of the masses. According to this *grand* history, knowledge is a fundamental popular right, and its development is integral to social and political welfare. This grand narrative is a drama with heroes and villains. Priests and tyrants are the villains of the piece, conspiring against the populace and reserving knowledge for themselves. The French Revolution and its modernizing aftermath are seen as breaking with premodern superstition and absolutism. At the same time modernity is proclaimed and popular education endorsed.

A more philosophical style of grand legitimation is traced to Berlin at the beginning of the nineteenth century. Lyotard sees the state as being implicated indirectly in this project rather than assuming an expressly directive role. He conceives of this grand narrative as legitimating the variety of fields of knowledge by specifying their common, interlinked role in developing the knowledge and education (*Bildung*) of a grand, all-encompassing subject. This subject is conceived as the inspirational telos of knowledge and reality, explaining all avenues of science and the impetus to legitimate them.

These two ideal types of grand narrative are distinguished schematically. The grand sweep of their perspectives is epitomized, for Lyotard, by the comprehensive theorizing of Hegel and Marx.[34] Lyotard sees Hegel's philosophical system as constituting the most elaborate version of the philosophical style of grand narrative. He takes Hegel as tracing all knowledge to its source and goal in the development of an all-encompassing Subject.

> Hegel's *Encyclopedia* attempts to realize this project of totalization ... It is here in the mechanism of developing a Life that is simultaneously Subject, that we see a return of narrative knowledge ... The

Encyclopedia of German idealism is the narration of the history of this life-subject ... The narrative must be a metasubject.[35]

For Lyotard, the Marxist grand narrative is an amalgam of the two designated ideal types. On the one hand, the bombastic propaganda of Stalinism advertises its political role in yoking education and science to the cause of popular emancipation. The Stalinist fraud whereby tyranny masquerades as emancipation underlines the potential for terror of a *political* grand narrative. The Party supersedes the university, the proletariat replaces the people, and official dialectical materialism directs science into politically approved areas. On the other hand, an alternative Marxist narrative is recognized by Lyotard. In this guise, Marxism perceives socialism to represent the fulfilment of knowledge, in which the proletarian advance in self-consciousness functions as the historical vehicle for and consummation of epistemological development. These idioms of Marxism, developed variously in Moscow and Frankfurt, exemplify contrasting blends of political and philosophical grand narratives emblematic of modernity.[36]

Lyotard sees these alternative Marxist grand narratives as collapsing in the context of a resurgent capitalism in the aftermath of the Second World War. The post-war world of technological innovation and rampant consumerism is taken by Lyotard to remove the conditions for secular emancipation. The unrelenting success of capitalism in its continuous commodification of activities, in its entrenchment throughout the globe and in its enrichment of the working class, is taken as eroding the Marxist myth of a proletarian revolution.[37] Lyotard sees the contemporary world's systemic exemplification of the technocratic logic of efficiency as rendering redundant the Hegelian paradigm of grand philosophical speculation and the Marxist model of proletarian emancipation.

He identifies internal incoherencies within Hegelian and Marxist grand narratives as contributing to their demise. Hegelianism is diagnosed as signalling its own deficiencies by its tendency to reduce absolutist claims to a mere perspectivalism, abandoning universalism for a rehearsal of 'positive', specific forms of knowledge. Comprehensive absolutist Hegelianism is explained as presupposing the development of the empirical sciences. A Hegelian overview of knowledge in its various guises, though, is taken as operating as a perspective in which fluctuating modes of knowledge are merely combined rather than elevated into a supervening general explanation. Lyotard perceives this perspectival viewpoint as flourishing and receiving its due formulation in postmodernism. Likewise, the Marxist narrative of political emancipation is diagnosed as suffering from internal contradictions. Lyotard sees Marxism as subscribing to Enlightenment reductionism: ethical discourse is reduced to a denotative discursive infrastructure. For Lyotard, the Enlightenment equation of emancipation with scientific knowledge mixes disparate and incommensurable forms of discourse. Lyotard indicts Marxism for misrecognizing the irreducibility of prescriptive statements to denotative ones. Hence, Lyotard sees the Marxist grand narrative of political emancipation as being internally problematic. Its misreading of the diversity of discourse is seen as spawning a diversity of Marxisms because Marx's successors are driven by the internal incoherence of their project to emphasize either an ethical or a scientific version of Marxism.

Lyotard perceives the internal tensions bedevilling Marxism and Hegelianism as highlighting the general problems facing all grand narratives. He is an obituarist for modernity. He takes the demise of absolutist explanatory schemes to signal the expiry of modernity and the postmodern release of heterogeneity. Lyotard condemns Hegelianism and Marxism for presenting unificatory discourses that override plurality and difference, and postmodernism is espoused for opposing absolutist unity and embracing difference. For Lyotard, a postmodern mentality recognizes the irreducible diversity of the discourses that maintain social connections. He notes,

> The social subject itself seems to dissolve in this dissemination of language games. The social bond is linguistic, but is not woven with a single thread. It is a fabric formed by the intersection of at least two (and in reality an indeterminate number) of language games.[38]

This critique of Hegelianism and Marxism is incisive insofar as Lyotard highlights their unacceptable tendency to assume a general unidirectionality to history which ignores the contingency of events and the contestability of their interpretation. It also exemplifies Lyotard's resistance to absolutist universal theorizing that is indicated by the phrase, 'the end of grand narratives'. The evocative aspect of 'the end of grand narratives' explains why it remains a feature of his standpoint even after his preoccupation with the narrative form wanes. 'The end of grand narratives' serves as an evocative formula for expressing his opposition to universal schemes of thought. Lyotard's critique of Hegel and Marx also reinforces the point of his own affirmation of postmodernism. Difference and inventiveness are threatened by theoretical standpoints that claim to subsume complexity and heterogeneity within their general frameworks of explanation.

Notwithstanding its insight into problems involved in their theories, Lyotard's critique of Hegel and Marx underplays the possibilities suggested by the variety of interpretations of Hegelianism and Marxism. Lyotard himself observes that Hegelian absolutism can be reduced to a mere perspectival arrangement of areas of thought and that Marxism has spawned a range of styles. Given the varieties of Hegelianism and Marxism, Lyotard's summary designation of them as *grand narratives* dedicated to absolutist forms of explanation, appears a compressed formula that is as misleading as it is enlightening. Hegel and Marx can be, and have been, interpreted in ways that do not see their theories as being closed, absolutist systems. Open and revisable modes of Hegelianism and Marxism are possible and they are neither to be dismissed lightly nor to be seen as symptomatic of chronic problems in Hegelian and Marxist schemes of thought. The condensed sketch of Hegel and Marx offered by Lyotard cannot be sustained as a definitive reading. In any event, more open readings of Hegel and Marx are worth exploring irrespective of their accuracy in registering what Hegel and Marx actually meant. Non-metaphysical interpretations of Hegel and non-deterministic, open variants of Marxism explore imaginative explanations of the tensions and possibilities maintained in and between social practices that cannot be dismissed as grand, absolutist strategies of legitimation.

The end of grand narratives?

Lyotard, in *The Postmodern Condition*, breaks with grand narratives, and in so doing takes the scope and power of philosophical explanation to be limited. He proclaims a postmodern departure from the project of providing large-scale explanation of the human condition. The central argument of *The Postmodern Condition* is an obituary for grand projects of legitimation that link science and politics to ideals of emancipation. For Lyotard, there is an irreducible multiplicity of discourses and practices. The condition of postmodernity rests upon an acceptance of this multiplicity and a reluctance to press for a theory commensurating differences between these discourses. Lyotard denies that there is an Archimedean point from which the totality of the world's meaning can be appraised. Lyotard sees neither a natural nor a socially contrived harmony between the indeterminate number of language games that form the social fabric.

The force and radicalism of Lyotard's commitment to break with generalizing perspectives that aim to establish unified explanations and shared values are exhibited in his opposition to Habermas's discourse ethic. Habermas is a self-consciously post-metaphysical theorist who abandons the Enlightenment aspiration to achieve a comprehensive, substantive philosophical explanation endorsing political emancipation. Nonetheless, he sees himself as continuing the Enlightenment project of valorizing reason, because he presumes that reason can serve as a procedural device to establish a rational consensus on a fair legal and ethical order. Habermas identifies a post-metaphysical notion of justification as arising out of modernity itself. In *The Philosophical Discourse of Modernity*, he notes, 'it (modernity) has to create its normativity out of itself'.[39] This entire concern to establish consensus, however, is abrogated by Lyotard who sees a continuation of the Enlightenment project as maintaining the generalizing perspective of grand narratives. Lyotard takes an absolute incommensurability between language games as foreclosing on social consensus and unity. For Lyotard, the valorization of unity epitomized by classic grand narratives and their successors is tantamount to terrorism in its overriding of difference. His absolute hostility to the Enlightenment project is stated bluntly in one of the letters composing *The Postmodern Explained to Children*. In 'Apostil on narratives', Lyotard observes, 'I would argue that the project of modernity (the realisation of universality) has not been forsaken or forgotten, but destroyed, "liquidated".'[40]

Lyotard's indictment of the very idea of consensus is a powerful challenge to the heirs of the Enlightenment due to its evocation of entrenched and irresolvable difference. The ideal of consensus appears benign in its optimistic assumptions about the capacity of human beings to see things the same way. Lyotard's challenge to the ideal of consensus and the commensurating capacity of reason, however, is powerful because his opposition does not derive merely from the evident difficulties involved in achieving the projected unity.

Lyotard objects to the very idea of unity as an ideal. For Lyotard dissensus is to be valued because it harmonizes with an incommensurability which is fundamental to the constitution of social practice. The mentality of agonistic inventiveness he commends is designed to intensify differences, and so register the possibilities latent within the social bond. For Lyotard, reality, as demonstrated by science and postmodern higher education, resists exhaustive schematized comprehension. Postmodern inventiveness and respect for difference are at one with his sense of a reality that is not amenable to unitary modes of rational explanation.

Lyotard's commitment to postmodernism and his criticisms of the unificatory rationalism exhibited by grand narratives and the pursuit of consensus are maintained in his later writings. In the collection of essays published in 1997 under the revealing title *Postmodern Fables*, Lyotard revisits the notion of modernity and the condition of postmodernity and reasserts a postmodern pluralism and the redundancy of the great narratives of modernity.[41] The fables that are rehearsed presume the truth of nihilism and the nullity of the emancipatory notions of progress maintained in classic modern narratives. In the essay 'Anima minima', Lyotard declares, 'The ideals of Western civilisation issuing from the ancient, christian and modern traditions are bankrupt.'[42] In the essay 'A bizarre partner', Lyotard reaffirms his commitment to the notion of a multiplicity of language games that thwarts the aspiration to establish a rational consensus amongst language users.[43]

The argument of *The Postmodern Condition* is radical, forceful, but elliptical and problematic. A host of themes are introduced and related together. A number of these themes suffer from being insufficiently developed and justified. For instance, Lyotard's advocacy of a postmodern conception of science embraces a paralogy that subverts processes designed to check knowledge claims. Norris, amongst others, is critical of Lyotard for jettisoning too easily more conventional notions of science that see scientific procedures, such as the careful and public testing of hypotheses, as indispensable indicators of the objectivity of scientific discourse.[44]

Lyotard's derogation of the self is arresting but puzzling. He observes,

> A self does not amount to very much but no self is an island; each exists in a fabric of relations that is now more complex and mobile than ever

before. Young or old, man or woman, rich or poor, a person is always located at 'nodal points' of specific communication circuits however tiny these may be.[45]

Lyotard's subordination of the self to diverse circuits of communication is unsettling, and requires sustained analysis and justification of the relations between selves and 'communication circuits' if it is to be clarified and legitimated. On the face of things, the derogation of agency is at odds with the role of reflective understanding in language and thought. Social practices, such as contracts, moral conscientiousness and market behaviour, assume the stability of individual identities. The cultivation of agonistic qualities would also seem to presume a degree of collected self-awareness that is at odds with the notion of a fragmented self.

The brevity of Lyotard's accounts of modernity and postmodernity causes concern. Lyotard himself subsequently counselled against the implicit temporal conception of these conditions. The sociological depiction of the contemporary world as harbouring a dichotomy between its incubation of a closed system dedicated to instrumentalism and the promotion of more flexible, imaginative attitudes is suggestive but abstracts from concrete specification of developments shaping contemporary theory and practice, such as ecologism, feminism, nationalism, civil society, the family and globalism. The linking of modernity to grand narratives also tends to abstract from the content of these narratives and hence the impact of, say, individualism and capital upon distinctively modern theory. The insubstantial character of Lyotard's notion of modern grand narratives informs his subsequent comments on the subject. For instance, his later suggestion that the great narratives of modernity are characterized by their drive to articulate the end of the separation of the self from itself remains undeveloped.[46]

The compression of Lyotard's account of modernity informs his critique of particular grand narratives, notably those of Hegel and Marx. He tends to read the theories of Hegel and Marx as being closed, absolutist schemes but in so doing does not allow for the variety of different ways in which their theories have been interpreted, such as readings which accent their philosophies as procedures of criticism rather than for positing the end of history.

Above all, *The Postmodern Condition* suffers from the paradox that its account of postmodernity and the end of grand narratives assumes the uninhibited certitude and unity that it takes to be the trademark of grand narratives. Lyotard's critique of metanarratives can itself be seen as a metanarrative. Lyotard implicitly acknowledges the force of this criticism in his late essay, 'A postmodern fable', in which he imagines social development as being dedicated to the task of developing thinking without a body so as to effect an escape from the destruction of life on the planet Earth. He maintains, somewhat uneasily, that his narrative of the developmental complexity of life, insofar as it claims neither to provide a final truth nor the emancipation of humanity, is not to be seen as a grand narrative. In this essay, however, as in *The Postmodern Condition* and other works, Lyotard rehearses a generalized account of social development that apes the unificatory universal style of social theories that he characteristically identifies as being emblematic of grand narratives.[47]

The provocative insights of *The Postmodern Condition*, and the tensions within its arguments, invite readers to consider their provenance in earlier writings of Lyotard and their revision and development in his subsequent writings. *The Postmodern Condition* has been treated as a maverick work, rehearsing a modish phenomenon.[48] It actually reflects, in its provocative radicalism, in its singular standpoints such as the espousal of undemonstrable judgements and in the tensions to which its arguments are subject, persisting features of Lyotard's thought.

In reviewing *The Postmodern Condition* twenty years on from its publication, it can be seen to possess more than a merely modish, passing significance. It highlights what are currently widely appreciated as severe problems besetting unificatory schemes of reason that affect to resolve the problems of social and political practice. A postmodern scepticism over the claims of generalizing social theory advanced in *The Postmodern Condition* is now a prevalent disposition amongst social theorists. In retrospect, however, substantive aspects of its argument appear deeply problematic. Its reading of modernity and postmodernity is superficial. The sharp break that is postulated as separating these conditions derives from a view of modernity that abstracts from its complexity and from an account of grand narratives that is tendentious in its reading of classic modern theories. Likewise, its perspectives on language, social practice and the self are highly elliptical, just as the promotion of a postmodern agonistic pluralism lacks supporting argumentation and justification while ignoring questions about the overall organization of social practices.

3 • The Development of Lyotard's Thought: From Phenomenology to the Game of Justice

Introduction

Lyotard is against grand narratives. He opposes the very aspiration to domesticate the world by bringing it under the rubric of an explanation. He sees the entire enterprise of connecting experience under the guise of its compatibility with universal concepts as denying the refractoriness of the real, and the volatility of events. The rationalist appraisal of reality is taken by Lyotard to effect an illicit withdrawal from the unmalleable materiality of events, from their 'happening' quality. From Lyotard's perspective, the disruptive character of happenings, discharging a multiplicity of particulars, cannot be seen in the distorting mirror of representational thought. Postmodernism, for Lyotard, celebrates the contingency of events and an inventiveness that is sensitive to and nurtures difference.

Lyotard's critique of the imperialist logic of 'grand' forms of rationalism is radical and underpins a political standpoint that questions the impulse to impose an external order on the distinct, unassimilable aspects of experience. His postmodern denial of an order of things and a unity of moral purpose is radical and unsettling. Its singularity is highlighted in Rorty's critique of what he takes to be Lyotard's melodramatic obituary for grand narratives. In 'Cosmopolitanism without emancipation', Rorty sees Deweyan pragmatism as happily dispensing with grand narratives. He concludes that the idea of universal answers consonant with grand narratives can be abandoned but yet liberal social democracy can be embraced and canvassed with a minimum of fuss. For Rorty the end of grand narratives is no big deal. It is merely a prelude to a pragmatic search for a consensus that is to be achieved by a sober endorsement of liberal political ideals. Rorty observes,

> one of the less important sideshows of Western civilization – metaphysics – is in the process of closing down. This failure to find a single commen-

surating discourse, in which to write a universal translation manual (thereby doing away with the need to constantly learn new languages) does nothing to cast doubt on the possibility (as opposed to the difficulty) of peaceful social progress.[1]

For Lyotard the very idea of progress is a mistake. It collapses different events together into a single frame of reference for evaluating progress. Lyotard is unremittingly hostile to manœuvres that endanger the individuality and discrete materiality of events. Rorty's comfortable espousal of liberal social democracy jars with Lyotard's insistence on incommensurable, unbridgeable difference. The presumptive ease of working out common rules and policies for a society runs counter to differences of, for example, language, sexuality and status that may call for contrary rules or even alternative designations for the individuals to be linked by the rules.[2]

Grand narratives, for Lyotard, fail because of the intractability of difference. Discourses are various and variously different, hence a generalizing discourse judging between distinct standpoints is ruled out. Moreover, pragmatic agreement douses the inventive spark that ignites a particular discourse or language game. Given his sensitivity to unresolvable difference and the 'it is happening' quality of a particular event, that stands for its irreducible individuality, Lyotard is set against all idioms of universality, even the avuncular variety maintained by Rorty. In his essay 'A bizarre partner' published in *Postmodern Fables* (1993), Lyotard rehearses a long-standing opposition to Rorty's commitment to establishing a pragmatic consensus. Lyotard highlights the plurality of reason, invoking Kant's notion of the heterogeneity of judgement and disavows the homogeneity of language. He observes,

> Despite the reasonable but misplaced objections that Rorty makes to my reading of Wittgenstein, I still think that the multiplicity of 'language games' sets up an analogous difficulty (i.e. to the Kantian notion of differential procedures of thought) *mutatis mutandis* to the principle of a homogenous language.[3]

In distinguishing his own position from Lyotard's in 'Cosmopolitanism without emancipation', Rorty gestures towards an explanation of Lyotard's radicalism by locating it within a French philosophical discourse. He takes a defining revolutionary nostalgia to inform French philosophy, rather than the down-to-earth practical moderation that shapes Anglo-Saxon philosophy.[4] While the terms of the contrast sketched by Rorty are debatable, the sharp separation between Lyotard and contemporary Anglo-Saxon philosophy and political theory is doubtless to be explained in part by the differences between their formative intellectual contexts.

Lyotard was a French theorist and the development of his thinking reflects political and philosophical currents shaping post-Second World War France. Unlike many contemporary Anglo-Saxon theorists, he matured politically and philosophically in an atmosphere where grand narratives, such as Hegelianism and Marxism, exerted a profound influence on political and intellectual life. Lyotard is linked with other theorists in France post-1945, such as Derrida and Levinas. Their philosophies express a similar opposition to stucturalism, an archetypal overarching theory that permeated French philosophy and social science. Lyotard's intellectual context is a web, and the breaking of the web marks his thinking.

Certainly, the radicalism of Lyotard's political theorizing, its disruption of conventional moderating notions characteristically maintained in Anglo-Saxon political philosophy, reflects and emanates from the radicalism of his writings preceding *The Postmodern Condition*. A radical, disruptive spirit engendering a revolutionary approach to both philosophy and politics is evident throughout the course of his intellectual development. *The Postmodern Condition* is not a bolt from the blue, conveying news from nowhere. Its standpoint reflects previous articulations of Lyotard's unease at representational conceptual schemes and false trails of universalism.

In this chapter, Lyotard's philosophical opposition to comprehensive rationalist explanations of reality will be explored, via analyses of his major theoretical works up to *The Postmodern Condition: A Report on Knowledge*. The severity of Lyotard's hostility to forms of rationalism will be highlighted: he explores a variety of vocabularies in expressing his anti-rationalism and the principal targets of his hostility will be shown to vary from work to work. His initial philosophical work, *Phenomenology*, considers a range of influential philosophical standpoints in post-war France, such as phenomenology, Hegelianism, structuralism and Marxism, which will all be successive targets of his philosophical critique of totalizing systems of thought.

Lyotard's key theoretical texts in the period 1954–79 will be examined. Given the extent of Lyotard's writings, this review will focus mainly upon *Phenomenology, Discours, figure, Libidinal Economy* and *Just Gaming*, though other writings will be invoked to support lines of argument and clarify aspects of Lyotard's development. The aim is to explore the basis of Lyotard's repudiation of grand narratives that is announced in *The Postmodern Condition*. Grand narratives in that work are the emblems of modernity that are renounced so that postmodernity can be embraced. Lyotard's dismissal of grand narratives is motivated by his critique of their universalism and his exposure of what he regards as their bogus absolutism. This abrogation of the claims of large-scale theory rests upon a persistently profound scepticism. The shifting formulas adopted by Lyotard in opposing hegemonic claims of reason, however, reinforce doubts about the argument of *The Postmodern Condition*. These doubts will be explored in what follows.

In interpreting Lyotard, an overall sense of his standpoint and arguments is useful, given the somewhat forbidding density of his more philosophical works. What is going on, for instance, in *Libidinal Economy*, can be obscured by the series of intricate and disturbing metaphors with which it expresses movements of desire. What motivates this 'evil' book and Lyotard's entire philosophy is a sensitivity to the distortive effects of totalizing theories that misperceive events by equating them with forms of rational representation. Lyotard's emphasis upon irrefragable difference has already been highlighted, along with his notion of the opacity of material reality to reason. These themes underlie his political radicalism and inform his major philosophical texts before *The Postmodern Condition*. The exalted status accorded to intentionality in phenomenology, the holistic theories of Hegel and Marx and the totalizing discourse of structuralism are objects against which the early formulations of Lyotard's iconoclastic anti-rationalism are directed.

Phenomenology

Lyotard's first book, *Phenomenology* (1954), the subject of his doctorate, prefigures many of his subsequent theoretical preoccupations. It is a dense and perplexing book, as the differences between interpretive studies of the text demonstrate.[5] Lyotard reviews the phenomenological approach to objectivity and subjectivity in relation to a variety of human sciences. Lyotard's assessment of phenomenology is ambiguous. On the one hand, he is sympathetic to aspects of the project, such as its concern to avoid obstructive and adventitious theorizing in its engagement with reality. On the other hand, Lyotard ultimately disparages what he takes to be its lack of materiality, exhibited in its location of the source of meaning in the interstices between the objective and the subjective rather than in the objectivity of matter.

Lyotard's *Phenomenology* discloses its empathy with the phenomenological approach through its extended review of Husserl's project of phenomenology and its relationship to sociology and history. Lyotard takes Husserl's phenomenology to be committed to avoiding incoherent conceptions of knowledge by framing the essential, logical conditions by which phenomena are apprised. Husserl is explained as understanding all consciousness of objects as proceeding from an originary, essential givenness of conscious experience. In conceiving of the ego and the natural world, Husserl in *Cartesian Meditations* is seen as limiting questions about the status of the natural world.[6] This topic is suspended so that the notion of the surrounding world, like the ego itself, is taken as involving phenomena of being, by which the self is in an originary intentional relationship with objects in the world.

The reduction of questions about the world and the ego to a relationship of intentionality between the ego and phenomena is seen by Lyotard as begging questions about the ego and other egos. He traces the trajectory of Husserl's thought whereby, in his last great work, *The Crisis of European Sciences and Transcendental Phenomenology,* Husserl is seen as locating the individual ego in the life world of inter-subjective culture. Lyotard relates his analysis of Husserl's phenomenological studies to contemporary variants of the human sciences. The phenomenological approach, by which an essential consciousness of an object is established, is compared favourably with positivistic human sciences that frame insufficiently examined notions of the *objects* of their investigation. Likewise, Lyotard is critical of accounts of the ego that misinterpret the self by assuming its transparency in introspection.

Lyotard's appreciation of the phenomenological project, with his respect for Husserl and admiration of the work of Merleau-Ponty, is revealed in the contrasts he draws between their insights and the fundamental misconceptions he attributes to Hegel and Sartre.

Lyotard is critical of what he takes to be Sartre's privileging of the mind, separating it from the body and social interaction. Lyotard regards Sartre as lapsing into an unsustainable reliance upon the introspective interiority of consciousness. He observes,

> We must admit, however, that 'the absolute interiority' invoked by Sartre in opposing consciousness to the objective body does not strictly follow the phenomenological tradition: interiority leads us to introspection, and we fall back into the somewhat dated dilemma of an untransmissable subjectivity and an objectivity lacking its object.[7]

In contrast, Lyotard recognizes that Merleau-Ponty construes physiology as interwoven with the originary contact with the world. Merleau-Ponty is explained as admitting a subtle role for perception in this contact with the world, and as avoiding the setting up of an unbridgeable gulf between individuals by taking the originary situation to be inherently social.[8]

Lyotard deploys Husserl's standpoint against Hegel to highlight what he takes to be Hegel's unsustainable rationalism. Husserl's sense of the originary, unquestionable givenness of essences in experience is contrasted with Hegel's imputed equation of being with meaning. This conceptual standpoint attributed to Hegel is seen as precluding any brute sense of mere givenness in experience. Lyotard identifies the contrast in the following terms: 'The double Hegelian proposition – that Being is already meaning and that there is no origin which founds knowledge – permits a clear distinction between Husserl and Hegelian positions . . .'[9] Lyotard evidently ranks Husserl's approach as superseding Hegel's because Hegel sinks reality into a conceptualized world of meaning. Husserl's project, though, is ultimately seen as being contradictory in that it assumes a prelogical being that is to be designated in language, and hence rendered unachievable. Intentional analysis is committed to turning reality into meaning even if this project is taken as never ending. Again, notwithstanding the sharp critique of Hegel, Lyotard refers fleetingly to the suggestion by Merleau-Ponty that Hegel's system might be taken as a militantly open, unfinished one, in which case it would converge on Husserl's notion.

Despite his generally positive reading of the phenomenological perspectives of Husserl and Merleau-Ponty *vis-à-vis* Hegel and Sartre and positivistic approaches to the human sciences, Lyotard ultimately condemns phenomenology. This emerges clearly in his discussion of

Marxism at the close of the *Phenomenology*. He highlights 'the *insurmountable* oppositions that separate phenomenology from Marxism'.[10] The crux of these oppositions is located by Lyotard in Marxism's materialism, that is, in the validity of Marxism's refusal to separate being from meaning. He takes phenomenology to be deficient because it is assailed by the contradictory notion of a world of meaning constituted by the intentionality of consciousness and an originary world that is a neutral world of becoming from which humans must be alienated.

Lyotard recognizes a more positive role for phenomenology in relation to Marxism than is acknowledged by Gane in his interpretation of *Phenomenology*. Lyotard considers that phenomenology can provide a benchmark for explorations of consciousness and the superstructure.[11] He canvasses an open version of Marxism, in which history is open and contingent and hence is not reducible to the tenets of a deterministic science. He takes phenomenology, in its exploration of aspects of consciousness, to be exemplary for this style of Marxism, because it provides a model for dealing with super-structural elements that are allowed autonomy.

Phenomenology is a carefully written, concise text that highlights key aspects of Lyotard's thinking that resurface throughout his career. He is attracted to phenomenology's commitment to realism through its imagining the originary forms of objects by consciousness. Throughout his career, Lyotard aims at a realistic perspective that avoids the distortions endemic within the positivistic accounts of human behaviour and forms of rationalism that the phenomenological perspective is designed to avoid. The phenomenological 'reduction' of questions about the status of the natural world, so that the world of objects is seen in relation to conscious egos, also undermines tendencies to inflate the role of the ego or self. On the phenomenological view, the self does not occupy a universal privileged site but is dynamic and tied to the objects with which it is engaged. A persistent feature of Lyotard's thought is his deflation of the essentializing, universalizing claims to self-identity.

In Chapter 1 of this book, Lyotard was taken to be a materialist, in that he envisages theory to be subordinate to the nature of things. The commitment of phenomenology to realism, and its affiliated sensitivity to the difference between distinct eidetic forms of objects, explains Lyotard's concern to consider it closely. Lyotard's *Phenomenology* also incorporates a critique of Hegelian idealism that informs his later work, and underlies his materialism. Lyotard's critique of Hegel's absolute idealism underlines his opposition to rationalism because Hegel is criticized for aiming to enfold reality within a discursive web of concepts.[12] His critique of Sartre's existentialism also reinforces his materialism, in that the Sartrean notion of a self's independence of a material setting is renounced.

While Lyotard's affirmation of Marxism in *Phenomenology* is abandoned dramatically in subsequent texts, the expression of a form of open Marxism, allowing contingency and difference within history, is reflected in his later renunciation of grand narratives. Lyotard's later repudiation of absolutist theories that purport to provide explanations of the course of historical development, which reduce diversity and contingency to a unifying identity determined by a general theory, is reflected in his insistence in *Phenomenology* that the course of history resists prediction.

Lyotard's espousal of Marxism at the end of *Phenomenology*, however, is somewhat disappointing in the light of the care and reflection that is bestowed on phenomenology in the preceding pages. His affirmation of Marxism and its core notions of materialism and the priorities to be assigned to production and the class struggle are asserted without being justified by argumentation. Lyotard is anxious to specify the need for a countervailing weight to be attached to super-structural elements and to insist upon history's openness, but his acceptance of core elements of Marxism remains problematic. The inadequacy of his positive standpoint in *Phenomenology*, in relation to the power of his critique of other positions, anticipates the character of his later works. Throughout his career Lyotard is most impressive in exposing the pretensions and undermining the claims of absolutizing theories. His development of a positive set of doctrines, though, tends to be entangled in tensions and to suffer from a lack of convincing argumentative support.

Figuring discourse

In the years after the publication of *Phenomenology* Lyotard devoted himself to *Socialisme ou barbarie*. His next major theoretical work, *Discours, figure*, was not published until 1971, fifteen years after *Phenomenology*. It deals with issues that are raised in *Phenomenology*, however, notably the capacity of rational signification to encapsulate reality. The title indicates its theme, which is to trace the relations between two distinct spheres. These are the sphere of discourse, reason, ordered signification, on the one hand, and a countervailing figurative sphere, of visual art, poetry and desire. Lyotard opposes a number of philosophical standpoints in the text. Indeed, its overall point, which is to undermine the sway of the discursive, may be styled the deconstruction of philosophy. Carroll takes the first part of *Discours, figure* to be directed most notably against Hegelianism. He observes:

> In the first part of *Discours, figure* the Hegelian dialectic seems to be the principal obstacle to heterogeneity and alterity, and Lyotard's disputes with Hegel are largely over Hegel's way of 'saying' the unsayable, that is Hegel's attempt to 'place it within a semantic field that links it to universality'.[13]

Lyotard, here, as in *Phenomenology*, takes the Hegelian project to involve incorporating the sensible into the conceptual holism of his system. Reality, on this basis, is coeval with thought. Lyotard reprises Merleau-Ponty's privileging of perception over language in taking the corporeal visual experience of the sensible to be different form the assimilation of meaning in conceptual thought. The separation of sense from meaning is taken by Lyotard to frustrate the dialectical impulse, because the sensible must be transformed into the meaningful before the operations of the dialectic can be made to function.

Discours, figure is also opposed to what Rojek has termed, 'the juggernaut of structuralist theorizing'.[14] Contemporary French philosophy and social science were influenced by Saussure's structuralist linguistics, which conceives of language as comprising a system of signs, so that linguistics is taken to be a science of the combinations of linguistic signs. Language as a system of representation is taken to function according to the logic displayed in its internal operations because the relation between signifier and signified is arbitrary and hence the system of signs can be analysed without reference to the signified. *Langue* is separate from *parole*. Lyotard, however, takes the figural to be disruptive of language as a stable system of signs. The processes of communication in acts of writing, the formulation of metaphors, the production of poetry and the dreaming of dreams disrupt organized channels of communication and the system of signs. Language as a system of signs is seen by Lyotard to refer to and exhibit a world of movement and experience with which it is implicated in cross-cutting commerce that overrides the systemic aspirations of structuralism.

Lyotard aims to show how the *figural* deconstructs the framework of linguistic signification and conceptual meaning. Readings observes:

> The figural is an unspeakable other necessarily *at work* within and against *discourse*, disrupting the rule of representation. It is not opposed to discourse, but is the point at which the oppositions by which discourse works are opened to a radical heterogeneity or *singularity*.[15]

Lyotard sees the figural in rhetorical figures. In *Discours, figure* a metaphor undermines the fixed character of referential meaning. A metaphor militates against the closure of meaning. The process whereby one word operates for another is not seen as an economical transfer of meaning from one to another but, rather, constitutes an ineliminable tension between the two, resisting neat identification in an ordered, closed system of meaning. Lyotard highlights the energetic depth that is provided by metaphor in countering its Lacanian reading:

> The depth produced by the movement of a term shouldering aside another and eliding it, a depth in which I understand that the subject must lose himself at the brink of constituting himself (as a speaking subject), is absent from 'metaphor' if it is accepted that, for the linguist, metaphor is equivalent in the order of tropes to the paradigm in the order of the structures of language, and to selection in the order of operations of speech.[16]

Lyotard perceives the text's occupation of physical space to constitute a figural disturbance of discourse, due to its simultaneous impact upon physical and conceptual space. The line on a page is not an indifferent, exchangeable mark, signifying merely an opposition between one unit of meaning and another. It is a physical delineation that the eye follows in the context of other physical signs, revealing the text to be a physical event that happens in time. The temporal, physical dimension of writing and reading texts is heterogeneous to the synchronic, homogeneous world of opposing signs imagined by Saussure. Lyotard's sense of a text as a burst of physical, psychical energy disturbs the structuralist image of a sanctified world of internally closed meanings. Writing is, as Bennington and Lyotard emphasize, an event.[17]

In *Discours, figure*, Lyotard develops his theme of figural deconstruction of discourse by attending to the aesthetics of language and expression. He sees the point of modernist art and poetry as being to evoke and explore the figural aspect of discourse. Mallarmé's poetry, for instance, is seen as experimenting with the opacity of words.[18] To Lyotard the physical succession of words in Mallarmé's poetry acts as a dissonant force of disorder that crosses the ordered world of regimented meaning. Likewise, for Lyotard, the experimental multiplication of artistic images of objects and events from divergent perspectives undermines the presumptions of the stability of representational meaning.

In his exploration of the disruptive play of differences between a visual field and linguistic signs, Lyotard draws upon the exploratory work of Merleau-Ponty, who tracks the perceptual world of depth and opacity that possesses a meaning that is not determined by language. Lyotard, however, is opposed to Merleau-Ponty's notion of an affinity between the worlds of perception and language that can be traced by phenomenological study. For Lyotard, there is no such affinity, the intercourse of the figural with the discursive is insusceptible of precise or remedial formulation so that language and the world cannot be aligned. The gap between language and the world, the endless deferral of referential verification of linguistic designation, engenders desire.

In turning to desire, Lyotard invokes Freud to suggest how desire connives with the figural to disturb the discursive. Desire is seen as unbounded and unattainable, transgressive against both figural perception and aesthetics as well as destructive of established orders and representational schemes. He highlights the Freudian hypothesis that dreamwork is

> a radical connivance between the figure and desire. It allows him [Freud] to establish a strong link between the order of desire and that of the figural through the category of transgression: the 'text' of the preconscious (day's residues, memory-traces) undergoes disruptions which make it unrecognisable, illegible: the deep matrix in which desire is caught thrives on this illegibility; it expresses itself in disordered forms and hallucinatory images.[19]

Lyotard examines the machinery of the complication of the figural in dreams, the *image-figure*, the *form-figure* and the *matrix-figure*. The first two figures transgress against figural forms, whereas the matrix-figure is difference itself. Lyotard depicts it as 'the "other" of discourse and intelligibility'.[20] Lyotard sees dreams, in their transgressive operations, *pace* Lacan, as operating extra-linguistically in their composition. A section of *Discours, figure*, entitled 'The dreamwork does not think', is dedicated to showing the work of dreams in transforming the symbolic rather than determining itself through signification.[21] Lyotard ends *Discours, figure* by highlighting that art and the critical discourse of his own philosophy are to aim at registering the unfulfilment of desire in its disruption of secondary discursive processes rather than at resolution.

Discours, figure is an unsettling work. Its point is to signal the discordant, transgressive interplay between the discursive and the figural. It is balanced in its deconstructive, critical discourse between the order of discourse and the *otherness* of the figural, which resists and transgresses against its representation. *Discours, figure* anticipates *The Postmodern Condition* in its scepticism over the explanatory powers of general theory and in its valorization of the dissonant. Like the later work, however, it is more effective in its critique than in its discursive deconstructive evocation of the interplay between figure and discourse. Its dualism threatens to undermine its discursive expression. Moreover, its valorization of the dissonant unfulfilment of desire, and the unresolvability of the interplay between figure and discourse, overburdens the notion of conflict and underplays the extent of communicative success. *Discours, figure* also tends to be reductionist in identifying tensions as deriving exclusively from primary figural processes rather than from secondary discursive ones.

After *Discours, figure*, Lyotard published *Dérive à partir de Marx et Freud* and *Des dispositifs pulsionnels*, in which reason and discursive order were subject to further critique. A significant image presented in the latter text is of the projection of representation as a theatre, a set-up, in which roles are assigned and the play of a combination of actors is staged. The former text collects together a series of essays, reflecting Lyotard's involvement in the events of May 1968 and his drift away from Freud and Marx. Lyotard's move from essentializing resolutive categories and standpoints is charted, as well as his subscription to a deconstructive revolutionary standpoint in which the role of art in breaking with the role of discursive hierarchy and order is highlighted.[22] In *Libidinal Economy*, Lyotard breaks decisively and abusively from Marx. The tensions of the dualism in *Discours, figure* are also abandoned for a positive assertion of desire.

Libidinal Economy, the economy of evil?

Lyotard's antipathy to Marxism as a general theory that dissembles its own distortions of reality is forcibly expressed in *Libidinal Economy*. The work blazes in denouncing the presumptions of representational thinking in misrepresenting the dissonant bursts of energy that constitute reality and which it celebrates. Lyotard himself subsequently depicted the text as evil. The projected 'evil' of the work consists in its deliberately provocative, amoral character. Lyotard aims to invoke without hypostatizing the *other* of settled orders of discourse, and to do so in a way that breaks with settled conventions of academic and representational expression. The hypostatization and dismissal of this otherness, the great zero, is effected by consciousness, the unified self, in manipulating signs so as to prescribe what is and what is not present. For Lyotard, the representations of the unified self do not capture libidinal intensities and singularities. Instead of operating with a system of signs that designate and represent 'reality', Lyotard invokes 'tensors' that are themselves conductors of libidinal intensities.[23]

Libidinal Economy aims at evoking what is not explained at the level of signification by traditional theory. Its point is to express and testify to the dynamic energy that forces its way through the desiccated forms of representational knowledge. It neither presumes nor aims to represent an intellectual object. The intellectual object is seen by the libidinal economist, namely Lyotard, as a fantasy. To the 'white terror of truth', Lyotard opposes the 'red cruelty of singularity'.[24] The libidinal economist invokes libidinal signs or 'tensors' that operate below the surface of intellectual discrimination, signalling forces and intensities, breaking out disruptively. The libidinal economy of movement and energy contrasts with the ordered political economies of markets and planned regimes, which respond to the 'rational' choices of self-conscious egos. The ordered reflective theories of political economy are contradicted by rushes of disruptive libidinal energy. Lyotard, though, aims to resist the temptation to valorize non-rational drives at the expense of reason and rationalizations. He models his notion of the interrelations between the power of reason and the force of libidinal energy on the interpenetration of the death drive and Eros canvassed in Freud's later writings.[25]

The opening passages of *Libidinal Economy* deliver its message. Lyotard imagines the skin of the body exposed, all of its folds opened out, elements dissected by 'polymorphous perversion', so that it can be seen as a site for unintelligible, pulsating libidinal forces.[26] This introduction is shocking and is meant to shock. It conveys a sense of ratiocinative theory yielding before disruptive energy. It intimates that the rhetorical force of the book, consonant with its notion of libidinal energy, aims to shock and to release energy, rather than persuade by its neat rational coherence.

In opposing the libidinal to rationalist theorizing Lyotard aims to recognize the interplay between them that is exemplified in the Freudian model of the interpenetration of Eros and the death drive. Marxism is the focus of Lyotard's exposure of the pretensions of representational logic. He is critical of representations of capitalism that take it as forming a global political economy that establishes a harmonious and mediatized order. In undermining this representation, though, he refrains from developing a critique. Rather, he envisages capital as offering opportunities, amidst its mediated networks of interactions, for intensities of force and singularity. In so doing, he breaks dramatically with the terms of his former Marxism, for he imagines that even the most conspicuous forms of exploitation and coercion allow opportunities for proletarian *jouissance*.[27]

In undermining the force of the Marxist critique of capitalism Lyotard abrogates the notion of critique itself, which is taken to be implicated in the terms and assumptions of its object. Marxism, for instance, is seen as standing on the same essentialist terrain as bourgeois rationalist apologetics. Alienation is denounced because it presumes an unsustainable phantasy of an essentially unmediated, unalienated society. For Lyotard, there is no such thing as a primitive or communist economy that is not political. He imagines the interfusion of libidinal and political forms of economy.

Lyotard aims at avoiding a critique of Marxist critique. Instead he aims at highlighting the libidinal force at work in Marx's laboriously constructed texts. Indeed, Lyotard identifies the very tortuousness and labour of Marx's theoretical tracking of the infinite circuits of capital as exhibiting his complicit, libidinous relationship with capitalism. Lyotard notes the endless, ever-to-be-postponed final theoretical reckoning with capital that Marx promises and agonizes over in his writings:

> Marx's inability to catch up with his book (a delay which is equally an 'advance' upon it, a form of temporal dislocation in any case), rather than being considered as an effect of masochism or guilt, should be compared with the way Sterne makes a theme of this delay in *Tristam Shandy*.[28]

For Lyotard, Marx's procrastinating postponement of a final reckoning with capitalism is the meeting point of libidinal energy and intellectual discrimination. Marx's endless theoretical engagement admits of no holier-than-thou explanation. It does not warrant another critique. The object of discourse, for Lyotard, is not reducible to rational signification. There is a gap, ontological and epistemological, between what is happening *now* and its intellectual apprehension. This gap that stands for what is most real in Lyotard's ontology is expressed in *Libidinal Economy*. In this text, Lyotard does not pretend to come up with a neatly turned argument about what is going on. Instead, he conjures signs of the libidinal intensities irrupting within political and theoretical economies.

Libidinal Economy, like *Discours, figure*, evokes forces disruptive of theoretical signification. These texts are related to Lyotard's *Phenomenology* due to their opposition to theories that valorize the rational. The phenomenological project is condemned for misrepresenting reality due to its inflation of the role of intentional consciousness. *Discours, figure* sets up a dualism operating between the order of linguistic signs and the transgressions of the figural. *Libidinal Economy* is to be seen as revoking dualism for an affirmation of the unrepresentable energy of desire. Though critical of Lyotard's repudiation of critical reason, Dews recognizes the force of *Libidinal Economy* in its consistent commitment to the project of overturning reason. He observes,

> In many ways *Economie Libidinale* must be considered as one of the termini of post-structuralist thought. Beginning with a challenge to the supremacy of semiology in *Discours, figure*, Lyotard is led to abandon the founding dualism of that book in favour of a metaphysics of libido, and then to think this metaphysics through consistently to the point of appreciating the futility of pitting 'good' desire against 'bad' desire,

'revolutionary' desire against 'fascist' desire, as Deleuze and Guattari still attempt to do in *Anti-Oedipus*.[29]

The very radicalism of *Libidinal Economy*, however, poses radical questions of Lyotard. For one thing, the omnipresence of desire, the reduction of the ethical to the libidinal, dismisses rather than deals with the dilemmas experienced by social actors facing situations in which moral and political decisions have to be made. Again, notwithstanding Lyotard's disparagement of theory and reason, *Libidinal Economy* presents an argument and urges the intensification of forces and singularities. At the close of the text, Lyotard raises the question of its truth. He asks:

> Will its red violence not be dissimulated by the white terror? Isn't it possible that it will be taken as a testimony, as a statement of the truth? And how in fact could this tension commit itself to the outside of rationality; ductility sheltered from regularity?[30]

Lyotard's answer to the question of the truth of *Libidinal Economy* is aggressively relaxed. He notes that Nietzsche can be shown to be a Platonist if the language of true and false is to be invoked. He aims at conveying the force, rather than the truth, of his position. He remarks:

> What would be interesting would be to stay put, but quietly seize every chance to function as good intensity-conducting bodies. No need for declarations, manifestos, organizations, provocations, no need for *exemplary actions*. Invulnerable conspiracy, headless, homeless, with neither programme nor project, deploying a thousand cancerous tensors in the bodies of signs. We invent nothing, that's it, yes, yes, yes, yes.[31]

Lyotard's sidelining of the question of truth highlights a problem that he dismisses without ever vanquishing, namely the problem of articulating an account of what subverts the enterprise of rational signification. The critical theorist, as Hutchings notes in her thoughtful study, *Kant, Critique and Politics*, will ask of *Libidinal Economy* questions that are not easily satisfied relating to the justification of its standpoint.[32] Its rhetorical force is undermined by its reductive valorization of libidinal intensity that abstracts from ethical dilemmas and social responsibilities. Notwithstanding currents within *Libidinal Economy*, Lyotard's valorization of intensity and *jouissance* is not to be seen as arising seamlessly in the text by appealing to libidinal force as foundational or from either the drift of history or the presentation of libidinal intensification as transcendentally given.

By the end of the 1970s, the drift of Lyotard's philosophy is set against rationalist theories purporting to explain reality. He repudiates the totalizing claims of reason, notwithstanding a countervailing move to favour the general claims of the non-rational and the transgressive. His philosophical vocabularies and strategies change as he strains to find terms to oppose the hegemony of reason and to depict the relations between the rational and the forces of its disruption. Lyotard's formulations vary but he offers a persisting critique of reason's explanatory powers and consistently valorizes the different and discordant at the expense of patterns of unification. This critique of reason motivates his abiding interest in aesthetics. His essays of 1977, *Duchamp's Trans/Formers*, celebrate the pointlessness and incommensurabilities of Marcel Duchamp's work. He celebrates Duchamp's production of restless processes of transformation that resist schemes of totalization.[33] Retrospectively, all of Lyotard's major texts can be seen as challenging the status of what he will term *grand narratives*. Even the equivocal *Phenomenology* urges an open, if firm, commitment to Marxism.

In *Just Gaming*, which was published in 1979, though based upon conversations in 1977 and 1978 between Lyotard and Thebaud, who acts as an interviewer, Lyotard adopts another vocabulary. This work aims at addressing ethical questions, thereby rectifying the amoralism of *Libidinal Economy*. Lyotard invokes the notion of paganism to embody a free-wheeling form of thinking that takes the Sophists as role models for the adoption of subversive, non-universalist perspectives that valorize difference rather than the pursuit of essentialized, Platonic knowledge. His invocation of a pagan deconstructive attitude towards reason and unified notions of politics is exemplified in the collections of essays of 1977, *Instructions païennes* and *Rudiments païens: genre dissertatif*. In two essays in *Rudiments païens*, 'Futility in revolution' and 'One of the things at stake in women's struggles', Lyotard explores how women and the feminine can serve the pagan cause of destabilizing forms of power and order.

In 'One of the things at stake in women's struggles', Lyotard observes that the feminist struggle can destabilize the supposedly universal perspective of theory and so expose the 'complicity between political phallocracy and philosophical metalanguage'.[34] In 'Futility in revolution', Lyotard highlights the role of women in the dechristianization movements in France of 1793–4. In this essay, he observes the tendency for a feminist movement to become entangled in an essentializing, entangling opposition to what it resists, virile power. The fugitive, transgressive pagan celebrations of 1793–4, however, appear subversively disconnected from power and reason. Lyotard underlines the subversive, pagan role of the movement in observing,

> what the unique presence of women in the dechristianization movements of 1793–4 does reveal, as a polymorphous presence located on the side of sublimated models as well on the side of the most devalued mobilities, is not so much (or not only) the emancipation of one sex oppressed by the other, but an attempt (here again with no apparent development) to transsexualize the social body, and thus to paganize it.[35]

Games of justice

Questions of justice and ethics are submerged in the torrent of energy unleashed and traced in *Libidinal Economy*. *Just Gaming* is a provocative work itself, but its motivation is to rethink the ethical and the political. The book is organized according to the order of days when the interviews with Thébaud were conducted. On the first day a theme is announced. Lyotard expresses his concern to distinguish the genuinely experimental in modern culture and art from the merely modish. In aiming to make this distinction, he refuses to rely on a consensus of informed appraisers. He observes, 'There cannot be a *sensus communis*... No we judge without criteria. We are in the position of Aristotle's prudent individual, who makes judgements about the just and the unjust without the least criterion.'[36] The style and object of this judgement invoke elements constantly at play in his writings. Lyotard is persistently exercised and fascinated by the experimental, the capacity to create and imagine new forms. What he means by experimental modernity here is subsequently depicted as the postmodern. This experimental capacity is what meshes with the figural, the unspecifiable, and motivates resistance to cultural conformity. Lyotard, in invoking the notion of a judgement without criteria, self-consciously draws upon his reading of Kant's notion of judgement elaborated in the Third Critique. The indeterminacy of judgement that strays beyond specific limits is a constant theme in Lyotard's work, and it is invoked in subsequent texts to express his notion of philosophical, aesthetic and political judgement.

At the outset of *Just Gaming*, Lyotard links this judgement on experimentalism to the ethical in designating justice likewise to be a practice insusceptible to formal criteria. He abrogates the notion of a rigid code of justice that, in its reflection of a determinate rational standard, undermines a sense of the divergent and discordant aspects of reality. Justice is a process of appraising without fixed rules; the experimental devises and acts. Lyotard's notion of justice is revealed in what is excluded from a self-consciously *pagan* perspective. The *pagan* operates in the way the postmodern performs in *The Postmodern Condition*. A *pagan* standpoint precludes reference to formal rules. It turns its back on the dominant traditions of Western political thought. It repudiates political theories that are affiliated to general philosophies, or what he terms grand narratives in *The Postmodern Condition*. On the second day of the interviews Lyotard expressly denounces the defining concern of Western political philosophy to found or ground justice in a determinate logical or denotative discourse. He opposes the false importation of metaphysical speculations or sociological observations into the inherently openended political and ethical arenas.

Lyotard repudiates founding a political order of justice on a preformulated theoretical revelation of the *truth*. In a long but important passage, he observes:

> I will state again, we are dealing with discursive orderings whose operations are dual, something that is characteristic of the West: on the one hand a theoretical operation that seeks to define scientifically, in the sense of the Platonic *episteme*, or in the Marxist sense, or indeed in some other one, the object the society is lacking in order to be a good or just society; on the other hand plugged into this theoretical ordering, there are some implied discursive orderings that determine the measures to be taken in social reality to bring it into conformity with the representation of justice that was worked out in the theoretical discourse.[37]

In *Just Gaming*, Lyotard objects to the preoccupation of Western political philosophy with establishing uncontestable criteria for a just regime. The lack of criteria alerts those involved in the game of justice to the indeterminate responsibility they bear to others. In the course of the conversations with Thébaud, he notes how modern political philosophy switches the alleged basis of ethical and political justification from an alignment of politics with a designated realm of 'objective' truth (as in Plato), to founding justice upon the conscious will of a set of people.[38] Modern notions of national self-determination and democracy are to be traced from a notion of expressive autonomy. For Lyotard, it is a false trail. The posited dichotomy between freedom and dependence, which this manœuvre self-consciously aims to overcome, presupposes a fundamental contrast between the addressors and addressees of language that Lyotard denies. He observes that traditional modes of narrative informing primitive cultures recognize and accept the givenness of stories and culture but still allow for creativity. In contrast, modern determinations of language and culture are seen as separating subjects into rigidly distinct spheres, setting up abstract notions of social life that demand equally misleading political solutions.

In the course of the conversations Lyotard affirms that prescriptive ethical language is a distinct type of language game. He notes, 'This social universe is formed by a plurality of games without any one of them being able to claim that it can say all the others.'[39] Lyotard rejects philosophical imperialism. He denies that philosophy can serve as a metalanguage into which all games can be translated. What he admits, however, is that he *is* recommending paganism. He prescribes a pagan style that valorizes the divergent and the inventive. His prescriptive standpoint, though, is self-consciously without epistemological foundations or a paradigmatic model of behaviour. During the fourth day of the interviews, when pressed by his interlocutor, Lyotard likens his celebration of paganism to Kant's conception of an Idea, a regulative conception or principle, that in the universality of its jurisdiction extends further than can be justified by determinate, sensible reference. Lyotard observes the incidence of pagan attitudes in the experimentation of modernism and intends paganism to operate as a Kantian Idea in its extension to phenomena beyond its experiential remit. Yet he insists that he is not setting up foundations or determinate criteria for ethics; he considers paganism to be neither an ethical nor an ontological truth.

On the fourth day, Lyotard is pressed over his repudiation of ethical foundations. He is asked if he would deny a fundamental injunction against killing. He denies its ethical necessity, recognizing the plurality of different attitudes, discriminations and qualifications that may inform judgements about killing. In the rest of the conversations

Lyotard elaborates upon his notion of the practice of justice. He rehearses the importance of experimentation to develop novel plural forms of justice. The aim of allowing for plurality, however, raises questions about the relations between games. The prospect of games encroaching upon one another's spheres is addressed by Lyotard on the last day in his delineation of the operation of a justice of multiplicity and a multiplicity of justices. The latter admits the prospect of a plurality of games being developed with their own rules and imaginative ruses.

The justice of multiplicity is deployed as a Kantian, regulative prescription that is designed to ensure the singular justice of each of the games and to guard against the terror that might be employed to achieve dominance in a game and over the range of games. The sense that this resort to regulative prescription might undermine Lyotard's pagan valorization of subversive difference is captured in his interlocutor's final comment that Lyotard is talking like 'the great prescriber himself'.[40] Lyotard's entire discussion of justice in *Just Gaming* is perceptive in highlighting the significance and problems of establishing justice without determinate criteria. Its projected practice of indeterminate justice, however, rehearses the problematic without resolving it. Its gestured combination of Kantian and pagan standpoints is uneasy, as Haber has observed, because it seems to imply a concern to regulate tightly the overall conditions of society while promoting a pluralistic and subversive experimentalism.[41] Questions abound over how this would work out in practice. The terms of a justice of multiplicity are inherently questionable and so cannot supply the assurance against terror that is implied in Lyotard's closing comments.

Conclusion: reason and incommensurability

Lyotard's philosophical career charts the paradoxically consistent dissident opposition to philosophical truth and closure. His writings prior to *The Postmodern Condition* exhibit a range of vocabularies and interests, but there is a persisting focus upon the limits of reason, the opaque fecundity of reality and the counterfeit quality of a theoretical resolution of discordance. The figural, the libidinal, and the pagan are adopted successively to signal the dissonance between reality and its discursive apprehension. The figural is invoked to specify the resistance of action in writing and dreaming that interrupts and transgresses against the presumptive power of discourse. The libidinal economy is counterposed to the mediating articulations of a political economy that it invades and subverts. Reality is depicted as pulsating unpredictably to the rhythms of libidinal energy: a pagan perspective, singular, disruptive and opposed to the Platonic search for absolutes.

From his first book, *Phenomenology*, Lyotard is committed to criticizing forms of thought that inflate their powers to subordinate difference and the givenness of experience to the specifications of a general theory. His critiques are numerous and vary in style and intensity, even assuming the disguise of an affirmation uninterested in critique. Hegel and Marx are the principal targets, but structuralism, classical political philosophy, phenomenology, existentialism, Baudrillard and a host of schools of thought in the human sciences are disparaged for their theoretical presumption. Lyotard's writings develop a forceful challenge to the standpoint of what he designates grand narratives in *The Postmodern Condition*.

Lyotard's sceptical probing of the presumption of generalizing theories, and his sensitivity to incommensurabilities between standpoints are effective deconstructive manœuvres against rationalist claims. His changes of vocabulary and invention of new formulations of his position in successive works, however, point to difficulties in establishing a secure platform for the discursive elaboration of a standpoint that is radically suspicious of discursive standpoints. These difficulties recur in Lyotard's later writings. Likewise, his later works exemplify his continuing difficulties in articulating an indeterminate ethics and a political standpoint that is sensitive to difference and to a sensibility that appreciates the value of an imaginative grasp of what cannot be formulated in dominant conventional discourses.

4 • Beyond the Postmodern Condition: *The Differend* and After

Introduction

Lyotard's *The Postmodern Condition* (1979) declared the end of grand narratives that purport to provide general explanations of the past and present, and valorized difference and inventiveness in announcing postmodernity.[1] In his writings subsequent to *The Postmodern Condition*, he reformulates his sceptical treatment of general theory and invents new terms for his espousal of difference. Lyotard retracts his depiction of the narrative form as an exclusive vehicle for false legitimations and for strategies of redemption.[2] Lyotard corrects the impression conveyed in *The Postmodern Condition* that the postmodern postdates the modern. In 'Answer to the question: what is the postmodern?', in *The Postmodern Explained to Children* (1986), Lyotard takes the postmodern to be a modality of the modern. He observes,

> What is the postmodern? What place, if any, does it occupy in that vertiginous work of questioning the rules that govern images and narratives? It is undoubtedly part of the modern. Everything that is received must be suspected, even if it is only a day old (*modo, modo*, wrote Petronius).[3]

While revising his formulation of postmodernity and retracting his inflation of the significance of the narrative form, Lyotard maintains a continued hostility to *grand narratives*, and repudiates the universalizing aspiration of theories that subordinate difference to characteristically modern projects of general explanation and prescription.

In this chapter, key texts of Lyotard's later thought are examined. *The Differend* (1983), a celebrated, philosophically sophisticated work, is analysed in detail. Thereafter, critical analysis is concentrated upon *Lessons on the Analytic of the Sublime* (1991) and *The Inhuman* (1988). These texts in interrelated ways develop and express Lyotard's later preoccupations. *Lessons on the Analytic of the Sublime* contains Lyotard's most sustained reflection upon Kant's Third Critique, which is drawn upon in *The Differend* and elsewhere to convey the character of the feeling of a sublime incommensurability that haunts discursive practice and which points to what exceeds rational deliberation. Lyotard's later thought perceives the development of a pragmatically successful *open* system in Western society as offering the prospect of an inhuman technological world in which man's openness to difference and sublime awareness of the inhuman conditionality of existence are compromised. This reading of the directionality of social development and its prospective effacement of a non-rational, inhuman sensitivity to the uncategorizable disruptivity of events is traced in *The Inhuman*. The late essays collected in *Lectures d'enfance* (1991) and *Postmodern Fables* (1993) expand upon Lyotard's aesthetic sense of an inhuman world that exceeds rational discourse in its amenability to a child-like undemonstrable sublime awareness. Lyotard's study of Malraux, *Signed Malraux* (1995), is devoted to elucidating an interest in the processes and relics of artistic creativity that are taken as defying the emptiness of an existence that cannot yield a meaning to rational contemplation.

Aspects of Lyotard's philosophy continue to remain problematic in his later writings. His commitment to the values of difference and inventiveness remains inherently contestable. This contestability is masked by the apparent minimalism of Lyotard's designation of what is demanded by this commitment. His focus upon the seemingly minimal requirement of recognizing difference and a sense of reality exceeding rational thought compounds rather than relieves the problems. It raises questions over the effectiveness of what is demanded. Lyotard's standpoint also remains vulnerable to the charge that its repudiation of grand narratives masks a resort to a generalizing perspective evident in his highly general account of contemporary social development.[4]

The *différend*

Norris, a trenchant critic of postmodernism and Lyotard, recognizes *The Differend: Phrases in Dispute* (1983) to be a significant philosophical work in the set of interweaving challenges it poses.[5] Just as *Libidinal Economy* revels in expressing the disruptive power of the libido, so *The Differend* expresses economically the limits within which linguistic expression operates. The notion of language in *The Differend* is framed upon a radical sense of its openness and contingency. At the same time, however, Lyotard sees an absolute incommensurability as separating and excluding discourses.

Philosophically, *The Differend* sets out what is at stake in language. Lyotard abandons the imputed anthropomorphic Wittgensteinian terminology of *language games*. He undertakes 'To refute the prejudice anchored in the reader by centuries of humanism and "human sciences" that there is "man", that there is "language," that the former makes use of the latter for his own end . . .'[6] Lyotard develops a new terminology designed to remedy an alleged instrumentality of language suggested by Wittgensteinian language games.[7] Lyotard identifies phrases as forming the basic units of linguistic meaning, rather than language games that invite the sense that they are coherent entities susceptible of unproblematic manipulation by game players.

The reality of phrases is taken by Lyotard to be indubitable. To doubt a phrase is to engage in phrasing, hence confirming the reality of phrases. Lyotard maintains that there is no escape from phrasing even in silence, because silence makes a phrase.[8] His presentation of the indubitability of phrases is turned against Descartes's identification of the cogito with an indefeasible foundation of knowledge. Lyotard's criticism of Descartes is not adventitious. His opposition to Cartesianism and rationalist introspection is signalled in *Phenomenology*, and is reinforced by his hostility to linguistic anthropomorphism. For Lyotard, phrases rather than the ego are the bedrock items that are insusceptible to doubt, because the nature of a phrase is given in its enunciation whereas the ego's identity, as a continuous, individuated substance, is not established in the act of thinking.[9]

Lyotard takes phrases to be fundamental, but necessarily incomplete. A phrase is always linked on to another phrase. A silence is either meaningful or consequential in respect of its linkage to what comes before and afterwards. For Lyotard, the indefinite plurality of phrases and their connectedness pose questions that simultaneously demand yet defy answers. The questions revolve around the interplay between the necessarily connected character of phrases and the absence of any uncontroversial criteria for determining how they are to be connected.

Lyotard takes a phrase to be necessarily connected to other phrases that shape how any individual phrase is to be taken. A phrase is thereby constituted by its fit with a set of rules determining a succession of phrases. Lyotard terms this set of rules a phrase regimen. Examples of distinct phrase regimens include reasoning, counting, describing and ordering. Phrase regimens are features of language that, in turn, are to be linked with other phrase regimens. They are seen as being connected by means of wider sets of linguistic rules. These wider patterns of linkage are styled genres of discourse: modes of communication such as dialogues and narratives that combine heterogeneous phrase regimens. A Platonic dialogue, for example combines philosophical speculation, with descriptions, jokes and questions.

Lyotard takes the mechanisms of linguistic connection to be necessary contrivances. However, he observes that there is no overarching set of rules determining the operation of genres of discourse and phrase regimens. Hence a phrase and a succeeding phrase are bound to happen, and yet there is no way of deciding how particular phrases are to be linked. Phrasing cannot be avoided but any particular constellation of phrasing must exclude other possibilities of phrasing. This exclusionary nature of language is diagnosed by Lyotard as constituting the bedrock problem of judgement.

Lyotard sees the necessity of linking and the inherent tendency for the exclusion of phrases and accompanying regimens and genres of discourse as signalling a *différend*. A *différend* occurs when something that may be said is not phrased, because of its exclusion by other phrases. This seemingly abstract linguistic preoccupation is taken by Lyotard as having profound political consequences. He remarks that 'the linking of one phrase onto another is problematic and that this problem is the problem of politics ... To bear witness to the differend.'[10] Lyotard's reworking of his conception of language in *The Differend*, in abrogating a humanistic vision of language, politicizes the operations of language.

The profound implications of what Lyotard understands by a *différend* is revealed in his evocation of the disturbing and apparently unresolvable character of a wrong. These implications are conveyed by the ordeal facing a survivor of Auschwitz who cannot testify to their experience. A wrong, for Lyotard, arises out of a conflict that does not admit of resolution, whereas a tort, at least in principle, can be settled according to a formula arising out of the common framework accepted by the litigants. Lyotard specifies a wrong as, 'a case of conflict between (at least) two parties, that cannot be equitably resolved for lack of a rule of judgement applicable to both arguments'.[11] One party in this situation is liable to be judged by the criteria of a different party and in so doing is seen as suffering a wrong. Lyotard observes: 'A wrong results from the fact that the rules of the genre of discourse by which one judges are not those of the judged genre or genres of discourse.'[12]

A tort is taken by Lyotard to refer to a dispute in which the parties involved speak the same language and can understand one another. In these circumstances damages can be accepted as having accrued, a compensatory award can be calculated and can be disbursed according to conventionally accepted scales. But where the two parties do not share a common understanding of what has happened, and how it is to be described, then any resolution of a dispute is liable to reflect one party's understanding and expression of it, and a wrong will have been committed. A wrong reflects the deep incommensurability that Lyotard identifies as running through language and reality. This incommensurability is what constitutes the *différend* between phrases.

To illustrate a *différend*, Lyotard imagines a worker, in dispute with a capitalist, who must accept a form of phrasing that treats his labour as a commodity.[13] A different sense of labour – for example a conception of it as an artistic statement, as a penitence and as a detour from the pain of thinking – is precluded, because the dominant linguistic regime of capital forbids alternatives to commodification. The ensuing frustration on the part of the worker exemplifies Lyotard's depiction of the *différend*. He notes, 'In the differend, something "asks" to be put into phrases, and suffers from the wrong of not being able to be put into phrases right away.'[14]

A *différend*, for Lyotard, is subject to the grim logic of the double bind, where two aspects of a situation are linked but one undermines the force of the other. A classic double bind is depicted in the novel *Catch-22*, whereby absence from combat is permitted only for the mentally unbalanced whose very act of seeking such a status expresses their rationality.[15] Lyotard offers the example of trying to verify the existence of a great novel for which there is no evidence in the public domain. The very condition of having to find the work, precludes its acceptance as a great novel.[16]

Throughout *The Differend*, Lyotard, relates the notion of a *différend* to Auschwitz, and the problems of proving its existence, testifying to it and imagining its place within a universal history. He refers to how Faurisson denies the Holocaust on the grounds of an alleged lack of verification of the death camps. Lyotard investigates the logic of this denial. He imagines an inventory of ways in which recognition of the holocaust may be avoided. He considers that historical evidence may be sketchy. He notes, however, that even if evidence is produced that is sufficiently strong to satisfy conventional criteria, the inveterate sceptic may resort to denying the validity of conventional criteria of historical evidence.[17] Lyotard sees the problem of verifying the holocaust as being compounded either by the possible death of all its victims or by the abjection of the survivors, precluding their testimony. Lyotard imagines a possible, ensuing, terrible *différend* whereby a victim is denied testimony to her suffering.[18]

Lyotard's account of holocaust denial is disturbing on a number of levels. He tends to run together a number of distinct elements that might underpin such a denial. Norris has rightly observed that Lyotard underplays the range and public credibility of the resources historians can marshal in adducing and appraising historical evidence.[19] While survivors might not be able to testify directly of their experience, historians are skilled in a eliciting a variety of forms of evidence to establish a record of the past. Ultimately, Lyotard sees the practice of holocaust denial as resorting to a blanket denial of the practice of history and the credibility of its procedures for obtaining and assessing evidence. This is a possibility, but the denial of the credibility of evidence authenticated by the practice of historians renders this *différend* more of a last-ditch defiance of rationality than the looming, plausible case of a *différend* pluralizing rationality that Lyotard's account is designed to imply. Lyotard's treatment of holocaust denial, then, is problematic, but its discussion highlights the drama of a *différend* in its evocation of the anguish of an inexpressible, undischargable trauma.

Lyotard's notion of a *différend* is interwoven with a theory of names and referents that reinforces his persisting sense that reality is not to be captured by a representational scheme. He outlines a theory of names that takes the objects of sense referred to in phrases to be designated by names. These names are blank proper names, lacking essential characters that facilitate discourse. The properties that are contingently ascribed to them are subject to fallibilist procedures of verification. Lyotard concludes that the reality accorded to names in heterogeneous phrases is necessarily subject to *différends*. This is because the *same* name is vested with contrary meanings and senses. Lyotard observes,

> Reality entails the differend. *That's Stalin, here he is.* We acknowledge it. But as for what *Stalin* means? Phrases come to be attached to this name, which not only ascribe different senses for it (this can be debated in dialogue), and not only place the name on different instances, but which also obey heterogeneous regimens and/or genres.[20]

He demonstrates how a proper name, such as Auschwitz, can provoke a feeling of the *différend*. According to Lyotard, the historian's characteristic engagement with a paraphernalia of cognitive procedures is challenged by the destruction and disappearance of records, and by the terror and awfulness of the happenings within the death camps. The sheer horror of the events, submerged by the detritus of historic processes and yet intimated to the historian, is seen as disturbing the rules governing the practice of historians, and is taken as liable to induce a profound sense of unease.[21] Lyotard evokes the possibility of a historian experiencing a possible *différend* over Auschwitz but it is conceivable that the historian could react differently. For instance she or he might undertake the historical research, provide a historical account and discuss the contemporary ethical implications of Auschwitz.

Auschwitz, and its exemplification of *différends*, is a theme of *The Differend*; its experiential extremity is invoked to highlight what can be at stake in recognizing a *différend*. To Lyotard, Auschwitz signifies an experience that undermines the Hegelian project of seeing history as possessing a unified meaning. Lyotard understands Hegel as unifying reality by perceiving it as a result of the process of eternal mediation undertaken by a universal subject, namely *Geist*. The posited universality of this spiritual subject and its universalizing activity is taken by Lyotard as allowing Hegel to conceive of the real as the rational.[22] For Lyotard, the real cannot be subsumed into the rational. He takes Auschwitz as providing evidence to the contrary. He concludes, 'We wanted the progress of the mind, we got its shit.'[23] Lyotard denies that Auschwitz and the death camps can be assimilated into a result for those who look on and judge the historical process. For Lyotard, we cannot, like Hegel, presume to be speculative observers of history, guardians of

Geist, who incorporate death camps into a notion of smooth spiritual ascent.[24]

In the section of *The Differend* entitled 'Genre, norm', Lyotard focuses upon the political dimension of the incommensurability between phrase regimens and the impossibility of arriving at an uncontroversial, commensurating genre of discourse to decide upon the linking phrases. He acknowledges that the characteristically deliberative politics of modern democracies, unlike traditional regimes, expose the incommensurability of the *différend*, though they are taken as dissembling its radical consequences by relying upon conventional procedures and policies. Lyotard remarks, 'In the deliberative politics of modern democracies, the *différend* is exposed, even though the transcendental appearance of a single finality that would bring it to a resolution persists in helping to forget the *différend*, in making it bearable.'[25] Lyotard's account of deliberative democracy is elliptical and enigmatic. Generally, he appears to oppose Habermas's optimism over the possibilities of establishing fair, consensual modes of rational, political deliberation. For Lyotard, there are abysses between differing perspectives that cannot be bridged. He observes: 'The deliberative is more "fragile" than the narrative ... it lets the abysses be perceived that separate genres of discourse from each other and even phrase regimens from each other, the abysses that threaten "the social bond".'[26]

Like *The Postmodern Condition*, *The Differend* offers no panaceas for its scepticism over the feasibility of general theoretical and political schemes. It is resolutely opposed to the idea of grand solutions to the predicaments it detects. The lack of a grand solution, however, does not imply the absence of a grand enemy to the spirit of heterogeneity it promotes. This enemy has a familiar name. It is capital. Lyotard sees capital as dictating a pattern to which all phrases must subscribe. The hegemony of capital, or what Lyotard refers to as the economic genre, is seen as committing a wrong in subordinating all phrases to the regime of capital. Lyotard imagines the domination of capital as manufacturing a *différend*, evinced in a feeling of unease generated by its exclusion of phrase regimens and genres of discourse that take activities and objects in ways that do not demand their commodification. Lyotard avers that his critique of the alleged bogus universalism of Marxism does not entail a break with its opposition to capital. He observes, 'This is the way in which Marxism has not come to an end, as the feeling of the *differend*.'[27]

In reworking a Marxist critique of capital, Lyotard takes the economic genre to be governed by the criterion of gaining time. He remarks, 'The heterogeneity of their regimens (phrases) as well as the heterogeneity of genres of discourse (stakes) finds a universal idiom in the economic genre, with a universal criterion, success, in having gained time . . .'[28] Given the putative governing priority of saving or accumulating time, everything is seen as being subordinated to this end. Hence work, in the context of capitalism, is seen as a means of acquiring time, when it could be undertaken for a variety of purposes, such as providing intrinsic satisfaction or wasting time. This exclusion of alternative notions of work is seen as constituting a classic *différend*. Lyotard sees the contemporary power of capital and its logic of time management as formidable. The only force capable of opposing it is seen to be attesting to the *différend* implied in its exclusion of perspectives other than that dedicated to saving time.

In concluding *The Differend*, Lyotard reasserts his opposition to grand schemes or narratives that purport to unify and commensurate the heterogeneity of phrases. He rules out the great 'philosophies of history' of the modern age by identifying disruptive events that undermine the claims of purportedly universal theories. Hegel's claim to recognize the symmetry of rationality and reality is held to founder amidst the death camps of Auschwitz. Marx's depiction of the proletariat as a universal, world-historical class is diagnosed as collapsing in the wake of Berlin in 1953, Budapest in 1956 and Czechoslovakia in 1968. Similarly, May 1968 is seen as refuting the myths of liberal democracy, the economic crises of 1911 and 1929 are invoked to undermine the assumptions of economic liberalism and the economic crisis of '1974–1979' is held to dissolve the pretensions of reformist capitalism.[29]

In a series of critical notices throughout *The Differend*, Lyotard invokes Kant's Third Critique as a model for negotiating the indeterminacy of appraisal requisite for areas outside determinate discursive frameworks. In particular, he sees Kant's notion of the sublime feeling arising out of the tensions between the imagination and reason, when confronted by events that frustrate the exercise of their powers, as constituting a paradgimatic expression of a *différend*. Lyotard reads events of recent history as signs of the sublime sorrow with which the end of grand narratives may be felt. Events such as the Prague Spring function as indeterminate signs that the spell of the

Marxist grand narrative is broken, and that grand theoretical syntheses purporting to direct social development are anachronistic.[30]

The characteristically enigmatic point of *The Differend* is encapsulated in its last sentence. Lyotard challenges the reader to consider whether they can respect the contingency and openness of what occurs. He asks, 'Are you prejudging the *Is it happening*?'[31] In *The Differend* he conveys a powerful sense of the limits within which reason and language operate, and in so doing rehearses persisting themes of his philosophy. *The Differend* testifies to Lyotard's persisting sensitivity to incommensurability. Lyotard's linguistic analysis sets up a gap between language and reality that undermines confidence in rationalist discourse. Phrases refer to objects and subjects, but only the names of these items can be assumed to possess a continuing identity. Their qualities are contingent; they depend upon a contingent succession of phrases.

The Differend, like Lyotard's preceding texts, harbours internal tensions to which Lyotard himself adverts. Just as *The Postmodern Condition* recounts a seemingly grand narrative about the emergence of postmodernity, so *The Differend* offers a general diagnosis of the condition of the contemporary world. In *The Differend*, Lyotard provides a critical reading of the current pervasiveness of the logic of gaining time in the circuits of capital. This general view of the present jars with the notion of the *différend* that designates the exclusion of a perspective rather than the elaboration of a general perspective on society. Lyotard himself wonders, 'Are "we" not telling, whether bitterly or gladly, the great narrative of the end of great narratives?'[32] He raises questions about the stakes with which he is operating in the writing of *The Differend*. He notes that *The Differend* is not a contingent, slapdash text, but a carefully constructed work that is designed to exert an impact on its readers. Notwithstanding the text's disavowal of a metalanguage which would ground the claims about the significance of the contingency and disparity of phrases and their genres of discourse, Lyotard admits that he is aiming to persuade readers of the significance of the singularity of, and differences between, 'events'. He admonishes himself: 'And to insist, as you do, on the indetermination of the linkings is still to function in terms of certain stakes, those of persuading your reader of the heterogeneity of regimens and of the preeminence of the occurrence.'[33]

The tensions that are harboured within the arguments of *The Differend* are epitomized ironically by a double bind maintained in

Lyotard's presentation of the *différend*. In their article, 'Lyotard and Kripke: essentialism in dispute', Sedgwick and Tanesini identify problems in the formulation of the notion of the *différend* that emanate from its contravention of Lyotard's conceptualization of the relations between names and their objects. Lyotard names the *différend* even though it cannot be phrased. Despite taking names generally to be rigid designators that do not reveal their objects, he takes the *différend* to name essential qualities. Sedgwick and Tanesini note: 'Lyotard avoids essentialism in the case of names, which are not differends... However, in the case of the differend we have a proper name that must by itself establish the reality of the referent.'[34]

It would seem that the *différend* is subject to the double bind of either possessing a credibility lacked by the notion of language on which it is based, or being incoherent but relating to a plausible view of language. Williams, in *Lyotard: Towards a Postmodern Philosophy*, highlights the same paradoxical aspect of Lyotard's account of the *différend* by identifying a double bind as arising out of a similarly discordant feature attributed to a *différend*. Williams locates the paradox as emerging out of Lyotard's notions of the presentation of phrases and their situation in phrase regimens. Lyotard's notion of a *différend* is held to derive from the contingency of the meaning of any phrase. The presentation of a phrase is held to under-determine its meaning, so that its sense is only determined by its situation fixed by ensuing phrases shaped by a phrase regimen. Williams observes, though, that it is impossible to articulate a freestanding notion of a presentation; for phrases are under-determined, and only fixed in meaning by their subsequent situations. The situatedness of any phrase begs the question of how Lyotard can fix the determinate notion of an under-determined presentation, such as is presupposed by his notion of a *différend*.[35] Williams sees Lyotard as attributing unjustifiable qualities to a presentation in his identification of a *différend*, where Sedgwick and Tanesini see the *différend* as possessing designated, but unsecured essential qualities.

The sophistication of Lyotard's argument in *The Differend* does not eliminate the tensions and problems to which his previous philosophizing was subject. In positing the *différend* as a determinate, general feature of language, Lyotard puts a strain on his own notion of language that precludes a generalizing discourse from determining particular features of the world. Any particular ordering of phrases, according to Lyotard, will be potentially exclusionary in that any concatenation of phrases excludes another possible concatenation. Lyotard's own discourse, dedicated to the general recognition of the *différend*, however, would seem to be implicated in these processes rather than to transcend them.

Philosophy, art and politics, for Lyotard, are spheres in which judgement lacks foundational criteria. Although Lyotard does not specify the tensions within his argument that are identified by Williams, and Sedgwick and Tanesini, his notion of a sublime feeling of a *différend* is defined in terms of its expression of unresolvable tensions. Lyotard's sensitivity to the problematic character of his argument is not in itself a solution. His standpoint is elusive and presumptive in the generality of its application, both in highlighting the general identity of *différends* and in his abstract account of the contemporary dominance of an economic genre of discourse that is dedicated to gaining time.

Lyotard's discussion of the procedures involved in identifying, corroborating and dealing with *différends* raises significant problems that are insufficiently considered. The process and consequences of identifying a *différend* are not focused upon in *The Differend*. Lyotard concentrates upon conveying the epistemological and experiential status of identifying and testifying to a *différend*. Questions relating to identifying and dealing with a *différend*, however, may be exhibited in exploring Lyotard's most dramatic example, Auschwitz. Lyotard highlights the singularity of the experience of Auschwitz. At the outset of *The Differend* he reviews the problems of proving the Holocaust, and in so doing he tends to underplay the role which historical and sociological investigation actually plays in revealing the circumstances and character of Auschwitz. Likewise, the meaning, consequences and ethical implications of Auschwitz are not exhausted by evoking an attestory feeling. Investigation into Auschwitz's circumstantial development and the undertaking of remedial, compensatory action towards both victims and perpetrators of the death camps are plausible responses to a confrontation with Auschwitz. Lyotard, however, inclines to a position where investigation of a perceived wrong or its discharge by remedial action are precluded by their perceived immersion in one-sided discursive perspectives. He does not press the fact that a feeling of a *différend* emerges out of the interplay between discursive perspectives that might be altered and developed by the acquisition of additional information.

Lyotard's entire project of establishing a fault line of incommensurability through language is universalizing to the extent that it abstracts from concrete practical experience. Consequently, Lyotard depicts *différends* in highly general if elusive terms that do not allow for a discriminatory exploration of the questions that are posed by individual *différends*. Concrete historical and sociological analysis tends to fade before a highly general vision of the domination of capital, and the ubiquity of a managerial-technical mentality.

The sublime and the inhuman

The Differend is a haunting piece of philosophical writing, and its evocation of insurmountable incommensurabilities between discursive perspectives is presumed and explored in Lyotard's subsequent work. On the one hand, Lyotard explores the character of the feeling that signals a *différend* by attending closely to Kant's aesthetics and, in particular, the Kantian notion of the sublime. The feeling of the sublime is invoked and examined closely, most notably in *Lessons on the Analytic of the Sublime*, so as to highlight its peculiar disruptive quality that precludes an impulse to construct discursive systems. On the other hand, Lyotard also develops his conception of the domination exercised by the *economic* discourse of saving time that is elaborated in *The Differend*. In *The Inhuman* and other later writings, Lyotard conceives of the technological, time-saving discourse as establishing an increasingly complex, developed society that tends to stifle the imagination and threatens to remove the very *inhuman* basis of experience, an embodied existence in the world, that stirs human beings to strain against their own imagination and reason, and feel the sublime. In texts subsequent to *The Differend*, therefore, Lyotard tends to present a melancholic reading of the prospects for and condition of a humanity poised before the possible annihilation of its capacity to sense the sublime.

In the essay cited at the outset of this chapter, 'Answer to the question: what is the postmodern?' (1982), Lyotard had signalled the increasing significance of Kant's Third Critique for his philosophy. In this essay he revises his image of the postmodern so as to distinguish it from the kitsch with which it is sometimes identified and to highlight its kinship with an avant-garde aesthetics of modernity. Lyotard valorizes a sublime, aesthetics that is opposed to an aesthetic realism favoured by totalitarian political regimes and in an alternate guise by the commodification of art under capitalism.[36] The effect of the essay is to reinforce the sense, evident in *The Differend* and in the later 'Note on the meaning of "post"', that the postmodern embrace of difference is not to be seen as a chronological, sociological development but as a sublime reflexive feeling.[37]

Lyotard's preoccupation with Kant's aesthetics in his later writings is exemplified in his brief but intricate treatment of Kant's notion of the community of feeling evident in judgements of the beautiful in '*Sensus Communis*'. Lyotard transmits his admiring recognition of Kant's identification and exploration of the character of the reflective, indeterminate style of judgement evinced in ascriptions of beauty. The judgement is not to be explained by a purposiveness or by relating it to notions of causal determination, but rather as turning upon the reflexive euphony between the faculties of understanding and imagination experienced in thought itself. It is an exemplary universal judgement in that the act of judgement does not refer outside itself for circumstantial or regulative support. The universal validity that Kant imputes to such judgements is interpreted by Lyotard as signalling and presupposing a transcendental harmony of the faculties that anticipates all determinate judgements and their critique. Lyotard rejects any suggestion that the universality of the judgement is to be established empirically. He observes, 'The beautiful doesn't get elected like Miss World.'[38]

Lyotard rehearses what he takes to be the essentials of his reading of Kant's notion of the community of sentiment that recognizes the beautiful. He observes, 'The essential is this: the feeling of the beautiful is the subject just being born, the first equalling-out of non-comparable powers. This feeling escapes being mastered by concept and will.'[39] Lyotard's sympathetic reading of Kant is also to be seen in his recurring exploration of the significance of Kant's notion of the sublime. In *The Differend* Lyotard refers to the sublime as playing an important role in Kant's assessment of history and politics. In *L'Enthousiasme: la critique kantienne de l'histoire*, he expands upon his preceding remarks on how Kant's notion of the progressive development towards the achievement of the moral law depends upon the sublime feeling emitted by the historical sign of the enthusiastic greeting accorded to the French Revolution. The enthusiasm exemplifies the striving towards freedom rather than its determinate achievement. Its indeterminate, unpresentable aspect is sublime and hence not translatable into a determinate mode of demonstrable reasoning. Lyotard's invocation of Kant's sublime reading of history, however, does not entail that he reads history's signs similarly. In the essay 'The sign of history', he relates how symbolic names of recent history, May 1968, Budapest 1956, Auschwitz, induce a feeling that history is not progressing to a definitive resolution, but do evoke the very sublime sense of these events attesting to incommensurability and heterogeneity. For Lyotard, therefore, recent signs of history confirm the very standpoint that looks for signs rather than determinate causality in history.[40]

Lyotard's most painstaking analysis of Kant's notion of the sublime is contained in his *Lessons on the Analytic of the Sublime*. He presents the text as being composed of lessons that 'have only a modest scope'.[41] The professed modesty, however, masks a tendentious reading of Kant and a demanding elaboration of how a *différend* may be registered. Lyotard provides notes to accompany lectures on Kant's *Critique of Judgement*. Given its significance as a manifest source of Lyotard's philosophy from at least the writing of *Just Gaming* onwards, it is unsurprising that Lyotard undertakes its textual analysis. Kant's *Critique of Judgement* can be seen as offering a bridge between the preceding Critiques whereby the gulf between causal knowledge of the possible conditions of experience and the realization of freedom under the unconditional moral law is spanned by the regulative Idea of the finality of nature. On this reading Kant secures the universality and necessity to aesthetic judgement so as to prepare the way for the validation of a natural teleology culminating in freedom.

Lyotard's reading of Kant, however, downplays the notion of natural, objective teleology to highlight the reflexive, indeterminate aspect of aesthetic judgement. For Lyotard, the regulative reflexive character of sublime judgement entails that categories of understanding and freedom retain their heterogeneity. The reflexive tautegorical quality of the sublime, in its maintenance of a tension between the feelings generated by the play between the faculties of knowledge and presentation, is not to be seen as a propaedeutic for a finalized teleological conceptual understanding of nature. Rather, Lyotard sees its tautegorical character, whereby the tension of the soul is matched by the disharmony between pleasure and pain in its object of judgement, as exhibiting the reflexive character of judgement that is central to Kant's entire critical philosophy. Lyotard refers to the Third Critique, 'as making manifest, in the name of the aesthetic, the reflexive manner of thinking, that is at work in the critical text as a whole'.[42] The critical project is thereby interpreted as resting on the *feeling* of judgement. The upshot of Lyotard's reading of aesthetic judgement is to highlight heterogeneity and indeterminacy in Kant's philosophy.

Lyotard tends to read Kant's critical investigation of epistemological foundations as exhibiting a postmodern heterogeneity. He sees the sublime as subverting unificatory aspirations in Kant's critical philosophy. He interprets the sublime as valorizing a feeling of radical disjunction both within and between reason and imagination. Schaper, in a recent article on Kant's aesthetics, observes: 'Sublimity transcends the grounds of sense and understanding.'[43] Lyotard rhapsodizes what he sees as this negative aesthetic of the sublime. It undermines rather than portends a reconciliation between nature and freedom. Lyotard notes, 'Sublime violence is like lightning. It short-circuits thinking with itself. Nature, or what is left of it, quantity, serves only to provide the bad contact that creates the spark. The teleological machine explodes.'[44]

Kant's notion of the sublime is taken by Lyotard to be the disruptive feeling engendered by a dissonance within and between the faculties of conception and presentation. It is an experiential vertigo occasioned by the incommensurabilities involved in straining to imagine in excess of what is presented and in contemplating an idea that supersedes the limits of the sensible. A feeling of beauty harmonizes presentation and understanding in the well-formed, the sublime shocks both understanding and the imaginative faculty of presentation. Lyotard emphasizes the duality of the shock:

> As it is expounded and deduced in its thematic, sublime feeling is analyzed as a double defiance. Imagination at the limits of *what* it can present does violence to itself in order to present *that* it can no longer present. Reason, for its part, seeks unreasonably, to violate the interdict it imposes on itself and which is strictly critical, the interdict that prohibits it from finding objects corresponding to its concepts in sensible intuition.[45]

Lyotard takes the imagination to turn to unbounded reason in its task but cannot present what supersedes the bounds of sense. The feeling of the sublime presses against the limits of reason and the imagination.

Lyotard shows the mathematical sublime as exhibiting the stress exerted upon the imagination by aiming to supersede the limits of the succession of increasing and decreasing numbers to imagine what reason offers but cannot substantiate, the notion of the infinite all at once and in opposition to any measurable magnitude. Similarly, he sees the dynamical sublime as expressing the tension, the unresolved mixture of pleasure and pain, that constitutes the sublime. The unpresentable idea of absolute causality inspires the imagination to pursue the impossible task of presenting it. The sublime is experienced in assuming the free agency of the subject to be a countervailing sign of the unpresentable infinite of reason.

Lyotard's *Lessons on the Analytic of the Sublime*, in interpreting Kant as expressing the heterogeneity and dissonance between the faculties, confirms his invocation of Kant as a precursor of his philosophical perspective. Lyotard's later writings employ a Kantian vocabulary to express a persisting sense of the limits within which reason operates and of the heterogeneity of discourse. The notion of the sublime testifies to the power of events to disrupt discursive schemes that is evident in *Discours, figure* and in the intensifications of libidinal forces of *Libidinal Economy*. The notion of sublimity expresses Lyotard's enduring sense of the incapacity of discourse to determine the indeterminacy with which events occur. The sublime expresses the *différend* whereby two discursive perspectives cannot capture one another's idioms, and an unresolvable conflict ensues. The sublime is the feeling of such a conflict; it is the profound, exquisite and painful realization of the unresolvable conflicts occasioned by imagination and reason in straining to imagine and compute at their absolute limits. Lyotard notes:

> The differend is to be found at the heart of sublime feeling: at the encounter of the 'two absolutes' equally 'present' to thought, the absolute whole when it conceives, the absolutely measured when it presents. 'Meeting' conveys very little; it is more of a confrontation, for in accordance with its destination, which is to be whole, the absolute of concepts demands to be presented.[46]

He invokes Kant's notion of the sublime to register the character of the feeling that recognizes the unbridgeable heterogeneity of categories and the limits of thought and the imagination. The Kantian sublime expresses the tension involved in testifying to a *différend*, the expression of an incapacity. Lyotard, in *The Differend*, also adverts to the dominance of the economic genre of discourse that threatens to subordinate the heterogeneity of discourse to the imperial purpose of economizing on time. His later writings are marked by a pronounced recognition of the ominous nature of the development of a one-dimensional culture predicated upon the technological logic of saving time in all activities. *The Inhuman* (1988), a set of commissioned lectures, presents this prospect of development in bleak terms. It articulates a profound pessimism over the prospects of social development and about the directionality of history. Notwithstanding the sociological and historical character of the lectures included in *The Inhuman*, they also invoke the disruptive feeling of the *différend*, and the sense of a reality beyond the limits of human conceptualization conveyed by Lyotard's invocation of the sublime. Later essays published in *Lectures d'enfance* and *Postmodern Fables* continue to counterpose the development of a successful system promoted by liberal capitalism to an aesthetic sensibility that is sensitive to what cannot be put into words neatly or be exploited easily for functional purposes.

Sim, in his generally insightful book, *Jean-François Lyotard*, takes Lyotard's introductory reflections on the lectures to be crucial for an interpretation of *The Inhuman*. Lyotard emphazises:

> The suspicion they betray (in both senses of the word) is simple, although double: what if human beings, in humanism's sense, were in the process of, constrained into, becoming inhuman (that's the first part)? And (the second part), what if what is 'proper' to humankind were to be inhabited by the inhuman?[47]

Sim sees *The Inhuman* as combating inhumanity on two fronts. One form of inhumanity is the developing techno-scientific displacement of humanistic goals by the absorption of human beings into goals of functional system-maintenance. Sim sees the other style of inhumanity as arising out of the pressures of socialization that insidiously force human beings to give up on their humanity. Sim concludes: 'It is against these inhumanities and their misappropriation of time, that *The Inhuman* is directed.'[48]

Sim misinterprets Lyotard's conceptions of humanity and inhumanity, as evidenced by the opening line of *The Inhuman*. Lyotard observes, 'Humanism administers lessons to "us".'[49] This sentence is ironic, and thereby highlights that Sim is misguided in taking Lyotard to be defending humanity against inhumanity. For Lyotard, an administered lesson is an oxymoron. Lyotard makes his meaning clear by observing that the lessons administered by contemporary theorists, such as Apel, Rorty, Habermas, Rawls, Searle and Davidson, invariably suffer from failing to interrogate the value that man is assumed to possess. Lyotard's entire philosophy is about interrogating an assumption and a commitment to humanism that Sim takes him to be defending. Lyotard, in *The Inhuman*, opposes the techno-scientific development of a systemizing functionalism, but he is not doing so in the name of humanity. He valorizes the second sort of inhumanity to which he refers in the passage cited by Sim. He defends the uncivilized aspect of inhumanity that is alert to the indetermination of reality which resists but is displaced in the processes of socialization and normalization that humanist theorists invoke to defend the norms of rationality by which human beings are to be administered.

Lyotard, in *The Inhuman*, explores the notion of the inhuman from these two angles. Hence, he takes the capacity to recognize the sublime, indeterminate aspect of an inhuman condition that supersedes the powers of human faculties to be threatened by the development of a technological/scientific culture that subordinates an openness to the experiential limits of human awareness to the imperatives of increasing effectiveness. The lecture 'Can thought go on without a body' is paradigmatic of the style of *The Inhuman*. It is composed of two declarations; one by HE and the other by SHE that in themselves express differential and unmediable patterns of discourse.

The statement by HE sets up the dilemma of the essay. HE imagines that things will come to an end, in that at some point in the future the sun will explode, and the nice questions relating to theory and practice will be obliterated. HE goes on to consider whether it will be possible to make thought go on without a body and hence replicate thinking existence and project it into some distant part of the galaxy. This is the quintessence of the drive underlying the ongoing technological development of humanity that is part of the wider processes of complexification or negentropy that the universe sets in motion. HE imagines that the project is complicated by the involvement of the body in processes of thinking upon which Dreyfus has commented.[50] His detached, abstractly philosophical consideration of the problems of thinking without a body are supplemented by the more radical, passionate thoughts of SHE.

SHE attests to the experiential dimension of thinking, its physicality that interweaves suffering and thinking in the tensions of imagining and conceiving. SHE takes thinking to be different from the external manipulation of data. It is a painful creative process that is indeterminate in its direction. SHE also emphasizes the significance of sex, and the demand of desire that energizes the flow of thinking. SHE retails the multiple insidious ways in which the body is inseparable from thinking, and expresses the positive sense of the inhuman, uncivilized, unprogrammed sense of the inhuman, 'in the secrecy of bodies and thoughts'.[51]

The lectures in *The Inhuman* are on various topics, but all testify to Lyotard's preoccupation with the theme of inhumanity in its two senses. In 'Newman: the instant', Lyotard explores the work of the avant-garde American artist, Barnett Newman. Newman's art is seen as expressing a notion of time in keeping with an inhuman receptivity to experience which is resistant to social, humanistic conditioning and opposed to the wholesale saving of time that motivates the technological/managerial developments in the contemporary world. The minimalist art of Newman is taken by Lyotard as registering the notion of time as an instant happening. Lyotard urges that Newman expresses the secret 'happening' quality of a world that exerts a strain upon human representation. It is in this sense inhuman. Lyotard observes that for Newman the very happening of occurrence is an irreducible flash. He urges that,

> Without this flash, there would be nothing, or there would be chaos. The flash (like the instant) is always there and never there. The world never stops beginning. For Newman, creation is not an act performed by someone; it is what happens (this) in the midst of the indeterminate.[52]

In 'Rewriting modernity' Lyotard rewrites his understanding of modernity and postmodernity. He repudiates a notion of postmodernity as a temporal displacement of a preceding modernity. He identifies the postmodern valorization of indeterminate experimentation with a style of rewriting. He explores a number of possible senses of rewriting, such as the aim of beginning anew or revising past mistakes, but dismisses them as being confounded by the impossibility of starting anew and the revisionist fallacy that misrecognizes the present desire to revise by sundering present inclination from past activity. Lyotard opts for a notion of rewriting modernity as akin to the aesthetic imagination articulated by Kant.

Lyotard takes the process of rewriting to be a concern to flow with and respond to what is given, so that it can meet with the individuality of experience masked in representational language and projects that interpose between the world and its representation. Lyotard observes that his fugitive sense of rewriting modernity may be taken as the postmodern. It is linked to what he depicts as an inhuman openness to the unmasterable givenness of experience. He explicitly counterposes this openness to indetermination to the inhuman modernist project of liberating humanity through science and technology. He maintains, 'Postmodernity is not a new age, but the rewriting of some of the features claimed by modernity, and first of all modernity's claim to ground its legitimacy on the project of liberating humanity as a whole through science and technology.'[53]

In late essays in the collections *Lectures d'enfance* and *Postmodern Fables*, Lyotard continues to express a sense of a developing social system which is successful in promoting complexity and in managing social and technical problems but which desensitizes men and women to the *thing* or the *other* signalled by a sense of a sublime incapacity to represent what is going on.[54] In the *Lectures d'enfance* Lyotard invokes childhood as a metaphor for an unsocialized openness to this sublime sense of an unmasterable, unknowable reality and highlights it in essays that deal with thinkers such as Freud and Kafka who have explored artistic and psychotherapeutic techniques to testify to this reality.[55]

The tone of the essays in *Postmodern Fables* varies from the playfully ironic 'Marie goes to Japan', in which a contemporary lecturer visiting Japan has to negotiate the market-place of cultural capitalism, to the melancholic retrospection of 'Unbeknownst', in which the inevitable demise of the events of 1968 is reviewed, and to the ominous sense of a notion of supra-human evil conveyed in 'A postmodern fable', in which the supersession of the human species in the apparently amoral development of complexity is considered.[56] In all the essays, though, Lyotard juxtaposes the aesthetic sense of attesting to what exceeds rational designation in art and writing with the systemizing of culture that takes place in successful capitalist development. In 'The intimacy of terror', Lyotard contrasts art to the social system in a way that encapsulates the spirit of all the essays: in a world in which 'the system silences noise in its promotion of consensus the creation of a work of art requires the artist to become inhuman'.[57]

Conclusion

Lyotard's work after *The Postmodern Condition* reinforces the notion that there are limits to what can be understood and represented in discourse. There is a profound continuity in Lyotard's explorations of the fecundity of the real which contrasts with the pretensions of discursive thought in aiming to master its unpredictable creativity. Lyotard's later writings also continue to affirm difference insofar as they resist the generalizing trend of theory and cultural development. His philosophical works subsequent to *The Postmodern Condition*, though, develop this philosophical perspective in new ways.

The Differend is a more sophisticated analysis of language and the limits of discourse than is presented in *The Postmodern Condition*, where questions about the individuation of language games and the functioning of incommensurability had not been pressed. *The Differend* is an austere, sophisticated study of language, which highlights the profound incommensurability of a *différend*, something that demands an expression but is not put into words because it cannot be accommodated by a prevailing pattern of phrasing. Lyotard's notion of a *différend* is evidenced by the uncomfortable feeling that accompanies the misbegotten, uncommunicative dialogue between interlocutors deeply divided by ideology. For example, a dialogue between last-ditch loyalists and fanatical republicans in Ireland or between fascists and liberals does not lend itself to a neutral means of communication allowing for mutual understanding.

There remain problems, however, with the view of language maintained in *The Differend*. The theoretical specification of a *différend* is a highly general identification of something that appears to transcend Lyotard's own specification of the particularity of patterns of discourse. It is also unclear what recognizing a *différend* is to achieve, because it might be followed up in a number of ways. Arguably, remedial, ethical action should be seen as warranted by the exclusion of a perspective. Moreover, as Frank observes, Lyotard's analysis of language, insofar as it is designed to diminish the sense that human beings are unified subjects able to reflect upon the discourses in which they are involved, seems to undermine the ethical force of Lyotard's sensitivity to *différends*.[58] Why does a *différend* matter if it is not to be linked to a sense of an individual's powers of autonomy and agency? Again, a view of language that minimizes the powers of human agents in linguistic processes begs the questions of how and why human beings are being presumed to show concern for *différends*.

In *Lessons on the Analytic of the Sublime*, Lyotard highlights the non-demonstrable tautegorical feeling of the sublime as registering how *différends* are experienced and recognized. Its designated indeterminate, incommunicable character rehearses but does not relieve the tensions to which rational analysis of a *différend* is subject. In *The Inhuman*, Lyotard contrasts the experiential indeterminate context into which human beings are born with the unidirectionality of current social development. He imagines the inhuman techno-scientific project of developing a smoothly operating complex system as liable to obliterate the stirrings of a sublime awareness of the incalculable nature of reality itself. This reading of contemporary social development, which Lyotard himself designates as banal, informs his later political thought that valorizes dysfunctional, inhuman individuality rather than the smooth-running system in which individuals are situated.[59] Lyotard's sociological reading of the present and his projection of an ominous future, however, has been characterized perceptively by Anderson as assuming the style of grand narrative generally deprecated by Lyotard.[60]

Lyotard's identification of the essence of reality with a non-discursive, melancholic inhuman feeling of its tensions and unmasterability is evident in *Signed Malraux*, a late work published in 1996. Lyotard's fascination with Malraux is expressed through the scholarship and imaginative empathy extended in this biography. Lyotard evokes and responds to Malraux's sense of the nihilism of Western civilization and his heroic, desperate concern to register the unresolvable tensions of being in the world. Lyotard reflects upon Malraux's adventurous lifestyle that courts danger and notoriety to leave a stamp on existence, a signing of his life that will supersede the unfathomable transience of existence. Likewise, Lyotard is impressed by the force of Malraux's extraordinary imaginative *Antimemoirs*, which is seen as expressing a way in which identity can be claimed or rather reclaimed from the ongoing press of events.

Lyotard recognizes a kindred spirit in Malraux, who has an aesthetic sense of how the imaginary museum of artistic, creative objects can testify to, without explaining, the imaginative spirit of events swept away by their endless succession and masked by their cultural affiliations.[61] From the opening chapter's evocative suggestion of Malraux's identification of death as the reality from which men flee and which women mourn, a sense of a profound *différend* between men and women and a feeling for the nihilistic finitude of existence that is seen as haunting Malraux's life are established as themes of *Signed Malraux*. Lyotard remarks, 'This phobic expression for the viscous discharge of lives and their consignment to the depths constantly returns to Malraux's writings.'[62] Lyotard traces the nothingness of civilization that spurs Malraux constantly to risk death and probe the surfaces of cultures to glimpse an underlying, but ultimately unknowable, reality. What remains for Malraux and indeed for Lyotard himself is an unanswered and unanswerable inhuman question: 'There remains the question . . . The question is the enigma.'[63]

Signed Malraux is a consummation of Lyotard's work in its melancholic, sceptical resolve to testify to the value of Malraux's assimilation of the nihilism of existence and in his affecting quest to testify to the mystery and unassimilability of events. It completes the sceptical, questing turn that marks Lyotard's philosophical perspective from the outset. In 'Limbo', the final chapter of *Signed Malraux*, Malraux is praised for his unflinching grasp of the singularity that marks Western civilization, that is, its inability to provide an answer to the meaning of a life.[64] Lyotard relates sympathetically Malraux's diagnosis of the West and declares, 'Once rid of ideologies and fashions, its singularity (i.e. Western civilization) becomes brute questioning. The only meaning left is powerlessness to respond.'[65] Lyotard's philosophy can be seen as climaxing in a melancholic reverence for what eludes human conception. The closing expression of his thought attests to what is inhuman in the human imagination, the sublime sense of what exceeds discursive articulation.

5 • Lyotard and the Political

Introduction

Lyotard reworks his political vocabulary and sense of the political throughout his career. New idioms are fashioned constantly in a manner that testifies to his commitment to the values of invention and difference. Just as there are persisting features of Lyotard's theoretical standpoint, however, so there are recurring preoccupations in Lyotard's politics. His politics are intimately related to philosophical imperatives that are encapsulated in his break from grand narratives and in his concomitant recognition of incommensurable difference, contingency and intractability. His politics trace an opposition to universalizing theories and a hostility to schemes designed to order politics according to general criteria. Even while a Marxist, Lyotard exhibits a sensitivity to singular events and a diversity of social factors that render practice intractable to the terms of a purportedly universal Marxist theory.

The interweaving of Lyotard's philosophical standpoint with his politics threatens the rationale of this chapter in that his very theoretical opposition to rationalism has political implications. Lyotard's politics are difficult to isolate.[1] They resist neat compartmentalization into a public sphere that may be treated as being independent from a private realm. The force of Lyotard's politics turns upon his opposition to generalizing forces that are theoretical as well as social and political. What animates his politics is a determination to resist closure wherever it is threatened. Consequently, he can see seemingly apolitical moves that disrupt or subvert established constrictive patterns as eminently political. Language for Lyotard is contingent and exhibits patterns of discursive variety. A threat to override the autonomy of a form of discourse, for Lyotard, constitutes an injustice, exclusion of a discursive perspective, that demands a political response.[2] In the context of the manifest success of liberal capitalism recognized by Lyotard in his later writings as assuring the successful development of society and ensuring the neo-totalitarian promotion of a systemic instrumentalism in Western societies, the very act of creative writing is seen as registering a sense of what exceeds a gathering social conformity.

While Lyotard's notion of the political resists conventional characterization, it can be understood as linking on to the categories that it intends to subvert.[3] Hence, the force of Lyotard's notion of the political can be highlighted by focusing on his confrontation with conventionally defined political events. This chapter will review Lyotard's politics by attending to his engagement with and reflection upon publicly recognized political events, as well as exploring the further reaches of his notion of the political. This review is divided into three sections. The first deals with Lyotard's essays on the Franco-Algerian conflict that were written for the journal of the Marxist group to which he belonged, *Socialisme ou barbarie*. The second section discusses Lyotard's essays that track his own involvement in the events of May 1968 and its aftermath. The final section is less focused upon a set of well-known political events, as Lyotard tends to withdraw from direct engagement in the public arena. It analyses Lyotard's political thinking from the end of the 1970s to his death in 1998, considering his development of a pagan politics of indeterminacy and difference, and reviewing his late standpoint in which he continues to valorize a dissonant alertness to indetermination while recognizing the inescapability of an instrumentalist liberal capitalism.

This analysis refers to a number of Lyotard's texts, but, where possible, the set of Lyotard's writings edited by Readings under the title *Political Writings* is drawn upon to illustrate themes. This book conveniently collects together many of his essays on the Algerian war of independence, the student revolt of 1968 and more recent essays on the 'political' role of intellectuals and the menacing qualities of a developing system that is seen as neo-totalitarian in its systemic promotion of the instrumental.[4] Lyotard's politics draw upon the terms and positions marked out in his major theoretical works. The distinctiveness of his politics, however, is highlighted by essays that focus upon specific social, cultural and political phenomena.

There is continuity and development in Lyotard's politics. A sensitivity to difference and a resistance to closure are recurring themes but they are formulated and accented differently during the course of his career. His distinctive sense of the political can be seen as emerging out of his reflections on the Algerian War. The conflict between France and insurgent, native Algerians posed significant political questions in post-war France. In his Algerian essays, which analyse the conflict and its effects in France as well as Algeria, Lyotard reveals a developing sense of the strains exhibited by the *grand narrative* of Marxism. The writings testify to his questioning of the explanatory reach of Marxism in its incorporation of anti-colonialism as an aspect of its totalizing vision.

Lyotard's active involvement in and celebration of the revolutionary events of May 1968 express his support for a dissonant, disruptive politics that challenges conventional political schemes. His drift away from Marxism is marked by the writing of his provocative *Libidinal Economy*. He reinstates a concern for justice and politics in *Just Gaming* and *The Postmodern Condition*, though his opposition to grand narratives of politics such as Marxism is pronounced. He embraces an indeterminate politics where the rules are neither to be assumed nor fixed. An aestheticized sensitivity to injustice is the focal point of *The Differend*, where justice is seen to depend upon a sublime testimony to the wrong that occurs when a standpoint or perspective cannot be expressed. Lyotard's later essays on politics tend to counterpose an inhuman sublime feeling of the conditionality of existence with the inhuman development of a technical-scientific system that, in its instrumentalist social intercourse, threatens to extinguish all traces of openness to being.

Lyotard's notion of politics is extraordinary and intense.[5] On the one hand, he sees politics as highly significant at all stages of his career. Resistance to the imperialism of grand narratives, and to the suffocating conformity induced by social development, as well as the ethical imperative to acknowledge difference, are vital matters that determine the very texture of life. On the other hand, he denies the availability of criteria for deciding political questions. The ensuing tension ensures that political questions are live, energizing ones that cannot be left to experts – usual suspects for the role of *experts* include political leaders, intellectuals and commentators. These candidates for controlling politics are denied authority by Lyotard on the radical grounds that there are no authoritative criteria in politics. The difference between Lyotard and mainstream contemporary political philosophy is manifest and is rightly acknowledged by Williams.[6] Conventional goals and values that are assigned to politics such as consensus, stability, peace and emancipation are either repudiated or relegated in status by Lyotard.

Lyotard's notion of the radically under-determined character of thought and action underpins his intensification of the political. For Lyotard, the exercise of creating something new and undetermined harmonizes with the indeterminate presence of reality. His valorization of formless creativity is the reverse side of his repudiation of rationalizing forms of closure, the grand narratives of humanistic liberation. His valorization of creative resistance to closure is expressed differently at different moments of his career. His early revolutionary Marxism is followed by an espousal of disruptive revolutionary action. Subsequently, he exhibits a playful agonistic promotion of plurality, and that is followed by a less optimistic concern to attest to *différends*. In his late essays this sensitivity to *différends* is combined with a melancholic, defensive resistance to, or independence from, absorption within a system demanding conformity.

Lyotard is opposed to forms of intellectual and organizational closure that aspire to domesticate the otherness of material reality and to thwart inventiveness. His sensitivity to the closure of even an 'open' form of politics highlights the paradoxically reactive aspect of his notion of the political. The characteristically transitive nature of his politics derogates from the indeterminacy that he imagines as constituting the secret inhuman core of reality. A political move for Lyotard is a counter-offensive rather than a piece of independent construction. His insistence on the incommensurability of standpoints operates so as to undermine or devalue the deliberative construction of shared rules and principles to order a public association of individuals. The political prescription of regulatory standards, the maintenance of public rituals and the codification, communication and enforcement of performances are taken by Lyotard as occluding and even threatening the profound, unrepresentable singularity of an event and the contestability of any prescription. The force of his politics resides in its philosophically inspired general resistance to conventional or enforced formulas.

Lyotard's general deprecation of the value of stable consensual norms and his dismissal of the collaborative construction of shared norms and practices are questionable responses to the complex contextual conditions inspiring concrete forms of resistance. Resistance in practice invariably lends itself to more than either a testimony to an injustice or a reactive quietistic affirmation of the indeterminacy of existence. The determination to construct a just and harmonious basis for social interaction is an entrenched social aspiration that challenges theorists to undertake constructive social theorizing. This impetus for practical and theoretical political construction should not be ignored due to a tendency for the social *system* to arrest the imaginative possibilities of political construction. A philosophical preoccupation with deconstruction is justifiable as a moment within a wider constructive political project; its pursuit as an end in itself is problematic.

The spirit of Lyotard's persistent uneasiness over the claims of consensus and political unity is allied to an evocative, sociological reading of the present that characteristically sees difference as being threatened. Grand narratives are condemned for subordinating difference to the achievement of general goals and he observes the contemporary development of a social system that incorporates difference and critique within its operations as being ominously recalcitrant to an alertness to what deflects from the requirements of system management. Lyotard's tendency to juxtapose an individualized notion of a resistant sensibility to a generalized conception of a vast and undifferentiated system is not altogether a happy one. His sociological and historical reading of the present and the recent past appears to emulate the grand narratives stigmatized in *The Postmodern Condition*.[7] The sweep of Lyotard's generalizing perspective ignores alternative standpoints and subverts his own commitment to epistemological openness. Again, later his melancholy testimony to the clash between an encompassing system and a fugitive world of inner resistance is a poignant aesthetic evocation of the sense of loss engendered by technical/scientific progress, but it fails to address a plurality of questions that might be asked about contemporary social and political practices and their consonance with the aspirations of individuals.

Lyotard's eschewal of constructive political theorizing and his valorization of disruptive difference and concomitant derogation of social ideals, such as trust, equality and distributive justice, encapsulate the limitations of his political standpoint. These deficiencies, however, are the reverse side of his provocative disturbance of the easy assumptions entertained in fashionable political doctrines that favour consensus or concentrate on establishing an equitable distribution of rights and goods. Lyotard's political perspective serves as a powerful antidote to the very idea of consensus as a virtue and it challenges the reasonableness of the distribution of publicly determined goods amongst individuals whose identities are assumed to be interchangeable so as not to impact upon the nature of the distributed goods.[8] Lyotard highlights disparate, incommensurable standpoints that require resistance to standardized formulas of the public good. His philosophy stretches conventional notions of the political. His notion of the *différend* itself serves to identify the *différend* expressed in his political thought.

Algeria

The development of Lyotard's notion of the political, and indeed the politicization of his notion of the philosophical, can be traced to his analyses of the Algerian conflict between native insurgents and colonial France, in a series of essays he wrote for the journal of the Marxist group *Socialism ou barbarisme*. This dissident Marxist group gave Lyotard responsibility for its Algerian section in 1955. He was disturbed by the dogmatisms of the French Communist Party and unimpressed by the relative orthodoxies of non-party Trotskyist groups. Lyotard's commitment to Marxism, even the unconventional and self-consciously *open* Marxism of *Socialisme ou barbarie*, shaped and circumscribed his approach to the Algerian question. He approached the politics of Algeria with assumptions and governing concepts drawn from a Marxist canon.

Hence Lyotard's Algerian essays can be seen as deriving from a particular grand narrative with circumscribed sociological, historical and political concepts. On the other hand, in the retrospective essay 'The name of Algeria', Lyotard explains how his engagement with Algeria was personal and experiential as well as being directed by a preformulated political standpoint. He explains how his teaching at a high school and personal contacts in Algeria opened his perspective to a sense of a *différend* between colonial France and colonized Algeria. While retrospect lends itself to an anachronistic misreading of the past in the light of the present, Lyotard's Algerian writings disclose a simultaneous adherence to Marxist ideology and an uncomfortable, half-acknowledged expression of a novel vocabulary exhibiting a post-Marxist framework of thought.

In the article, 'The situation in North Africa', Lyotard examines the brooding, conflictual atmosphere of North Africa in the wake of uprisings, riots and protests in Algeria, Tunisia and Morocco that had led to independence for Morocco, autonomy for Tunisia and simmering tension in Algeria. Lyotard examines the messy politics of these countries. He recognizes colonial control as vitiating class allegiances and as incubating nationalism due to its inciting of a spontaneous reaction against its apparatus of oppression. He recognizes the distinct absence in Algeria of a powerful indigenous bourgeoisie. He disparages the French Communist Party's concern to forge transnational links between France and the colonies, because he sees it as a ruse by which the interests of indigenous peoples are to be subordinated to the hegemonic control of France and the French Communist Party. He is critical of the assimilation of difference. Lyotard's complex analysis of the situation stretches the conceptual repertoire of classical Marxism. However, he does not break with categories that seek to impose a Marxist model of development on the situation in North Africa. He observes: 'Lastly, it is important to understand and to make it understood that the only solutions (the solutions that none in the struggle can provide) are class solutions...'[9]

Lyotard's distinctly Marxist perspective is also highlighted in his 1957 article, 'The North African bourgeoisie'. In this piece he focuses upon the power politics operated by the newly established regimes in Morocco and Tunisia and the prospect of Algerian nationalism overturning French imperialism. His critique of the new ruling classes in Tunisia and Morocco discloses a Marxist teleological narrative.

> Half-measures, reconciliation, reforms: as soon as the class struggle emerges from the nationalist swamp in the 'backward' countries, new ruling classes seek to stick it back there once more. But they cannot hinder their very efforts from demystifying the workers little by little and leading them finally to envisage the struggle in the light of their own interests.[10]

Lyotard's 1958 article, 'Algerian contradictions exposed', reveals a frank scepticism over the prospects for transnational class solidarity and a readiness to question and jettison Marxist nostrums. He recognizes the indifference of French workers to the situation of the colonized. 'When the concepts or schemas are refuted by historical reality over a period of forty years, the task of revolutionaries is to discard them without remorse and to replace them with others that make an effective struggle possible.'[11] Lyotard, in this essay, recognizes the force and appeal of nationalism in Algeria. He sees nationalism as overriding class and class antagonisms. While he continues to envisage class as a factor breeding antagonisms, he approximates a decidedly non-Marxist, non-reductive way of reading nationalism. He observes,

> The ideology that animates the nationalist movement, even if in the final analysis it is composite, is lived as a unanimous response to a situation unanimously felt by all Algerians (just as, for their part, all the Europeans of Algeria unanimously respond to their situation, despite the internal antagonisms that actually set them at odds).[12]

Rather than seeing nationalism as a smokescreen deployed opportunistically to achieve goals derived from class interests, Lyotard sees nationalism as an effective lived reality, which the insurgent FLN promotes and from which it draws support.

In 'Algerian contradictions exposed' Lyotard traces the impact on French politics and culture of the situation in Algeria. He notes the brutalizing effect of the barbarism practised by the colonial army on native Algerians upon the mentality of French soldiers serving in Algeria, and the radicalizing effect of colonial propaganda placed in the French press upon the attitudes of the French political right. He also highlights the absence of solidarity shown by French workers for the Algerians. On widening his argument to note the general lack of solidarity shown by European workers for anti-colonial struggles, he observes how classic Marxist thought 'remains abstract'.[13] French workers, according to Lyotard, are unmoved by imperialism and theories of imperialism, but are affected by the death of a friend or son.

The attitudes of the left towards Algeria are diagnosed as being insensitive to the challenge presented by a foreign, distant situation. He condemns the left for advocating compromises that would impose an alien judgement on Algerian resistance. The French Communist Party's willingness to accept imperialism is ascribed to its Stalinist preoccupation with retaining influence in Algeria. A French presence in Algeria is seen as suiting a Communist Party that aims at forestalling its prospective domination by American capital. French arms are rated as superior to American capital, because they allow for a lingering influence by the French Communist Party. Lyotard's antipathy to Marxist dogma is evident in his critique of the Trotskyist position. French Trotskyists are criticized for a dogmatic insistence on 'permanent revolution' in a context that Lyotard diagnoses as rendering the slogan irrelevant. He dismisses their standpoint as 'a stupefying example of the degree of false abstraction that a political reflection can attain when it is steeped in dogmatism'.[14]

Lyotard's essays on Algeria reflect a process of opening out to events as they are happening. They signpost his development of a distinctly post-Marxist standpoint. The essays show how his confrontation with a colonial situation engenders its comprehension along lines that are not dictated by a notion of class struggle. The events in North Africa inspire Lyotard to reflect back on what is happening in France, and to interrogate developed forms of capitalism and the contemporary character of capital and class in ways that stretch and challenge Marxist categories. Gane has rightly pointed to the significance of this aspect of Lyotard's reflections on Algeria.[15] Lyotard's 'The state and politics in the France of 1960' notes how the French left, in canvassing support for the French bourgeois regime against a fascist reaction, are beguiled by their ideology into misperceiving working-class attitudes and underplaying the prevalent mass apathy in contemporary France.[16]

Lyotard sees the Gaullist regime of the Fifth Republic of France as being primarily motivated to undertake the political modernization of France that is required by big capital. At the same time, Lyotard attends to persisting weaknesses within post-war France, notably its lack of functional mass political parties that could enlist support for the new regime, and the persisting uncertainties arising out of the Algerian situation. Lyotard concludes that France is entangled in an unwinnable war with the Arab population. Notwithstanding this analysis of the Algerian War, he is withering in his critique of the left's call for mass demonstrations and strikes to offset the prospects of a 'fascist' coup. He despairs at the left's reliance on anachronistic formulas, such as a popular front against fascism. He takes the term fascism to exhibit a similar redundancy to that of the concept of the working class. It is seen as a token of a failure to think anew and to recognize what is happening. Lyotard castigates the French Communist Party and other leftist organizations by remarking:

> They do nothing but chew over the old slogan of the union of the left; they would almost be thankful if fascism existed because it as at least a situation with which they are *already* familiar, for which they already have tactics prepared. The fact that these tactics have always failed matters little; at bottom, they cried fascism in order to bring to life, and

at the same time, to give life to themselves. This is no longer politics; it is the hypermemory of the dying.[17]

Lyotard expatiates on how the contemporary French working class no longer conforms to its classic Marxist identity. Its radical depoliticization, and indifference to any global project of emancipation, is recognized. Lyotard signals the need to 'open our eyes, to identify the immense transformation in the everyday life of the working class'.[18] He sees contemporary capitalism, operating in a variety of styles, including Fordism and Taylorism and a reliance on statist welfarism, as succeeding in incorporating the workers into its project of endless accumulation, production and consumption. The cost of this incorporation is exhibited in what is diagnosed as a profound and enervating alienation, which is discernible in the exteriority of work and the increasing externality of processed needs to the actual felt experience of living. Capitalism, according to Lyotard, is assimilating the proletariat. At the end of the essay 'The state and politics in France in 1960', he identifies the contextual challenge to revolutionaries: 'But the problem posed by this profound erosion of activities and ideals is precisely that of how to know by what means the revolutionary project can henceforth express itself, organise itself, fight.'[19]

Throughout his various essays on Algeria, Lyotard is ambivalent towards the FLN (the Algerian National Liberation Front). He combines a recognition of its success in welding together a revolutionary nationalist force, and a respect for its role in the surge towards Algerian independence, with a scepticism over what it will achieve in its post-independence future. In 'Algeria: seven years after' and 'Algeria evacuated', he catalogues his ambivalence over the post-independence regime in Algeria. He observes its lack of direction in the aftermath of independence and a concomitant reassemblage of the bureaucratic means of stifling revolutionary energy. In the retrospective essay of 1989, 'The name of Algeria', Lyotard designates this dualistic position an 'intimate différend'.[20] The evocation of the term *différend* highlights the relevance of Lyotard's overtly political writings to the development of his later philosophy. Notably, his political reading of the Algerian crisis and war contributes to his disavowal of the capacity imputed to *grand narratives* of mapping reality. Lyotard draws one single paradoxical lesson from his engagement with Algeria, namely that one cannot import a preconceived body of thought into a political situation. He observes, 'But thought must yield to the evidence that the grand narratives of emancipation, beginning (or ending) with "ours", that of radical Marxism, have lost their intelligibility and their substance.'[21]

1968

Algeria was the site of Lyotard's working through, or what in *The Inhuman* he terms as rewriting, an increasingly critical understanding of Marxism.[22] In the course of the Algerian struggle he recognizes how Marxism cannot assimilate the Algerian revolt. He sees it as misperceiving the nature and attitudes of the French working class. May 1968, the student revolt and its revolutionary vibrations, generates the conditions whereby Lyotard enacts and portrays a revolutionary political standpoint which drifts further from traditional Marxism. He expresses this standpoint in the appropriately entitled *Dérive à partir de Marx et Freud*.[23] In essays relating to the events of 1968 and its aftermath, Lyotard depicts revolutionary politics in acts that are defined by their refusal to fit with any preconceived practice or theory. A revolutionary act is thereby severed from a guiding theory or totalizing narrative.

The essay 'Preamble to a charter' stakes out a revolutionary notion of the role and organization of higher education that abjures the bureaucratization of universities and specifies the goal of 'deconstructing the institution'.[24] Lyotard celebrates May 1968. He represents it as the revolutionary 'spirit that shook the nation'.[25] In the essay's exhortation to the Faculty of Letters at Nanterre University to re-organize education at Nanterre, Lyotard draws upon the excitement generated by the events of May 1968 to register a counter-authoritarian educational manifesto. He highlights how the events of May 1968 challenge the entire system of cultural repression. He hereby departs from the terms of a classically Marxist account of repression, which focuses upon its alleged economic basis and political expression, to emphasize the significance of cultural repression. The cultural reinforcement of the systemic character of the status quo is what Lyotard takes the students of 1968 to be challenging. He sees the revolutionary *élan* of the students as being directed against the repression of desire that marks the Marxist East as well as the capitalist West. Desire, in its destabilizing motivation of energy, is invoked as the goal of a revolution that is to break with traditional political forms. Lyotard observes: 'This (the crisis of 1968) is not a will for political renewal but the desire for something different, the desire for a different society, for different relations between people.'[26]

'Preamble to a charter' takes revolutionary action to be specifically opposed to existing and preformulated notions of the political. Revolutionary action is seen as being dedicated to disruption and inventiveness. In this spirit of revolutionary politics, Lyotard summons higher education to break with power by urging radicals to make education undertake comprehensive criticism and secure the 'liberation of the power of expression'.[27] He calls for education to engage in 'critique as a whole', and in so doing, to engage in physical resistance as well as battles with words.[28]

In contrast to the heady revolutionary atmosphere enlivening 'Preamble to a charter', 'Nanterre, here, now' (1970) is an essay written in the aftermath of the repression directed against the student unrest. The tone of the essay reflects a retreat from the infectious revolutionary enthusiasm entertained two years previously. The focus is now upon coping with and reacting to the authoritarian politics that have been brought into play by the university and state hierarchies, as well as the leftist groups that mimic the authoritarian style of the public institutions. Marxism is seen as a stale replica of the establishment to which it is opposed. The classic Marxist political rhetoric of invoking a *sacred* name, such as Mao, Lenin and Marx himself, is disparaged by Lyotard as being as unimaginative as capitalist consumerism. Lyotard declares the redundancy of an organized assault on central power as epitomized by the October Revolution in Russia. He urges that a true revolutionary politics is not to be enacted as part of a script that has been rehearsed in advance. He advocates 'interventions of the *here and now* kind'.[29]

For Lyotard, a revolutionary politics consists in the staging of disruptive events, such as the boycotting of ticket punching in Metro stations. These events are seen as disruptive precisely because they eschew a logic either dictated by or against the system. The aim of revolutionary action is seen as breaking completely with aspirations to order, classify and control events. The distance that Lyotard has travelled from orthodox Marxism is marked in his evocation of a disruptive revolutionary politics that disparages the Marxist tradition of promoting political education and discipline amongst its members. For Lyotard, the opposite is to be upheld. He favours an apedagogy that intimates a break with all orthodoxies. In a subsequent essay, 'March 23', Lyotard testifies to the positive impact the events of 1968 exerted upon his own style and sense of revolutionary action. The essay serves as a memorial to the Movement of March 22, a revolutionary group in the thick of events at Nanterre. In writing about this movement, Lyotard abjures the notion of writing its history. The movement is celebrated for its very staging of disruptive events that broke with elaborate justifications or narratives that constitute historical writing. He explicitly praises the movement for extending critique of the system to areas which traditional 'big politics' had ignored.[30] Lyotard urges that the systemic character of bureaucratic systemic capitalism demands revolutionary action that will break with the very form of its organized power.

In the introductory essay to *Dérive à partir de Marx et Freud*, Lyotard sees the affirmation of desire as being revolutionary, in its refusal to engage with the system and in its disdain for engaging in rationalist critique that compromises its affirmative power.[31] In his elaboration of his contemporary theoretical standpoint in 'On theory: an interview', Lyotard denigrates traditional political organizations and takes deconstruction to be the only effective type of political activity. He sees deconstructive action as the form of politics that is directed against the repressive, concealing dimension of order. He refers to the exemplary revolutionary activities of the *'here and now* kind' of the Movement of March 22.[32]

The system, difference and 1984

The events of 1968 helped to shape Lyotard's sense of the political as being at variance with mainstream traditional politics of the left and right. Whereas in his essays on Algeria the traditional, supra-nationalist Marxist vocabulary was stretched by the admission of a radical difference between Algerians and the French, in the essays relating to 1968 a celebration of spontaneous, disruptive action is explicitly counterposed to Marxist orthodoxies. Lyotard's distinctive sense of a politics that is dedicated to punching holes in a system, the skin of which is tightly drawn across refractory desires and differences, is heightened by the experience of 1968. This sense of a revolutionary politics also connects with and helps to explain his most notable works of general philosophy. The repudiation of Marx and valorization of desire in *Libidinal Economy*, the celebration of heterogeneity in *The Postmodern Condition* and the recognition of absolute incommensurability in *The Differend* resonate with his repudiation of order and its counterpart, an oppositional order. Politics, for Lyotard, highlights a resistance to conformity and order. This notion of resistance lies at the heart of his philosophy.

The nature of Lyotard's political standpoint, and indeed his entire philosophy, lends itself to critique rather than construction, dissidence rather than solidarity. In the 1970s Lyotard adopts paganism as a name for an attitude that counterposes assertive particularity to totalizing theories and politics. Paganism is a deconstructive attitude that Lyotard detects in diverse quarters, including in the women's struggle. In the collection of essays, *Rudiments païens*, 'Femininité dans la metalangue' urges that feminism opposes the dominance of the unifying discourse presided over by men. Lyotard observes: 'If "reality" lies, it follows that men in all their claims to construct meaning, to speak the Truth are themselves only a minority in a *patchwork* where it becomes impossible to establish and validly determine any order.'[33]

In *Just Gaming* (1979) Lyotard takes paganism to comprise the formulation and enactment of justice without recourse to grand narratives. Justice is to be determined by indeterminate reflective judgement. Lyotard aims to press judgement beyond what can be justified determinately, by invoking a Kantian regulative judgement of reason as a model for establishing hypothetical, indeterminate criteria for justice. The upshot is that Lyotard sees justice as a matter of regulating indeterminately the practices within and between a plurality of different language games.[34] The indeterminacy of political judgement highlights the problematic character of a politics that is contravened by determinate general judgements, the trademarks of grand narratives, identified as definitive of modernity in *The Postmodern Condition*. In *The Postmodern Condition* Lyotard elaborates a politics of resistance that enjoins a postmodern expression of difference in resistance to generalizing grand narratives and to the development of a one-dimensional social system based upon technical, pragmatic efficiency. His espousal of variety between and invention within language games derives point from the prospect of enervating closure discernible within the development of this system, though he detects signs of a postmodern indeterminacy in scientific imagination and educational strategies for manipulating data.

In the essays of the early 1980s collected together in *Tombeau d'intellectuel et autres papiers*, Lyotard reviews social and political prospects in similar terms. In 'The differend' (1982), he looks at the prospective role of the contemporary French Socialist government as liable to gravitate to that of managing the capitalist system. He refuses to accord intellectuals a privileged political role, because he sees them as lacking a determinate political expertise. However, he does highlight the significance of a more circumscribed role that intellectual observers of the social scene can enact. They can testify to *différends* wherever an exclusion of a group or voice occurs. This resistance to closure and injustice is a characteristic formulation of Lyotard's politics, in its forswearing of grand narratives to focus instead on particular instances of oppression.

In the title essay, 'The tomb of the intellectual' (1983), Lyotard ruminates on the invitation extended by Max Gallo, the spokesperson of the contemporary French Socialist government, to intellectuals to open up a debate on how France is to emulate rival nations in terms of social and economic performance. Lyotard dismisses the appeal as exemplifying the constricted character of a governmental agenda. He takes Gallo's appeal to reflect the tendency to reduce *grand* intellectual questions to a form of system management that removes disturbing, imaginative questions from the agenda. Lyotard, however, also reflects on the essential redundancy of the traditional pronouncements of intellectuals on great public matters. This kind of politics, for Lyotard, expires with grand narratives. There are neither universalizing projects, nor universalizing intellectuals. He concludes his review of the redundancy of the traditional intellectual by observing that the decline of the universal role of the intellectual can 'free thought and life from totalizing obsessions'.[35]

In 'A svelte appendix to the postmodern question', an essay of 1982 published in the same collection, Lyotard indulges in a reading of capitalism that perceives it as releasing the infinity of desire. He sees capital and its valorization of desire as invading language in the developing post-industrial society. He disparages invoking the language of alienation because he sees such language as drawing upon either theology or a philosophy of nature to oppose this development.[36] Lyotard is firmly against totalizing political postures. He expresses no fear of the commodification of language, though he is mindful of how states might manipulate information machines. Instead, he commends a postmodern, svelte attention to particular possibilities of language, whereby the richness of language in its indeterminate forms is to be enhanced rather than reduced to the requirements of a one-dimensional system.

In the later 1980s, Lyotard's reading of contemporary society assumes a more melancholic air. Whereas his writings in response to the events of May 1968 show a revolutionary *élan*, and his embrace of paganism and of postmodernism are enacted with a *jouissance*, his later essays tend to betray a burgeoning pessimism. Justice, in *The Differend*, is seen as demanding a sublime attestation to the feeling of a *différend* that occurs when a standpoint or perspective is excluded from discourse. The pursuit of justice is misrepresented in a call for remedial action or a politics of assertion. As Drolet observes, a more assertive standpoint might itself violate the *différend*. 'Our sensibilities toward justice create within us an auto-critique; one that constrains us from making statements for fear they will violate the différend.'[37] A sense of disenchanted pessimism, acutely aware of the limits within which politics operates, is reinforced by Lyotard's preoccupation with Auschwitz and the Jews in his later work. In his study *Heidegger and 'the Jews'*, Lyotard takes the Jews to stand for 'jews', who represent all the marginalized figures of Western culture whose marginalization reflects the culture's failure to deal with difference itself. He remarks, 'The "jews", never at home, wherever they are cannot be integrated, converted or expelled.'[38] Heidegger's silence on Auschwitz and the Jews is condemned for its complicity in the injustice of forgetting to honour those who are excluded from Western history and its discourse.

In his later writings Lyotard juxtaposes the development of an inhuman technocratic society with the imaginative inhuman sensibility that recognizes the stirrings of being and difference that form the context of human experience. Recognizing the danger of closure inherent in the development of an increasingly one-dimensional society, Lyotard takes seriously and reanimates Orwell's critique of 'big brother'. He reasserts Orwell's admonitions in a postmodern idiom. The essence of Lyotard's standpoint is revealed in his 1985 letter to David Rogozinski, 'Gloss on resistance', in *The Postmodern Explained to Children*, that explicitly reflects upon the meaning and continued significance of Orwell's *1984*. In a subsequent interview,

Lyotard himself draws attention to its importance in signalling his conception of society and politics.[39] In considering *1984* Lyotard locates resistance in the act of writing itself. Totalitarianism is seen to be most complete when it suffuses the language that allows for expression, and it is to be combated by the formulation of new expressions that resist the language of Newspeak. For Lyotard, the act of writing evokes what is not already formulated. It is an *event*, a happening that resists location on a map of meaning. Lyotard also focuses upon Orwell's recognition of the body and its unique sensibility as attesting to a singularity that imaginary and real big brothers are set on effacing.

Lyotard recognizes that the threat posed by totalitarian states such as Nazi Germany and Stalinist Russia has receded, but he sees the totalizing tendencies evident in the actual year of 1984 to justify the admonitions of Orwell. Lyotard sees the real basis of this totalitarianism as now residing in the economic and the mass-mediatized spheres rather than the narrowly political.[40] He recognizes the prescience of Orwell by remarking:

> It is a commonplace to say that our situation in 1984 is not the one that Orwell foresaw. But such a denial is too hasty. It is correct at least for the West, as long as this situation is understood in a narrowly politico-logical or sociological sense. But when we consider the generalisation of binary languages, the effacement of the difference between the here-and-now and the there-and-then which results from the spread of telerelations, the forgetting of feelings in favour of strategies (concomitant with the hegemony of commerce), we can see that the threats levelled at writing, love and singularity, because of this situation, our situation, are essentially akin to the threats described by Orwell.[41]

Lyotard, in taking seriously the threat of *1984*, repudiates a general resistance to a totalizing society that would put its faith in an alternative set of social ideals opposed to big brother. He rejects the line of intellectual resistance that traces a path from the Enlightenment to Sartre and Foucault. Rather, he traces resistance to a recognition of the unconscious bodily stirrings of a singularity that registers something that is outside the system and its communicative network.

The notion of resistance that Lyotard considers in 'Gloss on resistance' is melancholic and defensive. In the essay 'The survivor' (1988), a discussion of Arendt that is included in *Lectures d'enfance*, Lyotard concludes that resistance to what he terms contemporary neo-totalitarianism cannot be effected by revolutionary action, but only in an attesting, lonely judgement.[42] The present and the future are portrayed in equally melancholy terms in 'The wall, the gulf and the sun: a fable' (1990), an essay highlighting the pessimistic tone of Lyotard's later essays and presented in slightly longer form as two companion essays, 'The wall, the gulf, the system' and 'A postmodern fable' in *Postmodern Fables*.[43] He reviews contemporary political developments, and notes the profound change that has overtaken the process of political critique. He observes that the end of grand narratives determines the demise of the politics of an alternative. The notion of political emancipation is declared to be over. Critique has been enlisted as part of the repertoire of techniques employed in the efficient functioning of the 'open' system of Western democracies.[44]

Lyotard undertakes an analysis of two exemplary contemporary events, the fall of the Berlin Wall and the Gulf crisis. The former signals the failure of communism. He takes the Gulf crisis to undermine the credibility of a liberal interpretation of the West's power. For Lyotard, the West's implication in the creation of Saddam Hussein's power through its imperialist ventures undermines its liberal self-image. The wider conflict between the Islamic world and the West, though, he sees as being destined to be settled on the West's terms. The reason for the West's ultimate victory is its capacity to outperform all rivals. The continuing success of the liberal capitalist democracies of the West in achieving the goals of the system will ensure victory over rival powers. Instead of developing a systematic critique of the Western system, Lyotard relates an imaginative story or fable. He retails a story in which man is not the hero. The development of the planets, life and evolutionary development, the success of human beings and the flexible capabilities of liberal democracies are traced in a line of development. This prodigious development, though, is imagined as facing the catastrophe of the collapse of the Sun and the star system.[45] The prospective ending of life is taken by Lyotard as leading to a systematic, managed research programme to discover ways of brains surviving outside the body elsewhere in the solar system. He ends the story enigmatically without evaluating the project. The implication, though, is that, shorn of the body and the connecting links between thought and corporeal reality, man loses touch with the silent springs of his own creativity and restless energy.

In the rest of the essays making up the collection *Postmodern Fables* (1993), Lyotard contrasts the development of a form of politics as effective system management with an anguished sense of how such social development distances men and women from the unmasterable givenness of experience that is only to be sensed through an open individual sensibility that eschews the conventional culture managed by the system. In 'Unbeknownst', perhaps the most beguiling essay in the collection, Lyotard looks back to the experience of May 1968 while reflecting more generally on politics. He notes:

> Politics never ceases calling for union, for solidarity; and, in the least bad of cases, it turns the manner of being together into the object of an open-ended negotiation, the object of a better-distributed justice or of a consultation that remains to be pursued. This daily fare of politics is not an easy matter. It is the art of Machiavelli.[46]

This conventional art of politics, however, does not take account of the 'thing', the unmanageable aspect of reality to which the Nazis endeavoured to put a face before exterminating. This 'thing' is what conventional politics can never master; it is the nameless, formless activating part of a human contact with reality that Lyotard elsewhere names as the inhuman. It is what Lyotard takes the entire experience of socialization to be engaged in effacing. It is what activates revolutions and yet is inevitably betrayed as revolutionaries assume power and govern. It is what, retrospectively, Lyotard takes the May 1968 events as honouring. He observes, 'The events of May 68 – once shorn of their hodgepodge of intentions, wills, strategies, and concilatory illusions, took on their luster, an intelligible luster really, from what they revealed of childhood.'[47] Childhood stands for the free engagement with unconstrained reality, rather than infantile regression. After 1968, Lyotard takes politics as resuming its work of managing the unmanageable. The rights that are accorded by the successful political system of liberal capitalism are to be respected and yet resisted in the name of the thing.[48]

Lyotard's contributory lecture to the Oxford Amnesty Lectures of 1993, 'The other's rights', also reveals his sense of how contemporary society, and indeed the conventionally political, tends to override sensitivity to the intractable nature of reality. The lecture is profoundly affecting. At first, Lyotard infers individual rights to be deducible from the shared membership of a speech community, in which the other is always implicated. Amnesty is seen as an organization that attests to the *différend* implied by the forgetting of someone's rights. Lyotard, however, goes on to suggest that the full justification of the right to speak and be heard is the annunciatory function that is to be discharged in speech. The sense of announcing something that has not been heard, something which resonates with the deep unheard otherness of experience is seen to justify a new discourse. A still silence is recognized to be a preliminary to speech, due to its role in evoking a message to be delivered. The significance of annunciation derives from its absence in contemporary society. Lyotard observes, 'It is the main function of the media today to reinforce the interlocutory consent of the community.'[49] He is sensitive to a sensibility that supersedes the power of rational speech. He announces, 'The power which exceeds the capacity of interlocution resembles night.'[50] The burden of his unhappiness with contemporary social development is that it limits the imagination. He observes, 'The discontent from which contemporary societies are suffering, the postmodern affliction, is this foreclosure of the Other.'[51]

Conclusion

Lyotard's political thought is challenging and original. It refuses to defuse the inherent contestability of politics. Questions of politics are not seen as answerable by theoretical knowledge, conventional wisdom or consenting adults. Lyotard's testimony to the significance of political questions, their ubiquity amidst the uncertainties of discourse, as well as the inherent contestability of the criteria by which they can be considered, is brought out in a postscript to Bennington's *Lyotard: Writing the Event*. Bennington observes:

> It would seem that the idea put forward in the Introduction, that Lyotard's thought is fundamentally political, has in a sense been vindicated. This is to be sure not a politics of programmes and prescriptions, and could almost be described as a systematic frustration of politics, through its refusal of the transcendental illusion which pretends to present in the real what can only, or at best, be an Idea of reason acting regulatively on political judgement.[52]

Bennington values Lyotard's political thought due to its simultaneous recognition of the significance of politics and its refusal to defuse the radical contestability of political questions. Lyotard's designated 'systematic frustration of politics', however, can be seen in a more critical light. In valorizing contestability and difference while deprecating consensus, Lyotard undervalues the achievement of a political order that can unite individuals in terms of their adherence to a defeasible but reasonable organization of rights, duties and practices. Lyotard's sublime attestation of *différends* does not provide resources for constructive political activity. Blaug, in an article entitled 'New developments in deliberative democracy', observes that postmodern deliberative theorists such as Lyotard are more comfortable with the critique of existing practices than they are in suggesting how power might be exercised legitimately.[53]

Lyotard is right to highlight the contestability of politics and to criticize grand narratives for purporting to provide universal answers. He is also perceptive in pointing to the possibility of incommensurable standpoints precluding the achievement of a consensual form of justice. Moreover, Lyotard's recognition in his late work of the simultaneous advent of the manifest success of liberal capitalism, in delivering a complex open system, promoting development and an extensive system of rights, *and* a regime in which creativity and dissonance are submerged in a neo-totalitarian conformity, resonates with the emergence of managerialist democracy, a global cultural market-place and political apathy.

Lyotard's dismissal of general theories and conceptions of politics, however, is too sweeping. It does not admit the possibility of invoking them in a critical spirit to generate feasible but contestable guides for guiding political action and a reflective form of public participation. A spirit of critical openness that allows for public consideration of a diversity of perspectives might allow for a sense of community while guarding against discursive oppressiveness signalled by Lyotard's notion of a *différend*. Moreover, Lyotard's general account of development and the pervasiveness of a logic of instrumentality that is emphasized in his late writings is itself highly contestable. Its generalized, melancholy image of mass conformity confronting an agonized sense of otherness appears insufficiently sensitive to the differences between social practices and institutions and the diverse opportunities and threats they pose to contemporary individuals. In late essays such as 'The intimacy of terror' and 'A bizarre partner', Lyotard contrasts the banality of the cultural market-place and conventional political practice with the imaginative terroristic force required by an individual, like himself, who engages in the act of writing.[54] This reflexive fixing upon his own activity, in its narcissistic abrogation of interest in the differential complexity and multifarious obligations of the social world, highlights the dangers involved in Lyotard's deprecation of theory and practice dedicated to establishing publicly acceptable forms of political order and norms of conduct.

6 • Hegel and the Critique of Closure

Introduction

Lyotard's philosophy reflects and derives from his critique of the closure he identifies within Hegel's system. This chapter undertakes an analysis and evaluation of Lyotard's conception of Hegel. It sets out a dialectic between Hegel and Lyotard in which Lyotard's image of Hegel as a closed, absolutist thinker is seen as itself an interpretive closure. Moreover, this interpretive closure is seen as blocking Lyotard's assimilation of what Hegel has to offer as a theorist who develops a subtle understanding of subjectivity and sociality in the context of modernity.

An overview of the relationship between Lyotard's and Hegel's philosophies is presented in the next section. This is undertaken in part by way of a review of Hegel's interpretation of the *Parmenides*, which highlights aspects of Hegel's philosophy to which Lyotard is opposed. Lyotard's disclaiming of the general Hegelian claim to provide an objective explanation of the rational nature of reality, with the affiliated claims to provide objective theoretical analyses of history and politics, is then reviewed. The following section undertakes a close textual analysis of the image of Hegel framed by Lyotard in the latter's theoretical texts. A persisting, negative image of Hegel as an essentializing absolutist is constantly invoked by Lyotard to throw into relief his own changing formulations of a sceptical philosophy that valorizes difference and indeterminacy. After the elaboration of Lyotard's view of Hegel, the chapter will conclude by assessing the impact of Lyotard's rejection of Hegel for the status of his own philosophy as an open testimony to difference and inventiveness.

Absolutism and the absolutism of absolutist interpretation

Hegel presents himself as an objective, absolute idealist. His philosophy makes a number of claims. He maintains that reality is essentially thought, and hence his dialectical examination of the logic of concepts is held to disclose the true nature of being itself.[1] Hegel also affirms the absolute objectivity of his thought, the token of its objectivity being taken to be the comprehensiveness of its explanation. Hegel urges that his system is absolutely systematic in explaining its own foundations and in circumnavigating reality by showing how thought pervades nature, underlies theory and practice and culminates in the reflexive self-consciousness of philosophical cognition. This reflexivity of Hegel's system is indicated in his conception of the Absolute Idea as being the whole system of thought of which it is itself the culmination.[2]

Hegel's general claims inform more specific ones, notably his suggestion that his *Philosophy of Right* provides an objective understanding of an ethical, political community. Hegelian claims to provide a comprehensive explanation of reality also underpin his ambition in the *Lectures on the Philosophy of History* to explain the directionality of history and his notion that his *Lectures on the History of Philosophy* show that the succession of historic philosophies form a system that mirrors the several parts of his own system. Hegel's approach to the history of philosophy is encapsulated in his remark that, 'Every philosophy has been and still is necessary. The principles are retained; the most recent philosophy being the result of all preceding and hence no philosophy has ever been refuted.'[3]

Lyotard aims to refute Hegel and to repudiate the very aim of providing a systematic explanation of reality that motivates Hegel's notion of philosophy. Lyotard is categorical in rejecting all the connected Hegelian claims considered above. A recurring theme within Lyotard's philosophy is his resistance to the closure of thought and the reduction of reality to what can be represented by a rational scheme. Hegel, for Lyotard, is the arch-rationalist and apostle of closure. Hence, Lyotard's own philosophy is defined in terms of an opposition to Hegel. What Lyotard objects to in Hegel and what he aims at achieving in his own philosophy can be indicated by considering the dialectical manœuvres of Plato in his dialogue, *Parmenides*.

The *Parmenides* is a later dialogue of Plato, in which a young Socrates is depicted as conversing with Parmenides and Zeno. In conversation with the elder Parmenides, Socrates affirms his belief in forms, rational patterns of thought removed from the particulars of sense experience that impart an attenuated reality to what is met with in experience. Parmenides, an experienced philosopher, questions Socrates' understanding of the postulated relationship between form and particular. Socrates is made to confront challenging questions relating to the forms, notably the third man argument, whereby the independent reality of the forms themselves is questioned. Notwithstanding his recognition of the problems involved in assuming their reality, Parmenides indicates his acceptance of a theory of forms, and offers a reflective exercise that is intended to serve as training to promote Socrates' philosophical development. Parmenides examines the conceptual implications for the One or Unity and for what is not One or Unity, when the One/Unity is and is not postulated. Parmenides draws a series of contrary consequences, inferring for instance, that if there is One or Unity then there cannot be plurality, and yet in another argument he contrives to show how the notion of Unity implies diversity, given that there is an implicit relation between the One and its signification that in turn implies an infinite set of relations between discourse and being.

No explicit general conclusions about thought and reality are drawn within the *Parmenides*. Its interpretation has exercised succeeding generations of Platonic scholars.[4] Hegel, though, is clear about the dialogue's meaning. He maintains that the *Parmenides* represents a systematic exploration of logical concepts, with Plato affirming the same dialectical interdependence of the categories of thought that Hegel himself undertakes to show in his *Logic*. Hegel ventures: 'If the *Parmenides* be taken along with the *Republic* and the *Timaeus* the three together constitute the whole Platonic system of philosophy divided into three parts or sections.'[5] Hegel's reading of the *Parmenides* is both plausible and contentious. Its plausibility derives from the similarity between Hegel's reading of Being and Nothing at the outset of his *Logic* and the contradictory consequences that Parmenides draws from postulating Unity or One in the *Parmenides*. In his *Logic* Hegel takes being to be indistinguishable from nothing and in registering this sameness infers a becoming or development of categories that issues in the unfurling of the totality of logical categories.

Hegel's notion of logic was undoubtedly influenced by a reading of Plato, hence the affinities between the *Logic* and the *Parmenides* can be read as allowing Hegel a unique insight into Plato's philosophy. Moreover, a number of Plato's later dialogues, notably the *Sophist*, explore the 'logical' interrelations of forms and hence confer a plausibility upon Hegel's reading of the *Parmenides*. On the other hand, the *Parmenides* can be read in a way that disavows a Hegelianized reading of its character. First, Plato in the dialogue characteristically draws no explicit conclusions about the forms, their relations or the nature of reality in the *Parmenides*.[6] What the dialogue undoubtedly reinforces is a sense of the paradoxes posed by conceptual thinking and the problems endemic to the task of establishing and justifying philosophical truth. The very nature of the dialogue form may be said to highlight the uncertain and contestable character of philosophical discourse. Again, the contradictions entertained in conceptualizing unity may be taken, *pace* Hegel, as signalling the profound opacity and ineffability of the real. Unity or the One, on this reading, is held to be at the limits or even beyond human understanding.

Non-Hegelian readings of the *Parmenides* can serve to register significant aspects of Lyotard's critique of Hegel, and indeed Lyotard's own philosophical position. If the dialogue is taken as inherently inconclusive, though serving to highlight the problematic character of philosophical understanding, then it can illustrate Lyotard's sense of the lack of foundations for philosophical explanation. Lyotard's characteristic notion of philosophical method is exhibited in his reading of Kant and the reflective judgement of the Third Critique, where thought is guided by its own internal feeling rather than by objective criteria. Moreover, Lyotard takes reality to be non-reducible to systematic conceptualization. Lyotard's notion of the inhuman limits of experience itself, which cannot be incorporated into the neo-totalitarianism of contemporary Western social systems, is evinced by a sublime feeling of the unpresentable character of being itself.[7]

Lyotard's notion of philosophy proceeding without rules, and without objective criteria, contrasts sharply with Hegel's conception of philosophical method that he attributes to the *Parmenides*. Likewise, Lyotard's notion of the opacity of reality is starkly opposed to Hegel's metaphysics. Hegel's own notion that a rationally demonstrable system of logical thought can achieve a complete explanation of reality informs his reading of the *Parmenides*. He assimilates the character of the thinking undertaken in this dialogue to his own style of dialectical logic, which purports to provide irrefragable truth. In so doing he also understands Plato's logical thinking, as demonstrated in the *Parmenides*, to constitute a necessary historical condition of his own system. The Hegelian philosophical system includes all other philosophies within its own system as moments of itself. This incorporative aspect of the Hegelian system favours a closed interpretation of a philosophical predecessor, such as Plato, for incorporation is facilitated by an interpretive procedure that underplays ambiguities and tensions, as well as standpoints that jar with itself. Lyotard, in rejecting Hegel, is opposing the notions of reality and philosophical system that Hegel attributes to the *Parmenides*. Lyotard denies that reality can be captured in a network of concepts, reading past and present as a closed system that has a discernible goal or result. He is against the closure of a philosophical system and the sense that the nature of reality can be grasped in a finalized way.

Lyotard and Hegel, then, are profoundly different in their conceptions of the object and method of philosophizing. Lyotard's dissent from Hegel's general claims to convey the objective truth of a *rational* reality and his more specific claims about the objective nature of history and politics will now be examined. Lyotard's notion of philosophy attesting to its own limits runs counter to the core Hegelian notion that philosophical explanation is holistic. This systematic aspect of Hegel is distilled into the following brief but key passage of the *Phenomenology of Spirit*: 'The truth is the whole. The whole, however, is merely the essential nature reaching its completeness through the process of its own development. Of the Absolute it must be said that it is essentially result ...'[8] For Lyotard, this holism presupposes a cosmic unity of reason with being, which is fundamentally at odds with the gap between being and thought that he highlights by asserting a dogmatic materialism in *Phenomenology* and by invoking the play of the figural in *Discours, figure*. Lyotard's opposition to Hegel's core notions of reason and reality sharpens his antagonism to more particular features of Hegel's philosophy.

In proclaiming the condition of postmodernity, Lyotard indicts Hegel for being a prime exponent of the grand narrative form that marks modernity by its subordination of difference to the requirements of a general scheme of supposed systematic philosophical knowledge. In his 'Apostil on narratives', in *The Postmodern Explained to Children*, Lyotard identifies Hegel as an arch-grand narrator, 'Hegel's philosophy totalises all of these (grand) narratives and, in this sense, is a distillation of speculative modernity.'[9] In *The Postmodern Condition* Lyotard condemns grand narratives for being essentializing modern schemes of legitimation and sees postmodernity, in contrast, as being conducive to a multiplicity of language games. The postmodern, for Lyotard, breaks with the holism of Hegel and modernity. Universal schemes for politics are to be abandoned in favour of local and transitory forms of agreement.

His opposition to unificatory grand narratives, and general schemes for organizing society, entails a rejection of Hegelian politics. Hegel, in fashioning a holistic system, claims to identify a rational state, consisting of a community of intersecting practices, in which the citizens, in adhering to a rational framework of law, acknowledge their unity as the teleological consummation of historical development. Lyotard, in *The Postmodern Condition*, repudiates a teleological reading of history that derogates from the contingency that he ascribes to language games. Moves in games are neither fixed nor predictable elements in the general development of games. For Lyotard, there are only contingent moves in distinct games. Lyotard also takes claims to establish the essential rational political organization of society to lack foundations. He valorizes difference that harmonizes with the indeterminacy of political judgement. Justice, in *Just Gaming*, is presented as demanding an inventive imagination that can operate without the criteria that an essentialist ethics requires.

Lyotard's hostility to Hegel is implacable. Throughout his career he opposes what he takes to be Hegelian closure and systematizing. In *The Differend*, and in related essays specifically devoted to Hegel, Lyotard identifies Hegel as a philosophical opponent who frames an imperial metalanguage to reduce the singularity and contingency of phrases and their regimens. Lyotard counterposes the contingency of phrases and their relations to Hegelian systematizing. In *The Differend*, and more particularly in the essay, 'Discussions or phrasing "after Auschwitz"', Lyotard points to 'Auschwitz' as constituting a *reductio ad absurdam* of the notion that all events can be seen as contributing to an essential, unproblematic course of historical development. The experience of Auschwitz is seen as unthinkable within the framework of a notion of history that takes historical development to provide a sense of destiny that explains and justifies the vicissitudes of historic experiences. Lyotard's invocation of the Kantian notion of the sublime in *The Differend* and later works, to register the undemonstrable feeling of a *différend* and the sense of the inhuman originary connection with corporeal, creative being, is radically opposed to a Hegelian determination to explain the totality of reality in terms of the coherent development of philosophical thought.

At all stages of his career Lyotard takes Hegel to be his significant philosophical *other* whose profession of certain, synoptic truth must be opposed. The terms of Lyotard's understanding of the relation between Hegel and his own standpoint are rehearsed by Williams in *Lyotard: Towards a Postmodern Philosophy*. Williams identifies a fundamental opposition between Lyotard and Hegel in remarking, 'So in opposition to Lyotard's uncertainty, Hegel puts forward the model of a certainty based on the exhaustive inclusion of whatever event we have to judge.'[10] Of course, Williams and Lyotard are right to highlight a contrast between Hegel's conception of philosophy as realizing a comprehensive, inclusive account of reality and Lyotard's sense of an irreducible multiplicity of perspectives and the indeterminacy of philosophical judgement. Again, Hegel's general objective idealism informs a claim, for instance, on the objectivity of ethics, while the achievement of a rational polity and a teleological view of history run counter to Lyotard's sceptical standpoint.

The relationship between Lyotard and Hegel, though, will not be grasped if Lyotard's perspective is to be endorsed uncritically. Hegel's reading of Plato's *Parmenides* was criticized earlier in this chapter for its assimilation of Plato to Hegel by abstracting from the dialogue's ambiguities and alternative interpretive possibilities. Similarly, Lyotard's Hegel assumes the identity of a caricatured, absolutist antagonist and his account is absolutist itself in disregarding the subtlety of Hegel's thought that allows for a multiplicity of possible interpretations. Lyotard's susceptibility to engage in absolutist interpretation of multi-dimensional philosophical figures is signalled in his remarks on Plato in *The Differend*, in which Plato is construed as a philosophical absolutist whose dialogues are lightly disguised dogmatism.[11] An acquaintance with the *Parmenides* and its interpretive history, however, exemplifies the complexity of Plato's thought and the hubris to which a commentator adopting a single line of interpretation is subject. Moreover, Plato's dialogues are dramas in which the depiction of questing for knowledge supersedes the transmission of knowledge itself.[12]

Connor detects an irony in Lyotard's account of modernity. He observes that Lyotard allows neither for alternative characterizations of modernity nor for rival interpretations of the theories he designates as grand narratives.[13] The upshot is that Lyotard's account of grand narratives appears to possess the absolute certainty and self-styled objectivity that he imputes to what he is impugning. The self-subverting character of Lyotard's generalized notions of modernity and postmodernity has also been noted by Jencks and Bernstein.[14] The puzzle is endemic in Lyotard's writings. The notion of a *différend* is presented as a universal feature within the radical contingency of discourse, and the notion of inhuman social development has been identified by Anderson as possessing the aspect of a classic grand narrative.[15] The absolutism of Lyotard's interpretation of Hegel and the generality of his images of modernity and social development disrupt the neatness of the supposed contrast between the synoptic absolutism of Hegel and the relaxed pluralism of Lyotard.

The multi-dimensionality of Hegel and his susceptibility to multiple interpretations preclude the rigidity of his categorization by Lyotard that is assumed by commentators such as Williams, Readings and Jameson.[16] While Hegel is a synoptic theorist who aims to achieve a comprehensive overview of reality, he has been interpreted in various ways. There is, for instance, a much discussed disagreement between metaphysical and non-metaphysical interpretations of Hegel. A non-metaphysical interpretation tends to view Hegel as adopting a more open, less closed perspective in which he is not seen as reducing human affairs to the necessary development of a supra-human subject, but is envisaged as tracing an intelligible systematic pattern in human thought and practice.[17]

The dispute over the metaphysical or non-metaphysical character of Hegel's thought defies easy resolution. On the one hand, Hegel's concern to see a definitive pattern in the development of history and his confidence in outlining what he takes to be a supremely rational organization of society and culture suggest a commitment to a notion of a necessary order to human affairs that underrates the contingency of human thought and practice. On the other hand, Hegel's consistent and emphatic sense of the mutuality of the finite and the infinite testifies to his repudiation of the notion of a supra-human meta-subject directing the course of human affairs.[18] Moreover, Hegel, in his political, social and cultural writings, displays a nuanced sensitivity to the particularity and subjectivity of the social and cultural practices of modernity.

Hegel's reading of modernity is not addressed in any detail by Lyotard. This is unfortunate on at least two counts. First, the character of Hegel's social theory is exemplified in his exploration of the culture of modernity. Second, Hegel's conception of modernity challenges Lyotard's in its evocation of the dilemmas posed by the interplay between subjectivity and social contextual practices that are insufficiently addressed by Lyotard. Hegel's sense of the complex burden and promise of modernity is ignored in Lyotard's highly general notion of modernity and its supersession.

Hegel sees modernity as being distinguished by its evocation and expression of forms of particularity and the free subjectivity of human agency. Protestant religion, romantic art, insistent and labyrinthine styles of individualistic morality, the endless production and consumption of commodities in free markets and the demand for representative government are seen by Hegel as testifying to assertive forms of particularity and individualism. These forms disturb the rhythms and unities of the social practices through which they emerge. The complexity of relations between subjectivity and inter-subjective practices precludes the wholesale and untroubled assimilation of particularity and subjectivity into the order of the political community set out in the *Philosophy of Right*.[19]

Hegel's recognizes that the force of modern individualism prohibits the resumption of the harmonious integrative culture of Ancient Greece. His awareness of the irrepressible dynamic of modern individualism, which threatens to unravel community ties and undermine ethical objectivism, has been seen by Plant and Hardimon as motivating his entire philosophical project of establishing an overall, synoptic philosophy that reconciles modern men and women to their fate.[20] The depth of Hegel's historical and sociological insights into the complex interplay between subjectivity and inter-subjectivity within modernity is not matched by the strict and inflexible austerity of Lyotard's insistence upon difference and incommensurability.

While Lyotard's absolutist dismissal of Hegel's absolutism is a justifiable critique of the metaphysical, unduly unified aspect of Hegel's conception of reality, it does not do justice to Hegel's subtle evocation of the tensions and possibilities generated by the dynamic interaction of principles, social practices and individualistic aspirations that shape the modern world. Lyotard's critique of Hegelian absolutism is as suspect as Hegel's own resort to a unilear notion of teleological development to frame his account of the emergence of a resolution to the dilemmas of history.

The grand inquisitor

Throughout his career, Lyotard acts as the grand inquisitor who aims to expose the unwarranted closure of Hegel's philosophical system. Lyotard's first major work, *Phenomenology* of 1954, directs a powerful critique against Hegel.[21] Hegel's phenomenological project is indicted for its pervasive rationalism. The *Phenomenology of Spirit* is a key text for Hegel, because it sets up the experiential conditions for scientific knowledge or his logical investigation of concepts. Logic, for Hegel, explains reality. Hegel's assumption of the unity of thought and reality is justified by the prior exploration of consciousness conducted in his *Phenomenology of Spirit*. A phenomenological approach is an unconditional review of a succession of ways in which truth is perceived by consciousness. A feature of any conscious formulation of the truth is shown to be that it must recognize the part played by consciousness itself in posing and fulfilling the conditions of truth. Hence, for Hegel, truth is to be seen as residing in self-consciousness, and it is this recognition that underpins Hegel's elaborate review of the alienated shapes of self-conscious misrecognition, as well as the final truth that reflective conscious thought is the basis of reality. For Lyotard, Hegel's phenomenological review of experience liquidates otherness in misperceiving the irreducible materialism of pre-linguistic experience.

For Lyotard, reason cannot explain reality exhaustively. In his *Phenomenology*, Lyotard abrogates what he takes to be the illicit Hegelian move of founding philosophy in the meaningful activities of consciousness. Lyotard observes:

> There is thus no answer to the question whether philosophy must begin with the object (realism) or with the ego (idealism). The very idea of phenomenology puts this question out of play: consciousness is always consciousness of, and there is no object which is not an object *for*. There is no immanence of the object to consciousness unless one correlatively assigns the object a rational meaning, without which the object would not be an object for.[22]

Lyotard, against Hegel, insists on the intractability of reality. The dogmatic assertion of materialism in his *Phenomenology* is a riposte to the imperialism he attributes to Hegel's quest for meaning. Acts of cognition, for Lyotard, rest upon a givenness of experience that cannot be subsumed in the acts of cognition themselves.

Hegel and Lyotard evidently assume differing perspectives in their conceptions of reality, consciousness, self-consciousness and thought. What is not clear, though, is the extent to which Hegel overrides the particular materiality of events in his dialectical investigations of the interdependence of forms of consciousness and categories of thought in conceiving of reality. Hegel's *Phenomenology of Spirit* has been read in a variety of ways. Bernstein, for instance, interprets it as functioning as a ladder to, rather than a demonstration of, the standpoint of science. Bernstein observes:

> Hegel is only attempting to provide a ladder to this standpoint because he believes that no demonstration or deduction is possible. Hegel's denial of the possibility of demonstration is premised on a simple logical insight: if what is presupposed as external to reason and cognition – material objects, other persons, language, social practices, history – are in fact *constitutive* conditions of them then a position whose premises are weaker than what it seeks to demonstrate ... must necessarily fail.[23]

A host of commentators, for example Burbidge and Flay, highlight how Hegel's *Phenomenology of Spirit*, far from attempting epistemological closure, aims at interweaving an openness to experience with the trajectory of explanation.[24] Moreover, Hegel's entire explanation of nature recognizes that its sheer externality is never to be mastered exhaustively by categorial understanding. The transition from logic to nature in Hegel's system is a move that testifies to the externality of thought. White urges persuasively that the dependence of thought on a conditional externality is acknowledged in the objectivity of the reflexive notion in the *Logic* itself.[25] Hegel, then, may be able to resist the charge of arch-rationalism that is levelled against him by, for instance, Michael Rosen, who takes Hegel to envisage thought as manufacturing the world out of itself. Hegel can be read as a more nuanced and more open theorist who recognizes difference as well as identity.[26]

Lyotard, in *Discours, figure*, follows the trail of his earlier *Phenomenology* in criticizing Hegelian rationalism. He counterposes a *figural* resistance to forms of intellectual representation. Rational schemes, like Hegel's system, which are taken as aiming to comprehend reality as a set of stable, rational relations between the elements of which it is composed, are repudiated. The act of writing on a page is not considered representable by a stable system of writing, and the figure of desire is not to be captured in its secondary representation.

In *Libidinal Economy*, Lyotard dismisses a concern for even providing a critique of the intellectual presentation of a system of signs. Hegel's rationalism is not to be subjected to complicit rational criticism. Instead, Lyotard aims at valorizing the operation of tensors that intensify forces and singularities of desire.

In *The Postmodern Condition*, Lyotard focuses his critique of Hegel upon what he takes to be the totalizing aspect of Hegel's philosophy. Modernity is defined by Lyotard in terms of the paradigmatically Hegelian project of providing a grand narrative to legitimate knowledge. Postmodernity, in contrast, is seen as implying 'incredulity to metanarratives'.[27] For Lyotard, the defining modernist project of absorbing all knowledge within a summative synoptic explanation exhibits the repressive character of modernity. Lyotard takes Hegel's systematic philosophy as epitomizing the speculative metanarrative of modernity, whereby the several modes of knowing are unified and legitimated by their portrayal as constituting the life history of a grand subject, Spirit. For Lyotard, this meta-subject operates literally, as a grand self that supersedes the selves and phenomena that it purports to explain.[28] Lyotard criticizes the putative Hegelian incapacity to do justice to the multiplicity and heterogeneity of language games in which selves are located.

Lyotard conceives of the self in postmodern terms that conflict pointedly with the universal, absolute meta-self he sees as unifying the Hegelian grand narrative. Lyotard observes,

> A self does not amount to very much but no self is an island; each exists in a fabric of relations that is now more complex and mobile than ever before. Young or old, man or woman, rich or poor, a person is always located at 'nodal points' of specific communication circuits however tiny these may be.[29]

Lyotard's derogation of the self and reflective subjectivity is not supported by a sustained analysis of how the self relates to its alleged dispersion in multifarious language games. Lyotard does not discuss if or how the self's involvement in multiple language games raises questions for the self of its own coherence and their identities.

As was signalled in Chapter 2 above, Lyotard highlights the unsustainability of the Hegelian enterprise by indicating that the absorption of the several modes of knowing within an encyclopaedia of absolute knowledge can easily slip into a mere perspectivalism, whereby the separate spheres of knowing are united not by a purported absolute standpoint but by a mere organizational perspective. This recognition of the possibility of a non-absolutist form of Hegelianism, however, does not induce Lyotard to relax the absolutist character of his interpretation of Hegel. He does not entertain the possibility that Hegel himself or at least a theoretical derivative might be read productively as providing an *open*, imaginative theory of the possible interrelations between practices and principles in the modern world.

Lyotard, in simply stigmatizing Hegel as the grand narrator of modernity, is remiss in refraining from examining in detail the image of modernity that is framed in Hegel's writings on history, politics and culture. Hegel provides a subtle understanding of modernity that is critical as well as reconciliatory. Dallmayr, in commenting upon contemporary social thought and its reception of Hegel, observes, 'What is neglected, in particular, is Hegel's role as both instigator *and* critic of the discourse of modernity.'[30] Hegel's agonized exploration of the destructive, divisive potential of modern individuality is instructive in highlighting the problems of modernity and the significance of the value of community in providing a plausible response to social atomization and alienation. Hegel recognizes that modern selves demand and express individuality and particularity in a variety of social practices, including moral and contractual practices as well as religious and artistic languages. Notably, however, Hegel identifies particularity as being promoted by economic practices that operate according to a logic of enlightened self-interest but which cannot ensure that all selves successfully pursue their interests. The intense modern expression of moral agency and individualistic economic self-assertion are also seen by Hegel as threatening notions of community and social trust that allow for the very expression of individuality. Hegel's recognition of these critical problems of modernity inspires him to perceive integrative social institutions, such as the patriarchal family, corporations, classes and political structures, as providing the bases of a countervailing sense of community that will allow modern individuals to align their notions of individual identity with a commitment to express the value of a sustaining sense of community.[31]

Lyotard's conception of the postmodern condition of society dispenses with Hegel's elaborate examination of the harmonies and tensions linking and separating selves in moral agency, contractual obligations, family life, economic practices, political participation and religious, artistic and intellectual experience. Lyotard counterposes a generalized image of instrumentalist performativity with a postmodern release of agonistic experimentation. He thereby tends to underplay the complex interplay between forms of subjectivity and social organization. Lyotard is justified in criticizing Hegel for conceptualizing social life in absolutist terms. Nonetheless, Hegel's comprehension of modern social life as revolving around the need to harmonize potentially dissonant elements, including practices for nurturing children, the flourishing of markets and the development of integrative ethical practices continues to be relevant to a present age that has not simply abandoned its *modern* character.

Lyotard's hostility to Hegel is continued in his writings subsequent to *The Postmodern Condition*. His most focused critique of Hegel is evident in his 1981 essays, 'Analysing speculative discourse as language game' and 'Discussions or phrasing "after Auschwitz"'. These essays, in taking language to consist in sets of phrases, express a standpoint that is resumed and deepened in *The Differend*. They show that Lyotard develops his most sophisticated philosophical analysis of language in opposition to Hegel. In 'Analysing speculative discourse as language game', Lyotard develops an internal critique of Hegel. Hegel's philosophy is diagnosed as being out of step with itself and the exposure of its contradictions is taken as pointing in the direction of postmodernism. Lyotard attends to the 'logic' of Hegel's *Phenomenology of Spirit* and *Logic* that is presented by Hegel himself as portraying the internal contradictions and immanent resolutions of, on the one hand, consciousness, and, on the other hand, the general categories of reason. Lyotard's procedure is to reveal how the manœuvres of Hegel's dialectical strategy obey the formula of a metalanguage, specifying the opposition of designated terms, their mutual implication and an ensuing generation of a new term. The abstractness of this dialectical procedure is seen as revealing an *external* teleology that subverts the advertised immanence of Hegel's dialectical, conceptual enquiry.[32]

The notion of language developed in 'Analysing speculative discourse as language game' conflicts with Hegel. Lyotard imagines any statement as co-presenting a number of universes, only one of which is actualized by a contingent follow-up statement. The looseness of the connection is distorted, according to Lyotard, by the speculative language game that imposes a notion of necessary development upon language. Language, for Lyotard, is not to be tamed or limited by external 'logical' criteria; it wants the infinite, and the infinite creativity of language is to be achieved by the inadvertency of 'moves'. The notion of the inadvertency of moves in and between language games contrasts pointedly with Hegel's subscription to the good infinite. Hegel's notion of the good infinite takes infinity to be best expressed by the finite exemplifying a sense of an infinite that completes rather than extends beyond the finite.[33] There is nothing inadvertent in Hegel's notion of the infinite, whereby 'the image of true infinity, bent back into itself, becomes the circle, the line which has reached itself, which is closed and wholly present which is beyond beginning and end'.[34] Lyotard's concluding comments in 'Analysing speculative discourse as language game' imagine postmodern, formless, uncategorizable experimentation as superseding the promise of a purely immanent account of thought and action purportedly offered by the Hegelian dialectic. The divergencies, incompatibilities and ineluctable creativity of language on this view cannot be subordinated to a general rational scheme; they can only be gestured at in a process of following their trail.[35]

A thoughtful if confrontational engagement with Hegel is also conducted in Lyotard's essay, 'Discussions, or phrasing "after Auschwitz"'. The phrase, 'after Auschwitz', is designed to invoke the bankruptcy of a totalizing dialectical discourse *after* the unique experience of suffering and inhumanity unleashed in the holocaust.[36] This experience is held to be unassimilable to traditional patterns of behaviour and discourse. Any continuation of speculative discourse after Auschwitz takes Auschwitz as forming part of a learning curve for a 'we' who constitute the subject of history. For Lyotard, the name of Auschwitz stands for the absolute discontinuity and incommensurability of phrase regimens. He invokes the unassimilability of Auschwitz to a general discursive standpoint to highlight his own respect for difference. For Lyotard there is no metalanguage to establish a common measure between phrases. Speculative reason, the Hegelian vehicle for tracing a pattern in self-moving thoughts, is diagnosed as reducing the flow and otherness of phrases by imposing upon them an external rhythm. Selves for Lyotard rehearse a fragmentary, mobile universe of contingent phrases and phrase regimens and there is no common language in which a self can trace a magnified reflection.[37]

The conceptual framework of 'Discussions or phrasing "after Auschwitz"' and its theme of radical difference are developed further in *The Differend: Phrases in Dispute*. Lyotard, in this work, sees the task of philosophy to be that of testifying to the *différend*, the sublime feeling of the unpresentability of a phrase that is excluded from discourse. Again, Lyotard takes Auschwitz to symbolize the exclusion of a unique experience from discourse.[38] Hegel's speculative discourse is taken as effecting the discursive closure Lyotard strains to avoid. Speculative language is seen as presupposing the convertibility of all discourse into a common currency that assumes that nothing is lost in the process of exchange. Lyotard complains, 'But this presupposition of the same (made by speculative discourse) is not falsifiable. It is a rule that governs metaphysical discourse as its closure.'[39]

Hegel, in his *Phenomenology of Spirit*, attests to the universality of thought, observing at its outset that terms such as 'here' and 'now', although asserting particular things, are actually universally transposable so as to refer to any particularity whatsoever.[40] Lyotard expressly opposes Hegel's reading of deictics such as here and now by allowing for names to function as rigid but empty indicators of reference. Lyotard observes:

> The name fills the function of linchpin because it is an empty and constant designator. Its quasi-deictic import is independent of the phrase in which it currently figures, and it can accept many semantic values because it excludes only those that are incompatible with its place in the network of names...[41]

Names, for Lyotard, facilitate discourse but they neither bear essential, universal properties nor signify reality; they are filled with content by distinct modes of discourse.

Lyotard, in *The Differend* and in the previously considered essays, 'Analysing speculative discourse as language game' and 'Discussions or phrasing "After Auschwitz"', indicts Hegel for operating with a closed notion of language that rules out inventiveness and openness from linguistic expression. The name *Auschwitz* is proffered as encapsulating a phenomenon that exposes the inadequacy of Hegel's closing of the gaps between phrases and experiences. A concentration camp, for Lyotard, cannot be incorporated unproblematically into a systematic review of the totality of experience. In pointed opposition to Hegel, Lyotard proffers a Kantian notion of the indeterminacy of philosophical discourse:

The stakes of philosophical discourse are in a rule (or rules) which remains to be sought, and to which the discourse cannot be made to conform before the rule has been found. The links from phrase to phrase are not ruled by a rule but by the quest for a rule.[42]

Lyotard's opposition to Hegel is confirmed in his later writings. The Kantian inspiration of his notion of the sublime signals his resistance to the Hegelian project of re-establishing the notion of reason as a force to comprehend reality. Lyotard sees the sublime as attesting to the dichotomy between imagination and reason, which is not to be bridged but is recognized in a feeling that is rationally undemonstrable. In his *Lessons on the Analytic of the Sublime*, Lyotard takes Kant's notion of the sublime to be a feeling of a *différend* and a *différend* of feeling. Lyotard perceives the sublime as registering the unease felt when imagination is discordant with conception, for instance, when an infinite object is imagined that contravenes the finite character that is reflectively attributed to objects. Lyotard takes this feeling of tension or unease as emblematic of the identification of a *différend* that obtains when the incompatibility of two types of discourse is felt but not translatable into another discourse.

In analysing this Kantian notion of the sublime, Lyotard categorically rejects a Hegelian reading of the dialectical subsumption of the finite into the infinite. He observes that there is a temptation to conceive of the tension between imagination and reason as being resolvable by Hegelian, dialectical thought. He observes, 'One is tempted to conceive of the finalization of this extreme discordance as a dialectical operation.'[43] Lyotard dismisses the Hegelian resolution in remarking: 'However, this (dialectical) reading is not the correct one. It is not critical but speculative. By this I mean it makes the two powers in conflict "homogeneous" in order to transform them into moments of a finalized process.'[44] Lyotard is opposed to the neutralization of the conflict to an objectifying process. He observes, 'A dialectical reading of this kind has no access to a sublime that is subjectively felt by thought as different.'[45]

Lyotard, in his discussion of the inhuman, invokes Kant against Hegel. He is concerned with two senses of the inhuman. On the one hand he focuses on the loss of a sense of an *inhuman* access to the very presence of reality and events, and he is also exercised by technological, instrumentalist development that threatens to subordinate all goals to its own logic of complexification. Lyotard urges that only a feeling of the sublime can attest to this transformation of experience. He also notes in the essay, 'Something like: Communication . . . without communication', that the impact of new technologies and instrumentalist communication on art destroys the sense of aesthetic communication of a feeling of beauty which Kant identified. He takes the development of art in a context of technologized communication to confirm Hegel's notion of the death of art in the context of increasing rationalization. Lyotard acknowledges the prescience of Hegel, while reflecting ruefully upon the commodification of contemporary art. He remarks, 'The art-industry would be a completion of speculative metaphysics, a way in which Hegel is present, has succeeded, in Hollywood.'[46]

Conclusion

Abbinnett, in his engaging book, *Truth and Social Science: From Hegel to Deconstruction*, urges that Hegel's notion of social ethics is not to be dismissed by deconstruction. While this view is commendable, he tends to overplay the reasonableness of Hegel's standpoint. He argues against an objectivist, absolutist reading of Hegel's *Philosophy of Right*. He observes: 'even (the) *Philosophy of Right* articulates no more than the conditions under which self-consciousness articulates its concept as the *demand* inscribed in the constitution of a rational state authority'.[47] This interpretation of Hegel's *Philosophy of Right* abstracts from Hegel's insistence that a philosophical rather than a historical treatment of law is absolute rather than relative in its judgements.[48] The absolutist aspect of Hegel's philosophy provides a justification for Lyotard's persisting critique of Hegel. Differences in perspective cannot be assimilated uncontroversially into an objectivist account of rational social ethics, framed upon the notion of a directionality to history that culminates in the political culture of northern Europe at the outset of the nineteenth century.

Lyotard's interpretation of Hegel, however, is as absolutist as the rigid metaphysical system that he attributes to Hegel. It ignores possibilities of interpreting Hegel in a non-metaphysical, more open way, that might deliver a more plausible, less restrictive Hegelianism. There is an ambiguity in the way Hegel can be interpreted and

Lyotard ignores this ambiguity in the interests of framing an image of Hegel that functions as an absolute *other* for Lyotard's thought. His opposition to Hegel and speculative discourse is unreserved and impacts upon Lyotard's politics as well as his philosophy. As Bennington observes, 'For Lyotard it is not that speculative discourse is "wrong" in the sense of being incorrect, but in the sense of being unjust.'[49]

Lyotard's rejection of Hegel is unfortunate in that it involves a dismissal of what can be learned from Hegel's painstaking study of modernity which tracks its contradictions as well as its achievements. In particular, Lyotard's work suffers from its lack of detailed consideration of Hegel's subtle evocation of the intricate interaction between forms of subjectivity and inter-subjective practices that shape society and the state in the modern world. Hegel perceives individual subjectivity, in the forms of conscientious moral agency and the economic man of modern markets, to be shaped by the social practices in which they are situated. He diagnoses the problems and possibilities of modern life as arising out of the complex interplay between social practices and individualized aspirations that are promoted by these practices. The complexity that Hegel perceives in the social world is overlooked by Lyotard, who tends to draw an abstract contrast between mass society and agonized individual attestation to sublime experience. Hegel's image of modernity as a complex condition also runs counter to Lyotard's late designation of great narratives as promising 'the end of separation'.[50]

O'Neill, in an engaging essay, 'Lost in the post: (post)modernity explained to youth', observes that Lyotard tends to underplay the interdependence between subscription to a social practice and individual identity. He observes: 'The choice between conformity and individuation merely results in two oppressive solutions, i.e the reduction of politics to aesthetics or the repression of aesthetics by politics. What is missing is the dialectical mediation of conformity and individuation in a civic society.'[51] O'Neill concludes that Hegelianism, in its articulation of the need to secure a mediated political community in which social institutions allow for a sense of social harmony while permitting individualism, has more to offer than Lyotard's unmediated valorization of difference. Notwithstanding the historically outmoded character of Hegel's specification of a rational political community that maintains patriarchal family relations and an undemocratic state, Hegel's reading of modernity and the general character of his designated resolution of its tensions remain of persisting value. They certainly offer a rich counterpoint to Lyotard's sense of dispersed subjectivity and the underplaying in Lyotard's work of the role of reflective agency in inter-subjective social practices.

7 • Marx and the End of Emancipation

Introduction

Lyotard's engagement with Marx reflects and inspires the changing idioms of Lyotard's thought. In this section the trajectory of the images of Marx maintained in Lyotard's thought is traced, and the significance of Lyotard's break with Marxism is focused upon by means of a review of his 'A memorial of Marxism: for Pierre Souyri'.[1] Thereafter, as a prelude to a detailed treatment of Lyotard's relations with Marxism, the general sense of Lyotard's way of handling Marx, both as a believer and a recusant, will be considered.

Lyotard's early philosophical and political career was Marxist. His *Phenomenology* (1954) culminates in a resolute affirmation of Marx and materialism at the expense of a phenomenological approach to which Lyotard was evidently attracted.[2] Lyotard was a member of the Marxist group *Socialisme ou barbarie* from 1954 until 1964, and another Marxist group, *Pouvoir Ouvrier*, until 1966. His political writings for the journal of *Socialisme ou barbarie* develop a sophisticated understanding of political events from a Marxist perspective. These essays on Algeria, however, express a tension in Lyotard's commitment to Marxism, in that they recognize the force of nationalism and working-class embourgeoisement. Lyotard's participation in and reflections on the events of 1968 testify to a drift away from definitive Marxist notions.

Libidinal Economy (1974) revels in breaking from Marxism, though Marxism is invoked as a negative register of a libidinal perspective. The work launches a torrential, radical assault on Marxism in framing a libidinal alternative to Marxist political economy. Subsequent to *Libidinal Economy*, Lyotard's essays and theoretical works tend to distance themselves from Marxism in developing their standpoints. *The Postmodern Condition* takes Marxism to be an archetypal grand narrative of modernity, narrating a universal history that is to be consummated by proletarian victory. *The Differend* highlights the contestability of discourse in contrast to a discursive imperialism imputed to Marxism. Lyotard's late preoccupation with the development of a one-dimensional system is especially melancholy because he takes the emancipative theories of modernity, epitomized by Marxism, and the affiliated notion of committed, engaged intellectuals, typified by Marxists who read past, present and future from the corpus of Marxist texts, to be hopelessly anachronistic.

The impact of Marxism on Lyotard is conveyed in his moving testimony of 1982, 'A memorial of Marxism: for Pierre Souyri'. Marxism, for Lyotard, is the epitome of a grand narrative, a theory that purports to explain all and demands total commitment. His memorial to his former friend and erstwhile Marxist colleague, Pierre Souryi, conveys the sense of total commitment that Marxism meant for Souryi and also for himself. Lyotard declares, 'Marxism had probably been for both of us a universal language, capable even of accepting within itself under the name of dialectical logic, the rupture and opposition of universals which were abstractions, and the paradoxical and infinite movement by which they are concretely realized.'[3]

The emotive power of Lyotard's testimony turns upon its evocation of the rupture in a close friendship occasioned by Lyotard's break with Marxism. The rupture is designated by Lyotard a *différend*. This designation is instructive in that it throws light on the meaning of a key term in Lyotard's later philosophy. Given the impact this break with Marxism is revealed to have exerted upon his personal and theoretical/practical orientation to the world, its instructiveness is in part to be explained by its instrumental role in forging Lyotard's sense of a *différend*. Lyotard observes that what was at stake between Souryi and himself was whether or not Marxism was the means by which the world could be understood and transformed.[4] He defines the problem as fundamental, superseding a question of interpreting evidence in this way or that. He observes:

> The problem was one of logic. A differend is not a simple divergence precisely to the extent that its object cannot enter into the debate without modifying the rules of that debate ... Our differend was without remedy from the moment that one of us contested or even suspected Marxism's ability to express the changes of the contemporary world. We no longer shared a common language in which we could explain ourselves or even express our disagreements.[5]

Lyotard describes how the routine machine of Marxist dialectical logic, whereby alterity was to be overcome by negation and particularity was to be conjured out of universality, had broken down due to this change in perspective. He depicts how rhetorical figures, for example, being labelled a political regressive, lost their power to undermine him. Lyotard remembers how the movement of his thought freed him from a powerful emotional force. He explains the trajectory of his thought by recalling the process of questioning that led to his abandonment of key positions and attitudes. He describes how he came to question absolutes presumed in his previous Marxist allegiance, such as the maintenance of a unified non-contradictory perspective, and the sense that history had to be unfurling a pattern. He recalls posing the following disruptive questions:

> What if history and thought did not need this synthesis (of apparent contradictions); what if the paradoxes had to remain paradoxes, and if the equivocacy of these universals, which are also particulars, must not be sublated? What if Marxism itself were in its turn one of those particular universals which it was not even a question of going beyond – an assumption that is still too dialectical – but which it was at the very least a question of refuting in its claim to absolute universality...[6]

'A memorial of Marxism' is an affecting memorial to Lyotard's friend, and an evocative remembrance of the pain involved in a profound reorientation to the world. An index of this pain and its negotiation, is given in Lyotard's account of the split in *Socialisme ou barbarie* that was precipitated by Castoriadis's submission of radical but plausible revisionist theses to the group. Souyri was against this revisionism. It clashed with his fundamental commitment to Marxism as a theory and political cause. Lyotard reveals how he found himself, illogically, throwing in his lot with Souyri and the old-guard Marxists who began publishing *Pouvoir Ouvrier* after the schism. Lyotard explains that his paradoxical allegiance to the old guard at the very time he was experiencing profound doubts about Marxism's grand narrative was due to his sense of the existential significance of Marxism's expression of a *différend*. Hence, notwithstanding or more probably because of the painfulness of the *différend* Lyotard felt between the old-guard Marxists and himself, he supported the old against the new-style Marxism. He recalls that his support for the old guard arose out of an appreciation that they were incorruptible existential champions of a *différend*.[7] Beyond questions of theoretical complexity and argumentative coherence Lyotard avers that the old guard appeared to affirm, better than the revisionists, an alternative discourse from that maintained by capitalism, one of class, that disputes the hegemony of capital.

At the outset of 'A memorial of Marxism', Lyotard disparages his own capacities as a historian.[8] The disclaimer is apposite because it is unwise to read a memoir as an unproblematic account of the historical record. His rewriting of his break with Marxism in terms of a *différend* reflects a vocabulary and standpoint that were only developed subsequently. Nonetheless, it is plausible to read the break with Marxism as a spur to the development of this very vocabulary. The emotional turmoil that Lyotard recalls about the episode registers something of the anguished experience of deep conflict between perspectives that the notion of a *différend* is expressly designed to capture. If the pain of Lyotard's break with Marxism can plausibly be seen to inform his conception of a *différend*, it can also be seen to shape his repudiation of grand narratives. The repudiation of grand narratives is a defining aspect of Lyotard's post-Marxist philosophy and politics. What Lyotard rejects by the phrase 'the end of grand narratives' is adherence to and manipulation of totalizing theories purporting to provide a comprehensive and absolute insight. The memoir of his own commitment to and break from Marxism reveals Lyotard to have subscribed to Marxism as a total form of explanation of the social world. It is this commitment to a totalizing picture of the world that explains the disorientation involved in its rejection.

Lyotard's absolutist commitment to Marxism is evidenced in his *Phenomenology*, published in 1954, the same year as his subscription to *Socialisme ou barbarie*. Marxism is presented as maintaining a materialist perspective that provides an absolute revelation of the real, as opposed to the closet idealism of phenomenology. The force of Lyotard's conviction is not matched by argumentation. Despite canvassing a revisionist, non-determinist Marxism, Lyotard is dogmatic on the fundamentals of Marxism. It is this subscription to a totalizing perspective that is challenged by his confrontation with events in his essays on the Algerian question. The awkwardness exhibited in Lyotard's Marxism in these essays is compounded by the liberating enthusiasms of the essays inspired by the events of May 1968, which exemplify his drift from Marxism. He revels in the freedom of the revolutionary atmosphere and departs radically from the rigidities of a dogmatic framework.

The sense of breaking with a dogmatic, restrictive belief system fires the exhilarating, destructive rhetoric of *Libidinal Economy*, in which a libidinal economy is pointedly contrasted with a Marxist conception of a political economy. The animating drive inspiring Lyotard's repudiation of all representing logics is an animus against the absolutizing Marxism of the Althusserians as well as his own Marxist past.[9] This assault on Marxism, and its supposed bogus absolutizing claims, is evident in his conceptualization of grand narratives and in the energy of his repudiation of their universalizing pretensions. In *The Postmodern Condition* Lyotard identifies Marxism as a paradigmatic grand narrative of modernity that purports to legitimate science through a narrative of political and philosophical emancipation. The rejection of modernity and the concomitant embrace of the postmodern is announced by way of an obituary for Marxism and its absolutist mode of universalizing theory.

The energy propelling Lyotard along a path of critique that breaks with absolutist theory is generated by Lyotard's own Marxist path and by his sense of the constitutive entailments of Marxism. The essence of Lyotard's critique of grand narratives, and the focus of his critique of Marxism, is that its closed, self-referential circle of purportedly universal concepts cannot capture a contingent world, susceptible to many divergent perspectives. This critique is both forceful and plausible. The human world is a world of socially situated reflective, discursive agents, who understand themselves in divergent, unpredictable ways that cannot be encapsulated in a single perspective purporting to chart the flow of historical development.

Highlighting the unacceptability of Marxist claims to embody a comprehensive and unique explanation of the world, however, does not entail that Marxism is necessarily to be rejected absolutely. The absolutism of Lyotard's rejection of Marxism imposes an unduly restrictive interpretation on how Marxism is to be understood. The idea of an open Marxism that might be susceptible to multiple interpretations and contribute to a variety of plural perspectives is signalled, though not acknowledged, in Lyotard's own writings subsequent to *The Postmodern Condition*. In *The Differend*, Lyotard sets out a linguistic perspective that underpins his sense of the profound divergencies of view that rule out the general, universalizing perspective that he attributes to Marxism. In so doing, he articulates an understanding of the perspectival imperialism of the economic genre of discourse, whereby economic imperatives of efficiency and profit are seen as overriding other discourses. This notion of the discursive domination of capital is clearly drawn from Marxism. Lyotard, however, neither addresses sufficiently the provenance of his conception of the economic genre of discourse in Marxist theory nor provides a convincing account of how his notion of the dominance of the economic genre is to be seen as avoiding the pitfalls of totalizing explanation which he identifies as characterizing the Marxist grand narrative.[10] It is a sensitive but under-theorized aspect of Lyotard's position that he fails to specify the boundaries of an intellectual tradition. Hence he ignores the question of how his own theory may be understood as emerging from but not participating in a repudiated grand narrative. Lyotard's late work, in its aestheticized pessimistic reading of the present and future, would seem to mark an unarguable severance from Marxism. The sense of a systemic incorporation of all aspects of society into a pattern of development driven by performance optimization, which informs much within Lyotard's later writings, however, can be seen as developing out of Marx's notion of capital's self-reproducing infinity of development.[11]

Breaking with a grand narrative

In the closing sections of his *Phenomenology* Lyotard discusses the meaning of the third way, by which he means the possibilities of a union between phenomenology and Marxism, rather than designer socialism or Blairite renewal. These sections exhibit Lyotard's subscription to Marxism as a grand narrative, explaining reality and history, though they also reflect an aspiration to interpret Marxism in a flexible, open manner. Lyotard provides a bifurcated conception of Marxism. On the one hand, he aims at presenting a form of Marxism that is neither narrowly deterministic nor economistic, and on the other hand, he presents an uncompromising and relatively unsupported defence of materialism and the class struggle.

Lyotard's very detailed study of phenomenology reflects a concern to open Marxism to other styles of thought. He quotes approvingly from the work of Thao, who reads the priority to be assigned to the economic infrastructure as not depriving superstructural elements of truth and significance, and as allowing for an influence of phenomenology upon Marxism. Lyotard, notwithstanding the contrary interpretation of his standpoint professed by Gane, concludes by recognizing a positive role for phenomenology.[12] Lyotard observes:

> There is thus room at the heart of Marxist analyses for phenomenological analyses bearing on consciousness, and allowing us precisely to interpret the dialectical relation of this consciousness, taken as source of the superstructures, to the economic infrastructure where it finds itself engaged in the final analysis (but *only* in the final analysis).[13]

Allied to the relative autonomy that Lyotard attributes to the superstructure, he is also concerned that Marxism should allow for freedom and contingency in history. He stresses, 'we must therefore escape this impasse of equally total freedom and necessity'.[14]

Lyotard's review of relations between phenomenology and Marxism and the status of his non-deterministic, non-reductionist Marxism is ambiguous, however, for he asserts the absolute, objective truth of Marxist materialism and the class struggle. In highlighting the indubitable, uncompromising character of Marxist materialism, Lyotard refers to 'the insurmountable oppositions that separate phenomenology and Marxism'.[15] He takes Marxism to disclose the 'meaning of history' in identifying its basis in class struggle.[16] He repudiates the phenomenological originary constitution of the world. It is seen as rendering reality neither objective nor subjective, but ambiguously neutral. In contrast, Marxism is taken to affirm unambiguously and correctly the materiality of reality. Lyotard pronounces, 'Marxism is a materialism: it holds that matter constitutes all of reality and that consciousness is a particular material mode. This materialism is dialectical.'[17]

In *Phenomenology*, Lyotard's affirmation of Marxism is an uneasy depiction of it as an open theory, allowing for freedom and superstructural independence and yet absolutely insulated from the quasi-idealism of phenomenology. Lyotard's condensed defence of Marxist materialism lacks argumentative support. Leaving aside questions relating to the general validity of a materialist standpoint, his account is highly problematic as a reading of Marx's theoretical position. Marx's hyperbolic materialist pronouncements in *The German Ideology* are related to a rhetorical overplaying of his differences from other Young Hegelians.[18] Marx's most considered methodological reflections are contained in the introductory sections of the *Grundrisse*, where he contrasts his approach with Hegel's idealism, but still maintains the relational character of social reality and observes that these social relations 'can be grasped, of course, only in ideas'.[19] Marx's materialism, then, is by no means as straightforward as it is portrayed in Lyotard's *Phenomenology*. It serves as a reminder of the complexity of Marx's thought and the possibilities for interpretive pluralism allowed for by his texts.

The tension evident within Lyotard's defence of Marxism in *Phenomenology* informs his political essays on Algeria. In his autobiographical *Peregrinations: Law, Form, Event*, Lyotard rehearses the intensity of his commitment to the Marxist cause during the period in which he wrote these essays. He avers:

> A sense of how important to my soul my allegiance to the cause of combatting exploitation and alienation was can be gotten from the fact that for fifteen years I neglected all forms of activity and sensibility other than those directly connected to this cause ... Writing was authorized only as a contribution to the common cause.[20]

What emerge in the essays, and what are documented in Chapter 5 above, are Lyotard's identification and analysis of features of the political situation in Algeria and in France that do not fit easily with his Marxist commitment. Lyotard fixes upon the irreducibility of insurgent nationalism to a determining infrastructure and the clash between the nationalist and consumerist attitudes and behaviour of the French working class and the proletarian internationalism demanded by Marxism. In a retrospective essay, 'The name of Algeria', Lyotard observes with a possibly anachronistic clarity: 'The differend showed itself with such a sharpness that the consolations then common among my peers (vague reformism, pious Stalinism, futile leftism) were denied to me.'[21]

If the *différend* of Lyotard's movement away from a soulful commitment to Marxism informs his essays on Algeria without being expressly pronounced, then Lyotard's essays on the events of May 1968, *Dérive à partir de Marx et Freud*, display a clear drift away from Marxism. In 'On theory' he acknowledges the force of Marx's general formula for capital, and, against Althusser, he highlights the need to retain the concept of alienation, not as a component of theory, but as a matter of lived social experience. He registers his movement away from Marxism by remarking, 'in the situation we know today, and have known for at least a decade, in fact, traditional

Marxism isn't wholly satisfactory from a theoretical point of view'.[22] He is sceptical of the claim of Marxist theory to project the necessary development of a revolutionary proletariat. He disavows a clear identifiable locus for revolutionary change, and looks to the deconstructive aspects of modern art as being exemplary revolutionary acts. Moreover, he dissents from a view of revolutionary acts as fitting a preconceived framework to achieve a distinct outcome. He points to actions of the 'here and now' kind, which are inherently disruptive, as being exemplary revolutionary actions.

In 'March 23', another essay included in *Dérive à partir de Marx et Freud*, Lyotard, in retrospectively reviewing the Movement of March 22 with which he was involved, expressly distances himself from a revolutionary Marxist party. He celebrates the politics of disturbance that shatters the ordering and channelling of events that is undertaken by parties of order and parties (like Marxist ones) of counter-order. He declares:

> The explicit question of the March 22 movement is the critique of bureaucracy, not only of the state apparatus set against society, not only of the (revolutionary) party that confronts the masses, not only of the organisation of productive labour against free creativity, but also of alienated life as a whole against – what?[23]

The extent of Lyotard's drift away from Marxism is adduced in his introductory essay to *Dérive à partir de Marx et Freud*, 'Adrift', written shortly after 1968, and reflecting on those events and his drift from Marx and Freud. In it Lyotard observes, 'Everyone knows that socialism is identical with kapitalism. Any critique far from transcending the latter reinforces it.'[24] In a partial anticipation of his subsequent *Libidinal Economy*, Lyotard valorizes libidinal energy rather than laborious and carefully formulated critique of the capitalist system. His writing reflects the zestful, revolutionary energy unleashed in the events of May 1968 and the turn against organized Marxism. While praising nihilistic destructive revolutionary energy, he notes: 'In its practice, the young generation occasionally anticipates this destruction, acts and thinks without consideration for equivalence, takes as its sole guide, instead of a potential return, affective intensity, the possibility of decoupling libidinal force.'[25]

Political and libidinal economies

Lyotard valorizes libidinal energy absolutely in breaking free of his commitment to Marxism in vitriolic fashion by writing *Libidinal Economy* (1974).The book is a wild, wilful, rambunctious celebration of the libidinal and an abandonment of all modes of rational and critical representation that aspire to explain or master the unpredictable coursing of libidinal energy. Central to the writing and argument of *Libidinal Economy* is Lyotard's discrediting of what he takes to be the counterfeit, oppositional, representational logic of Marx. Marx is seen as claiming to capture reality in the network of categories specifying the contradictory movements of capital and history. Lyotard takes Marx to be setting up an unsustainable dichotomy between the phenomenal world of capitalism and an allegedly *truer* reality denominated by Marx as communism that is destined to supersede an alienated form of existence.

In criticizing the Marxist formulations of his erstwhile colleagues in *Socialisme ou barbarie*, Lyotard aims to break with the language of critique and opposition to capitalism constructed around the fantasies of unalienated communism and an unalienated pre-capitalist society. He observes, 'To restart the revolution is not to rebegin it, it is to cease to see the world alienated, men to be saved or helped, or even to be *served*, it is to abandon the masculine position, to listen to femininity, stupidity and madness without regarding them as evils.'[26] Lyotard cites Marx's publication in the *Deutsche-Französsische Jahrbücher* of extracts from Feuerbach's *On the Essence of Faith in Luther's Sense* as evidence of Marx's sympathy for Feuerbach's advocacy of immediacy against mediated notions of reality. For Lyotard, a simple immediacy is neither external to nor supersedes a sphere of mediation. The libidinal and the mediated world of political economy are intertwined.[27]

Lyotard's libidinal standpoint is self-consciously directed at exposing and effacing the dualisms of Marx and his successors. He insists, against Baudrillard, that there is no primitive society in which desire can operate cleanly without intersecting with the mediating, complicating elements of a political economy. He indicts Baudrillard for replaying Marx in assuming that a primitive society can model the clothes of an unalienated society. For Lyotard, Baudrillard is invoking primitive societies as 'the role of a reference (lost, of course), of an alibi, (which cannot be found), in his critique of capitalism'.[28]

Lyotard's libidinal fury at the dualism of critical, representational theory is let loose on the political economy of capital. He is committed to closing the critical gap between capital as an object of analysis and a preconceived great zero outside capital, from where analysis allegedly takes off and returns. He invests the notion of a political economy with libidinal energy, just as he takes non-capitalist economies to be political. He sees capital, in its cycles and mediations, as posing routes of intensification for the circulation of libidinal energy. The upshot is that there remains no space for ethical, critical judgement. Lyotard contrives to see a rush of libidinal energy amidst the exploitation and suffering of the English workforce during the industrial revolution. In reviewing the operations of capital, he suggests that an imaginary interlocutor might object:

> But you will say it gives rise to power, domination, to exploitation and even extermination. Quite true, but also to masochism; . . . And perhaps you believe that 'that or die' is an *alternative*?! And that if they choose that, if they become the slave of the machine, the machine of the machine, fucker fucked by it, eight hours, twelve hours, a day, year after year, it is because they are forced into it, constrained, because they cling to life? Death is not an alternative to it, it is a part of it, attests to the fact that there is a *jouissance* in it, the English unemployed did not become workers to survive, they – hang on tight and spit on me – *enjoyed (ils ont joui de)* the hysterical, masochistic, whatever exhaustion it was of *hanging on* in the mines, in the foundries, in the factories, in hell, they enjoyed it, enjoyed the mad destruction of their organic body . . .[29]

Lyotard, then, sets up *Libidinal Economy* as a text that is opposed to the whole business of critique. For Lyotard there is only libidinal energy and its unpredictable transmissions. In line with this removal of an authorial access to a critical truth outside his or her orbit of analysis, he accordingly disparages the notion that he himself has access to distinct rational criteria to provide grounds for his standpoint. *Libidinal Economy* is not seen as a work that supersedes or criticizes Marx according to rational criteria separate from the flows of libidinal energy that it takes to form reality. Lyotard sees *Libidinal Economy* as a libidinal investment, rather than a critique. He affirms: 'Let's repeat it over and over again, we are not going to do a critique of Marx, we are not, that is to say, going to produce the theory of his theory, which is just to remain within the theoretical.'[30] For Lyotard, reality and theory are expressive of an ungovernable desire that energizes and produces effects. He sees his own text as libidinal, just as he takes Marx's theory to be empowered by the libidinal forces at play in workers' labour, conformity and disputes.

Lyotard understands Marx as undertaking a libidinal study of capital. He sees Marx's protracted analysis of capital as being a libidinal investment. Marx's endless stalling on completing his critique of political economy is seen as a token of Marx's endless pleasure in dedicating his life to capital's movements and ruses. Lyotard, himself, rather than concentrating upon the detailed textual analysis or the theoretical tricks of the Althusserians, sets up a deliberately provocative rhetorical figure to present the libidinal sense of Marx's standpoint. He imagines Marx's work as being constituted by an extraordinary interplay between the old man, Marx, and the young girl, Marx.

The libidinal interplay turns upon the old man Marx providing a critical, theoretical alternative for the young girl Marx, who recoils in horror from the prostitution involved in the mediated, commodified world of capital. The notion of an unalienated world of communism where relations between the sexes will transcend a crude possession of women that is proffered by Marx in the *Economic and Philosophical Manuscripts* is repudiated by Lyotard as a fantasy.[31] The old man Marx is depicted as rescuing the young girl from Bataille's image of *Madame Edwarda*, God figured as a public whore and gone crazy.[32] Lyotard maintains it is not capital's presumed denaturing of relations between man and woman and man and man that disturbs Marx but capital's displacement of inherited order and its insane pulsions of sexuality.[33] In a highly provocative abandonment of his former Marxist standpoint, Lyotard muses on the fascinating libidinal possibilities offered by capital:

> Now we must completely abandon critique ... we must take note of, examine, exalt the incredible, unspeakable pulsional possibilities that it sets rolling, and so understand that *there has never been an* organic body, an immediate relation, nor a nature in the sense of an *established site of affects*, and that the (in)organic body is a representation on the age of capital itself. Let's replace the term critique by an attitude closer to what we effectively experience in our current relations with capital, in the office, in the street, in the cinema, on the rods, on holiday, in the museums, hospitals and libraries, that is to say a horrified fascination for the entire range of the *dispositifs* of *jouissance*.[34]

In *Libidinal Economy*, Lyotard breaks decisively with the substance and form of Marxism. The content of Marxism, its laborious, tortuous, unfinished critique of capital, is exchanged for an ambiguous recognition of the libidinal possibilities that are offered by capital's multitudinous mediations of desire. The libidinal is valorized at the expense of a fixation on critique of economic exploitation. Equally, Lyotard turns against the very form of a Marxist critique. He renounces the notion that reality can be represented by a reflective analysis that is separate from the pulsions of the real. He denies that Marxist critique can establish the outline of a truly human reality to supersede the tangled relations of capital. For Lyotard, the only reality is libidinal; libidinal movement energizes theory and practice.

The rhetorical force of Lyotard's exposure of Marxist critique is appropriately shocking and affecting. The reader of *Libidinal Economy* is forced to attend to disturbing aspects of the very idea of a critique of political economy. Lyotard highlights Marx's actual fascination with the intricate mediations of capital, and he casts doubt on the possibility of an essentialized critique of political economy that counterposes a tranquil, coherent world of unalienation to the labyrinthine excesses of capital.

Lyotard's break with the very idea of proposing a generalized critique of and alternative to capital is maintained in his subsequent writings. He dismisses the idea of an essentialized critical theory of society and thenceforward is antagonistic towards the possibility of a schematized general emancipation of society. However, he is critical subsequently of what he perceives to be the reductionism of *Libidinal Economy*, whereby all phenomena are understood as expressing libidinal energy. Distinctions, notably between reason and desire and ethics and power, are overridden in the valorization of the libidinal within *Libidinal Economy*, and Lyotard's subsequent writings acknowledge the need to recognize the autonomy of distinct spheres of activity. In *The Postmodern Condition*, he is highly critical of Marxism. He sees its general critique of capital as being undermined by the incorporation of the working class within a system of development that is driven to maximize performativity. He also indicts what he sees to be the essentialism of Marxism, which is contrasted with a postmodern pluralism.

Lyotard, Marxism and the *différend* of a grand narrative

The Postmodern Condition entrenches Lyotard's opposition to Marxism that is declared in *Libidinal Economy*. It represents an obituary for Marxism as well as for modernity. Marxism is seen to be an exemplary, but redundant grand narrative of modernity. Marxism is identified and condemned for purporting to provide a universal theory of necessary social and historical development, in which the contingency of history and the diversity of language games are ignored in the interests of a unifying mythology. Lyotard distinguishes between two tendencies within the Marxist grand narrative. He assumes that classic modernist grand narratives tend to be configured either philosophically or politically. On this view, Marxism as grand narrative lends itself to being justified either as a 'scientific' Marxism, in which the end of history is to be documented by a Muscovite Communist Party that has a monopoly of truth, or by a countervailing tendency to see history as a dialectic of consciousness that will be consummated by the proletariat becoming for itself.[35]

Marxist grand narratives in either of these styles designated by Lyotard suffer from their presumption that a single co-ordinating truth is to be realized in history. For Lyotard, the notion of the social bond cannot be reduced to an essentialized unity. He understands the social bond as being composed of a diversity of incommensurable language games. This notion of incommensurability is highlighted by the gap that Lyotard fixes upon as separating prescriptive from denotative language games. Marxism, insofar as it mixes these two modes of operating, is subject to confusion. In criticizing the political style of grand narrative, Lyotard avers: 'There is nothing to prove that if a statement describing a real situation is true, it follows that a prescription based upon it (the effect of which will be necessarily a modification of that reality) will be just.'[36]

Lyotard sees Marxism as purporting to provide a theory of the universal operation of society and of the directionality of history. He takes this theoretical style to constitute an anachronistic grand narrative. In assessing the status of Marxism as a critical ideology, Lyotard sees its anachronistic character as being highlighted by the course of contemporary history. He takes the totalitarian practice of Eastern European communist regimes and the incorporation of critique as part of the programming of society in the 'open' system of Western societies as signalling the redundancy of Marxism. The refined, careful critique that is preserved in the sophisticated critical models of the Frankfurt School and *Socialisme ou barbarie* are viewed as undermining the force of Marxism in their blurring of class analysis.[37] Lyotard's recognition of different versions of Marxism in *The Postmodern Condition* suggests that his generalized depiction of Marxism as constituting a grand narrative is questionable. He does not attend to the variants of Marxist interpretation and practice in sufficient detail to justify his conclusion that all variants are irrelevant to contemporary society.

In *The Differend*, Lyotard articulates a notion of language as expressing incommensurable modes of discourse that determine the linking together of contingent phrases. The differences between phrase regimens and genres of discourse testify to the inexorability of difference, and the injustice of Marxism as a mode of discourse, given its determination to encompass contingent and differentiated historical and social events within a synoptic discursive perspective. Lyotard counterposes the contingency and incommensurability of phrases and discourses to the unjustifiable necessity and essentialism that Marxism allots to the historical and political role of the proletariat. The Marxist notion of the proletariat, for Lyotard, represents a Kantian idea of reason, in its outstripping of actual experience, and in its incarnation of attributes and duties that supersede actual instantiations. Lyotard unfurls a series of names that signify historic events that symbolize the vacuity of Marxist claims. Berlin 1953, Budapest 1956 and Prague 1968 are seen as self-evident counters to Marxist myth.[38]

Notwithstanding his critique of Marxist universalism, Lyotard himself draws upon and transposes Marxism. He understands Marxism as itself testifying to a *différend*. He remarks, 'Marx tries to find the idiom which the suffering due to capital clamours for.'[39] Lyotard, though, takes Marxism as aiming to remedy this *différend*. He sees Marxism as tracing a counterfeit resolution through its imputed necessary, historical redemption of the proletariat. According to Lyotard, the only justifiable response is to evince the signs of suffering.[40] In *The Differend*, Lyotard can be seen as resuming and continuing Marxism by his depiction of the linguistic imperialism of the economic genre. He takes capital to be imposing a discursive monopoly on phrases. All phrases under capital are seen as being subject to the logic of saving or accumulating time so as to maximize efficiency in the pursuit of profit. Work, for instance, can be conceived in a variety of idioms; it can serve, for example, as a therapy, a diversion, an aesthetic act, but, for Lyotard, under capitalism work is reduced to a matter of gaining time. He remarks: 'Working conditions in a capitalist system all result from the hegemony of the economic genre, in which the issue is to gain time.'[41]

In *The Differend*, capital, the economic genre of discourse, is seen as unjust insofar as it silences other possible modes of phrasing. Lyotard remarks upon this commodification of phrases:

> Under this condition, phrases can be commodities. The heterogeneity of their regimens as well as the heterogeneity of genres of discourses (stakes) finds a universal idiom in the economic genre, with a universal criterion, success, in having gained time: and a universal judge in the strongest money, in other words the most creditable one, the one most susceptible of giving and therefore reviving time.[42]

Lyotard's conception of the dominance of capital and its investment in language and preclusion of other discourses is attested to in the essay, 'A svelte appendix to the postmodern question', that was published in *Tombeau d'intellectual et autres papiers* in 1984. Here he imagines capital as testifying to an infinity of the will that is restlessly opposed to its fixing in any determinate state. Lyotard cites the *Manifesto of the Communist Party* as registering a sense of the infinity of capital, though it is the *Grundrisse* that invokes this very notion of capitalism's infinity that Lyotard discusses.[43] There, Marx observes: 'The immortality which money strove to achieve by setting itself negatively against circulation, by withdrawing from it, is achieved by capital which preserves itself precisely by abandoning itself to circulation.'[44] Lyotard, in 'A svelte appendix to the postmodern question', highlights how what he terms the 'big deal of the past twenty years' is 'the transformation of language into a productive commodity'.[45] He maintains that the commodification of language is not to be opposed by an essentialized notion of alienation drawn from a theological or metaphysical discourse.[46] Lyotard, though, is aware of the threat posed by the prospective domination of discourse by an instrumentalist notion of performance optimization. What he offers in resistance to this threat is a svelte, postmodern sensitivity to paradox and difference. Postmodern resistance is seen as distinct from the Marxist paradigm of essentialist opposition despite Lyotard's identification of Adorno as a precursor of this standpoint.[47]

Development and the end of emancipation

Lyotard's break with Marxism is an upheaval that ruptures an erstwhile commitment to a universalist scheme of thought. He desists from viewing reality according to an essentialist perspective. The entire commitment to a scheme of thought that resolves differences and elides gaps in the historical record is renounced by Lyotard in his evocation of a *différend* that leads him to abandon Marxist commitment for a standpoint that is marked by scrupulousness for discriminating *différends*. This difference with Marxism is accompanied by Lyotard's transformation of the Marxist notion of the operations of the capitalist political economy into a notion of the development of a system that expresses the economic discourse of an instrumentalist concern with saving time. Whereas, in *The Postmodern Condition*, Lyotard was excited by the prospect of the postmodern undermining the one-dimensionality of the system, in his later essays he conceives the development of the system based upon performativity as being so remorseless as to preclude its supersession in a social or cultural revolution.

Lyotard's repudiation of the prospects for large-scale emancipatory change and, in particular, his conception of the redundancy of Marxism as a redemptive philosophy, are evident in his late essay, presented as 'The wall, the gulf and the sun: a fable' in Lyotard's *Political Writings* (1993). He remarks:

> What was ultimately at stake for Marxism was the transformation of the local working classes into the emancipated proletariat ... capable of emancipating all humanity from the disastrous effects of the injury it had suffered ... society was viewed as being possessed by the *mania*, haunted by a ghost, doomed to a tremendous *catharsis* ... The rights of the workers were the rights of mankind to self-government, and they were to be fought for through class struggle. I mean class against class, with no reference to nation, sex, race or religion ... The mere recall of these guidelines of Marxist criticism has something obsolete, even tedious about it. This is not entirely my fault. It is also because the ghost has now vanished dragging the last critical grand narrative with it off the historical stage.[48]

Lyotard's reading of Marxism in 'The wall, the gulf and the sun: a fable' is elegiac but decisive in its rejection of the very possibility of social emancipation. In the essay, he pours scorn on the recently overturned Marxist regimes of Eastern Europe and sees the West as inviolable to radical critique. Western liberal democracies are perceived to operate as effective open systems that assimilate critique in their ongoing instrumentalist development. Lyotard's postmodern fable sees development as a supra-human phenomenon of the complexification of the universe that will only be threatened by the explosion of the sun. He imagines that this contingency will, in turn, promote a development of audacious complexity, the development of thinking without a body. This scenario underlines that development, for Lyotard, should not be seen as a humanistic project, susceptible of analysis in terms of human agency and fulfilment.

In his essays of the later 1980s and 1990s Lyotard moves emphatically away from resisting the system by emancipatory rhetoric to seeing resistance to a prevailing systemic instrumentalism as being effected, if at all, by an openness to the sublime feeling of the limits of experience, the conditionality of existence, that is achieved in the suffering of writing and the sense of the corporeal, sexual nature of thinking. This identification of resistance by means of non-demonstrable, aesthetic awareness of the *inhuman* limits of experience prohibits the very idea of collective action to achieve fundamental social change. He emphasizes this corollary in his critique of Arendt's notion of resistance to totalitarianism, in an essay of the late 1980s, 'The survivor'. In this essay, Lyotard stresses how contemporary neo-totalitarianism operates by assimilating the powers of judgement, imagination and anxious, inspirational thinking to the suffocating business of one-dimensional performativity. He repudiates tellingly his own Marxist past, as well as Arendt's nostalgia for public, political action, in derogating the capacity for inspirational renewal of the revolutionary workers' councils set up in Hungary in 1956.[49]

Conclusion

Carver, in a recent book, *The Postmodern Marx*, in contrast to Lyotard, urges that the development of postmodernism has allowed for a perspective on Marx that can discard previous certainties, so as to appreciate the indeterminate, plural and fragmented character of Marx's writings.[50] Carver notes that the open, ambiguous character of Marx's work is now susceptible to interpretation according to freer criteria than the mid-twentieth-century imposition of certainties upon the texts. Lyotard's rejection of Marxist absolutism is justified, and he has contributed to the critical atmosphere in which the very notion of a general reading of necessary historical development is no longer credible. Ironically, however, in Carver's plausible reading of Marx, the very popularization of the postmodern perspectivalism entertained by Lyotard can be seen as undermining his own absolutist interpretation of Marxism.

Lyotard's treatment of Marx throws up anomalies. In *Phenomenology* and in the style of Marxism embraced in *Socialisme ou barbarie*, which is reflected in his essays on Algeria, Lyotard aims at adhering to a Marxism that is open to events and prepared to revise traditional Marxist standpoints. At the same time, though, his Marxism is held as an absolute commitment, governing his entire way of seeing the world. The ambivalence in his *Phenomenology* between a readiness to admit a phenomenological influence on understanding super-structural developments, and an absolute commitment to a materialist standpoint, taken as excluding a phenomenological perspective, highlights this problem. Likewise, Lyotard rejects Marxism with absolute and shocking language. The decisiveness of the rejection of Marx advanced in *Libidinal Economy* is not retracted, and yet Lyotard draws on Marxist ideas throughout his career.

Lyotard's later thought is melancholic in its elaboration of a one-dimensional system whose instrumentalism is taken as pervading the social world without admitting the prospect of social emancipation. The pessimism of this perspective is reinforced by recognition of how dissent and criticism are incorporated within the operation of the system so as to promote its development. Lyotard observes that social development allows only for a fugitive expression of radical imaginative resistance to its one-dimensionality. The fugitive character of this resistance, though, is matched by the lack of conceptual and empirical elaboration of the nature of the system that is depicted. Lyotard's rejection of an essentializing style in Marxism that hypostatizes the working class and views the social world in essentialist normative terms is apposite. Marx's texts, however, offer a detailed and elaborated conception of capitalism and its contradictions that contrasts with the sketchy nature of Lyotard's identification of the system. Lyotard, himself, in *The Inhuman* and elsewhere, refers to his characterization of development and the system as banal.

Given its putative role in giving up on social emancipation, there is a strong case for regarding the banality of Lyotard's reflections on the sociology of the present as highlighting a major weakness in his thought.

8 • Conclusion

Introduction

Initially, in this chapter, the motivation for and grounds of Lyotard's break from grand narratives are reviewed. The repudiation of grand narratives is seen as plausible, given the variety and contestability of perspectives about the social world and its comprehension. Problems involved in Lyotard's critique of general theory, however, are also recognized, notably the reflexive question of the justification of his own theoretical position. Indeed, Lyotard's very rehearsal of a definitive end to grand narratives tends to presuppose and involve a general conception of theory and practice that itself is susceptible to the problems of justification attributed to grand narratives. A sense of the tensions to which his own sceptical ideas are subject is arguably a motivating factor in the changing idioms deployed by Lyotard to establish a convincing expression of his standpoint.

The relevance of Lyotard's critical standpoint to politics and political theory forms an important dimension of an evaluation of Lyotard. Hence, this chapter reviews the impact of his postmodern analysis on the conceptualization and assessment of politics. Again, the verdict cannot be univocal. On the one hand, Lyotard's repudiation of an absolute perspective on politics and his valorizing of differences are valuable counterpoints to theories that merely endorse pragmatically successful and conventional forms of politics. On the other hand, his deprecation of the ideals of community and consensus is questionable. Likewise, his displacement of questions of distributive justice, equality and democracy by a preoccupation with promoting difference is as tendentious as his relatively unexplored theory of one-dimensional social development.

Lyotard's standpoint can also be assessed in the light of his treatment of Hegel and Marx, because Lyotard identifies these theorists as the principal exponents of grand narratives. His studies are insightful in their denial of the absolutist claims of the social and historical theories of Marx and Hegel. The construal of history as the site for a summative realization of reason by Hegel and Marx's projected redemption of humanity by means of the proletariat are prime candidates for Lyotard's debunking of the claims of theory. Moreover, Lyotard's sense of the refractoriness of particular events and standpoints to the generalizing sweep of theory serves to undermine confidence in the unificatory theoretical and practical ambitions of Hegel and Marx.

Lyotard's antipathy to system in theory and practice highlights blind spots in the perspectives of Hegel and Marx. His reading of Hegel and Marx, however, like his general reading of the nature and demise of grand narratives, is contestable. His tendency to absolutize a reading of Hegel and Marx as representing an uncontentious truth is tendentious, because the texts of Hegel and Marx lend themselves to a multiplicity of interpretations. They can be read in a variety of ways, including ways that confound Lyotard's reading of them as articulating closed systems of thought. Lyotard's sensitivity to closure serves as an antidote to readings of Hegel and Marx that completely ignore its presence in their works, but his absolute dismissal of Hegel and Marx is perverse.

However Hegel and Marx intended their texts to be read, they can certainly now be read in ways that undermine absolutist assumptions. More *open* readings of Hegel and Marx reveal blind spots in Lyotard's own perspective. Hegel's philosophy, like Lyotard's, is crucially concerned with the nature of modernity and the achievement of justice in a pluralistic world that is subject to the systemic fostering of instrumentalism. Hegel's reading of modernity, while problematic and superseded by the impact of subsequent events, is nonetheless instructive on aspects of the modern world that Lyotard tends to ignore, such as the socially constituted but insistently individualistic force of subjectivity.

Lyotard rejects Marx decisively, but Marx's reading of the global reach and generative power of capital is an important source of Lyotard's sense of the dominance of the economic genre of discourse. Moreover, Lyotard's generalized reading of the development of the present and prospects for the future is disturbingly shallow. It is evidently inspired by Marx's understanding of capitalism, but lacks the comprehensive and focused power of Marx's sociology that presses insightful questions and highlights revealing empirical observations even where its explanatory logic may be criticized. Consideration of Lyotard's treatment of Hegel and Marx, then, highlights two sorts of problems in Lyotard's rejection of grand narratives. On the one hand, it is based upon, and in turn reinforces, one-sided readings of major theorists, whose works are susceptible to a plurality of interpretations. On the other hand, the perspectives of Hegel and Marx offer ways of interpreting social structures and modes of individuality that either raise questions about or enhance Lyotard's substantive theorizing.

The end of grand narratives: delegitimizing theory

Lyotard's philosophy is a kaleidoscope of changing patterns, vocabularies and formulations. Husserlian phenomenology, Freudian drives, Wittgensteinian language games, the Kantian sublime and avant-garde art are featured on the trail of discovery, while Hegelian and Marxist syntheses, consensual politics and the 'open systems' of liberal democracies are deprecated as constituting blind alleys or one-way avenues of historical misadventure.[1] Amid the maelstrom of Lyotard's ceaseless conceptual experimentation, the critique of grand narratives functions as a metaphor for inflationary products of the theoretical imagination that must be rejected. Lyotard expressly declares the end of grand narratives in *The Postmodern Condition* (1979). They are seen as legitimating relics of a modernity that is renounced in favour of relaxed postmodern pluralism. The end of grand narratives is elaborated as meaning the redundancy of general, explanatory schemes that purport to underpin and legitimate the rational development of thought and action in their various guises. Lyotard maintained that these schemes do not work; they misconceive the nature of things.

Throughout his career, Lyotard's theoretical explorations identify gaps between theory and its object. For him, the theoretical presumption that reason can encapsulate the disruptive energy of events is misguided. Events happen so as to disturb the notion of a premeditated and representable rationale. Moreover, the rhetorical force of theory itself eludes its self-referential construal in rational terms. Lyotard's antipathy to universalizing theories and his critique of their claims to achieve *grand*, comprehensive forms of explanation is a continuous feature of his philosophizing. Hence, throughout his career, by his commitment to a radical scepticism over the status and powers of reason, Lyotard can be seen as opposing the comprehensive claims of reason that serve as identifying marks of grand narratives.

CONCLUSION

Lyotard's first major work, *Phenomenology*, affirms a commitment to a grand narrative, namely Marxism. The affirmation of Marxism is an index of the absolute nature of Lyotard's commitment to the cause of Marxism that is documented in *Peregrinations*.[2] The very ardour of this conviction serves as a guide to the significance that Lyotard attaches to a break with holistic, absolutist theories. The break with Marxism, and the affective force mobilizing this break, is of existential moment, and the energy of Lyotard's apostasy is released in subsequent texts, notably in the rhetorical incandescence of *Libidinal Economy*. *Phenomenology* is an indicator of Lyotard's persistent commitment to materialism as well as a token of a faith that will be renounced. Its grounds for adhering to Marxism and rejecting phenomenology are the uncompromising materialism that is attributed to Marxism, and the ambiguous status it identifies as constituting the phenomenological originary standpoint. Lyotard's support for Marxist materialism is problematic. The meaning of materialism is as questionable as the attribution of materialism to Marx. In considered methodological moments, Marx recognizes reality to be relational, acknowledging that relations cannot be understood save by a conceptualization that derogates from the absolute independence of material reality from theoretical concepts posited by materialism.[3] Nonetheless, and notwithstanding the problems that Marx highlights as being associated with imagining material reality outside of its human conceptualization, Lyotard consistently maintains the primacy of the materially given to secondary processes of its representation.

Lyotard's materialism is connected to his presentation of the limits of reason and the opacity of its object. Reason is unable to capture reality in its conceptual net, because the composition of the net is fundamentally different from the material it aims to contain. The material of reality is particular; it is distinct and fundamentally different from the general nature of concepts. Figural disturbance transgresses against discursive articulation. Names of objects in *The Differend* are seen as rigid designators because in themselves they cannot assign properties; there are no essential, discursive properties.[4] In *The Inhuman*, Lyotard suggests that thought cannot go on without a body. He sees the corporeal character of experience as linking human beings to that which supersedes a humanistic reliance on man's allegedly essential rationality. Sex and the bodily foundation to thinking impart imagination and creativity to a process that thereby resists reduction to iterative mechanical operations.[5]

Allied to Lyotard's consistent stress upon the material opacity of reality is his sensitivity to the irreducibility of difference. Difference is not to be submerged in a unifying identity because the material opacity that resists enclosure in the universals of thought signals the particularity of what is different from conceptuality. For Lyotard, difference is a feature of the unpredictable flows of dynamic energy detectable within the apparently exclusively rational order of theoretical conceptualization.[6] It is thereby linked to invention that subverts rational structures. Difference and invention are features of the silence that attends the process of listening. It presages creative thinking and admits the positive right to speak, which is tied to the articulation of something new and different.[7]

Lyotard's investigations of language reinforce his sense of difference as constituting a fundamental, irreducible feature of experience. Discourses, for Lyotard, however they are to be conceptualized, are plural and resist reduction to a general formula governing their operation.[8] Ways of speaking are various. Jokes are made to make people laugh whereas books on political theory and philosophy do not intend to do so. Patterns of discourse determine the way in which the world is experienced, so that it is misguided to endorse or reject particular streams of communication. Moreover, the rules governing patterns of discourse are subject to change, for there is no fixed way in which the world should be addressed. Lyotard's interest in art, in its various forms, reflects his sensitivity to the reflective inventiveness of artistic expression.[9] In an age of the mechanical production of images, art is depicted as essentially about the question of art's identity.[10]

The persisting features of Lyotard's philosophical perspective contribute to the emphatic, unqualified nature of his rejection of grand narratives that receives its classic statement in *The Postmodern Condition*. Grand narratives evince the very qualities of an explanatory scheme such as universality, finality, absolutism that Lyotard, on breaking with his own commitment to an absolutizing Marxism, takes to be repressive fictions. Lyotard identifies modernity in terms of its development of a rationalist mentality that aims at providing comprehensive and absolute theoretical schemes to underpin an intertwined commitment to reason and the pursuit of progress.[11] He perceives Hegel and Marx as offering contrasting synoptic perspectives that affect to comprehend the diversity of experience in terms of unified theories of social and historical development. Hegel and Marx are significant figures in Lyotard's own intellectual development, but he alludes to a plurality of modern theories that combine unity and certainty in equal measure, amongst which are utilitarian models of economic man, reformist socialist doctrines and structuralist linguistics.

Lyotard's objections to totalizing explanatory schemes that purport to reduce the diversity of actual and possible phenomena to the unifying terms dictated by their own models are well-founded. Lyotard's identification of a plurality of patterns of discourse admitting of a variety of distinct criteria governing communication poses obstacles for a unified explanation of social phenomena. While Norris and Luntley (and even Lyotard himself) refer perceptively to the stable criteria governing a number of theoretical practices that thereby admit relatively undisputed forms of knowledge, there are a range of practical activities and theoretical practices whose informing criteria are the object of seemingly chronic contestability.[12] Art, politics, ethics and social science are forms of practice whose nature and development are sufficiently contentious to undermine definitive claims to explain and guide them. Lyotard himself specifies how the fundamental perspective of Rawlsian justice is inherently contestable.[13]

The indeterminacy of the rules structuring significant discursive practices and the contingency that is generally assumed in performative practice combine to rule out theories purporting to explain an essential line of historical development. The conceptions of the practice of historians traced by Collingwood, Oakeshott and Aron highlight an assumed contingency within history and its insusceptibility to general forms of explanation. These delineated postulates of history reinforce Lyotard's objections to the claims of generalizing theories. A common assumption in the practice of a historian is that change ensues from the interplay between historical actors pursuing contingent goals amidst intersecting frames of social meaning.[14]

Lyotard, then, adduces a range of features to undermine the claims of generalizing theories to provide conclusive explanations, notably the prevalence of difference, contingency and contestability in discursive practices. Notwithstanding the effectiveness of this aspect of Lyotard's critique of grand narratives, problems are associated with the assumptions and execution of his critique that signal tensions within his philosophy. Lyotard's opposition to general theories of explanation suffers from an insufficiently nuanced identification of its target. The broad, undifferentiated characterization of the critique and its target signals the radicalism of Lyotard's hostility to schemes of thought and explanation. His resistance to the very idea of providing schemes to order, explain and unify practices is so implacable as to be indifferent to the discrimination of grounds supporting the schemes and the degrees of provisionality with which they are expressed.

Throughout his writings Lyotard fails to provide a clear specification of the constitution of a grand narrative. For instance, he discriminates neither between the levels of generality nor the ranges of applicability of different forms of grand narrative. This lack of informing clarity is part of a wider problem of identity in his analyses of language. In *The Postmodern Condition*, Lyotard explains the social bond as being composed out of an indeterminate number of language games. The processes by which these games either are individuated or may be individuated are not specified. A grand narrative is defined in terms of its tendency to override the autonomy of other games, but Lyotard fails to individuate these subordinate games and to map their linkages with one another and grand narratives. Moreover, matters are clarified neither in *Just Gaming*, a contemporaneous text, nor in subsequent texts, where the individuation and operation of the theoretically designated key terms, such as phrase regimens and genres of discourse, are not specified precisely.[15] The upshot is that Lyotard's opposition to grand narratives merges with a wider hostility to a recourse to reason in theory and practice. The very idea of aiming to reach a unifying consensus, no matter how provisional and tolerant of recalcitrance, is deemed authoritarian.[16] The radicalism of this opposition to unity entails that provisional, consensual forms of community are rejected as delusions of unificatory grandeur along with infamously repressive totalitarian projects.

Lyotard's opposition to grand narratives, then, abstracts from differences in the way they may be held and promoted. He tends to see grand narratives as being absolute and comprehensive explanations of theoretical and historical development. His reading of Hegelianism and Marxism in *The Postmodern Condition*, however, notes a tendency for Hegelianism to slide into a perspectivism and he recognizes a diversity of tendencies in Marxism. Lyotard neither attends closely to the variation in the way general theories have been interpreted, nor considers the possibilities of how they may be taken.

CONCLUSION

His rhetorical ploy of absolutizing their tendency to make illicit claims serves his own purpose, which is to dramatize the unacceptability of such claims.

The absolutizing aspect of generalizing theories is matched by the absolutism of Lyotard's critique of grand narratives. The absoluteness of his rejection of grand narratives appears a mirror image of their designated, absolutely unacceptable rationalism. Lyotard's scepticism over grand narratives is part of a wider critique of the claims of reason. His critique of reason and theory is neither partial nor provisional. His various theoretical texts subsequent to *Phenomenology* are designed to frame absolute limits to reason that are not to be transgressed by discursive exploration, no matter how provisional or tentative. The problems consequent upon this design are signalled in Dews's study of post-structuralism, *The Logics of Disintegration*. His judgement on Foucault and Lyotard in 1972 applies equally to the subsequent career of Lyotard. Dews notes:

> There is one obvious difficulty which theories such as those of Foucault and Lyotard, which espouse a perspectival account of truth, and – futhermore – attempt to ground a conception of political practice in this account, must confront: the problem of their own status and validity as theories.[17]

In setting absolute limits to theory, Lyotard theorizes in an uncompromising style that apes the putative grand narratives to which it is opposed, though he evidently cannot rely upon the discursive grounds that he aims to discredit. This situation engenders a series of tensions within Lyotard's thought that exert a strain upon its credibility. A dramatic way of destroying the claims of theory is to valorize desire as the primary all-encompassing force that is to be seen as motivating and underlying theory. This tactic infuses the coruscating *Libidinal Economy*, engendering a text that is written so as to lend itself to rhetorical libidinal excess rather than considered rational thought. The upshot is a text that is unremittingly radical in its strategy of superseding the dichotomy of critiques that trade upon, while aiming to refute, representational thought. Lyotard's writing of a shocking book in which theory is twisted into a rhetorical monistic extravagance rather than functioning as a means of establishing a considered truth, though, is unconvincing as well as unsettling.

In presenting everything as libidinal energy, discriminations, judgements and justifications are suspended so that Lyotard leaves most readers of *Libidinal Economy* reeling but unpersuaded by its rhetoric. To the extent that Lyotard ascribes a libidinal rush to workers during the industrial revolution who were experiencing exploitation and physical exhaustion, as well as to the capitalists who were manipulating stocks and shares, he deprives language and experience of an ethical register. Ethics and discriminating judgement can only be reduced to the libidinal at the cost of an abstraction from the complexity of reality.

If *Libidinal Economy* is Lyotard's most adventurous, polemical assault on reason, the subsequent revision of his standpoint is an express recognition of a preceding failure to deliver on the ethical side of experience. *The Postmodern Condition* and the associated *Just Gaming* are texts that aim to account for ethical and political judgements while directly repudiating grand narratives. These texts are problematic, however, in that their scepticism over grand narratives expresses an absolute opposition to essentialized prescriptions promoting ideals of unity and consensus, while inventiveness and pluralism are prescribed without reservation or considered justification. There seems to be an unrelieved tension between the promotion of heterogeneity and the deprecation of grand narratives. To recognize the fact of diversity neither justifies nor grounds an absolute commitment to its valorization over ideals of consensus and unity.

The Differend is a sustained and considered meditation upon language that rehearses Lyotard's profound scepticism over the possibility of achieving shared, unificatory forms of understanding. Phrases are radically contingent and under-determined and are organized by distinct discourses that admit of no common unificatory discourse. This conception of difference, though, rests upon a notion of a *différend* between genres of discourse that is assumed to be the same across styles of discourse, and to demand ethical testimony. There is a tension in Lyotard's standpoint here, which is displaced rather than relieved by his frank recognition of the incommunicable nature of a *différend*. A *différend* reflects Lyotard's understanding of Kant's notion of reflective judgement, whereby judgement operates by means of its own reflexive feeling. It is exemplified by the gulf in sublime feeling between the presentation and understanding of an object that occasions an incompossible conjunction of pleasure and pain. The rational and communicative indeterminacy of an unfolding of *différends* is a polar opposite of the universal discursive rationality displayed by grand narratives. Nonetheless, the judgement of a *différend* is presumed to be absolute even though its absolutism cannot be supported by demonstrable reasoning.

The notion of the sublime and the significance of reflective judgement in the making of all judgement is developed in *Lessons on the Analytic of the Sublime*. In this text, Lyotard develops an understanding of the intransitive, tautegorical character of reflective judgement as it is expressed in sublime feeling. Lyotard's exploration of Kant is invoked to show how a *différend* constitutes the limits of the expressible in signalling deep incommensurabilities that cannot be joined discursively. This working through of the notion of the sublime confirms the absolutism and the inarticulacy of his resistance to generalizing modes of thought, but at the cost of universalizing an incommunicable silence. The upshot is unsatisfactory, as Drolet observes,

> Viewing silence as a pronouncement of the sublime sentients of pleasure and pain saves the name of the differend. However, any modern idea of a discursive universe – in which individuals are conceived as engaged in the construction of a just regime – is thereby shattered. Whilst this conforms to Lyotard's political intent (because the construction of such a regime is founded upon an *a priori* truth pronouncement) it implies a retreat into solipsism.[18]

These problems of solipsistic inarticulacy are compounded by their articulation in a work of discursive complexity, which in its turn can only appeal to reflective judgement that is to be justified through its own experimental indication of a sublime aspect within the very notion of judgement itself.

Lyotard's preoccupation in later essays with the significance of an openness to a sense of the unmastered indeterminable nature of being, and the prospective suppression of this feeling by the determination of techno-scientific social development, is highly evocative. Its suggestiveness, however, lacks convincing argumentative support. Lyotard's invocation of a child-like openness to the non-determined singularity of contingent events is an arresting image, but tends to arrest the imagination in a nostalgic reverie rather than admitting and inviting critical discussion. His depiction of the malaise of the present and corporeal stirrings of a sublime awareness of the incalculability of experience is a suggestive testimony to a disquiet about facile complacency in technological progress and the cultural marketplace. It tends, however, to overlook multiple possibilities of openness and discovery in dialogue and interaction with others. Moreover, as Anderson observes, it appears to depend on a narrative that is at least as grand as those rejected by Lyotard.[19] In the late essay, 'A postmodern fable', Lyotard himself acknowledges how his fable of the development of complexification assumes the guise of a grand narrative. His exculpatory arguments to avoid this charge adduce aspects of the form and content of his narrative that are held to run counter to classic grand narratives of modernity. These aspects, though, do not deflect from the generality of the purportedly explanatory role played by the notion of development in this fable and throughout Lyotard's late work.[20]

Politics

Lyotard's political thought emerges out of his engagement with grand narratives. His politics are of interest because they provide a critical review of the extent to which politics may be conducted and thought about in terms of general theory. The strengths and weaknesses of Lyotard's political thought, as is the case with his general philosophy, turn upon the radicalism of his break with theories that aim to structure society according to general criteria. The effect of his repudiation of the susceptibility of politics to reflective theories of what should be done is that it promotes a politics of vigilant opposition and alert counterpoint to imperialist theory and enervating conformity. Lyotard's political standpoint alerts him to perceptible dangers facing individuals and groups whose status and interests are not favoured by a dominant political discourse. His awareness of the pretensions of theory, and the possibilities for an illicit silencing of possible discourses and standpoints overlooked in the press of social development, sharpens his sensitivity to politics being played out on a plurality of terrains. His resistance to oppressive unificatory idioms of politics is accompanied by the positive assertion of a politics of difference and the significance of activities that are different from those that promote consensual development.

Lyotard's politics arise out of a commitment to Marxism. His essays on Algeria 1956–63 track a reading of the politics of Algeria and France that stretches beyond the limiting vision of a particular grand narrative. Lyotard understands the Algerian conflict as exhibiting the irreducible force of nationalism, and the complete absence of French working-class revolutionary internationalism. His engagement with Algeria alerts him to what he will subsequently refer to as a *différend*, a sense of the dichotomy between an Algerian perspective and the view from France.

During his involvement in the events of 1968, Lyotard promotes a revolutionary politics of disturbing the status quo so that it reverberates with challenges to its assumptions and practices. In *The Postmodern Condition* and in the related *Just Gaming*, Lyotard supports a plurality of discourses and calls for a pagan adoption of an agonistic inventive mentality that arises out of and fosters difference. His espousal of difference is accompanied by a sensitivity to the countervailing one-dimensionality of the system. He develops the Marxist notion of alienation, so that he sees society as tending to promote conformity to a governing logic of performativity.[21] The political aspect of his notion of the *différend* turns upon its identification of the possibilities of injustice consequent upon the exclusion of a minority discursive standpoint. The late essays of Lyotard maintain the themes of difference and resistance to the pressures of cultural conformity, but the tone of the essays is distant from the revolutionary *élan* of earlier years. He displays a scepticism over the possibilities of radical public co-ordinated action. While acknowledging the significance of maintaining rights and a concern for distributive justice in the public arena, Lyotard attests to the significance of a melancholic individual recognition of what cannot be said and assimilated within the system.

Lyotard's political thought throughout his life shows him to be concerned in a variety of ways with the politics of difference. He contributes significantly to the theoretical exploration of notions of difference and identity that have been invoked in the study and practice of politics in recent years. Theoretical sensitivity to questions pertaining to the recognition of *different* identities harmonizes with the practical emergence of a politics of identity, evident in the women's movement and the campaigns of cultural minorities.

What is of particular value in Lyotard's analysis of politics is his elaboration of the cultural pressures exerted by normalizing patterns of discourse that threaten to override the peculiar creative aspects of different identities. Connolly, in his book, *Identity/Difference: Democratic Negotiations of Political Paradox*, highlights the fragility of an individualized identity in the context of normalizing social pressures. He notes:

An identity is established in relation to a series of differences that have become socially recognized. These differences are essential to its being. If they did not coexist as differences, it would not exist in its distinctness and solidity. Entrenched in this indispensable relation is a second set of tendencies, themselves in need of exploration, to congeal established identities into fixed forms, thought and lived as if their structure expressed the true order of things.[22]

Lyotard opposes the notion of a discursively representable objective order of things, and he is sensitive to the normalizing pressures of successful Western societies that function according to an instrumentalist logic which demands conventional behaviour and identities to make the system work. In maintaining a consistent opposition to the system, and in embracing a radical notion of difference whereby identities are to be forged by opposing prevailing normalizing tendencies, Lyotard displays a consistent political radicalism. The radicalism of Lyotard's political imagination marks him out from contemporary mainstream Anglo-American political philosophy which nonetheless shares his sense of the lack of uncontestable criteria to assess and order politics.

Rennger, in his book, *Political Theory, Modernity and Postmodernity*, highlights how contemporary Anglo-American political philosophy is notable for its presumption that controversy can be settled by appealing to the conventions and settled convictions exhibited in actual institutions and practices. He notes that both sides in the debate between liberal and communitarian political theorists consider that epistemological and political matters are to be resolved by turning to what is exemplified in practice. In referring to these aspects of the debate, Rennger observes: 'Each (side of the debate) depends upon the same general assumption, to wit that quarrels in moral and political theory can only be settled or resolved through the proper understanding and/or reshaping of our *existing* moral convictions and political institutions.'[23]

This recognition of the limits within which contemporary Anglo-American political philosophy tends to be conducted is significant because it throws into relief the singularity of Lyotard's position. Contemporary liberal and communitarian political philosophers are aligned with Lyotard in breaking with grand theory. They are opposed to a notion of political philosophy as providing universal foundations for a general conception of what constitutes a good polity.[24] Liberals tend to support the rights of individuals because individual rights are seen as putting less of a strain on justificatory theory than a defence of the public good, and because rights appear to accord with the settled convictions of reasonable citizens.[25] Communitarians are characteristically opposed to supra-contextual theorizing, and criticize liberals for misperceiving the crucial role played by communities in the shaping and ordering of values. They urge that the significance of actual communities and traditions in facilitating social interaction and in fostering values should be respected.[26]

Both liberals and communitarians, then, in practice and theory, in forsaking universalizing theories, tend to look to standard notions of what is politically reasonable that are operative in individual convictions and the practices of mainstream communities. This tendency to valorize mainstream (male) opinion and to accept the *normalizing* paradigms of the liberal individual or the community-minded citizen of contemporary liberal democratic states is absolutely opposed by the political imagination of Lyotard who, throughout his career, is hostile to mainstream processes of political normalization.

The contrast between Lyotard and the general run of contemporary Anglo-American contemporary political philosophy is epitomized by the distance separating his work from Rawls's *Political Liberalism*. Rawls is the most celebrated exponent of contemporary Anglo-American political philosophy, and his *Political Liberalism* rehearses this tradition's tendency to limit the imaginative scope of theorizing. In this text, Rawls reworks his notion of justice as fairness so that it is presented as a specifically political conception of justice. The effect of this manœuvre is to elicit the principles of justice from the practice of liberal democratic political cultures and to limit the application of these principles to a circumscribed political domain.[27] Justice is seen as adherence to principles applying to the basic structure of society, enabling fair co-operation between reasonable individuals whose comprehensive notions of the good are envisaged as overlapping around a constructivist, political notion of the good. Elaboration of a comprehensive scheme of justice is dismissed as too problematic an enterprise to underpin a credible political philosophy. Rawls envisages that his specifically political conception of justice fits with the requirements of a liberal polity in which there is reasonable disagreement on comprehensive notions of the good.[28]

Rawls's emphasis upon the limits within which political philosophy must operate assumes that observance of these limits is uncontroversial, and that there is an uncontentious area of public, political concern clearly divisible from a private realm in which individualized notions of the good can operate. Lyotard challenges these assumptions while maintaining a reasonable suspicion against universalizing discourses that would impose notions of the public good. What Lyotard highlights is the prospect that the unintended effect of corralling and reproducing standardized forms of social, public interaction, even in seemingly benign liberal democracies, will promote processes of normalization that suppress difference and inventiveness. For Lyotard, the constitutional protection of a private domain of individual rights cannot ensure that *différends* between perspectives and rights will not occur. Moreover, Lyotard is also a critic of a notion of a consensual political system that in its very reasonableness allows for the oppressive impact of a ubiquitous logic of performativity and stifles creative, inventive speech and action testifying to difference and otherness, that is the very stuff of the inhuman architecture of reality.[29]

Lyotard's political standpoint, throughout his career, is radical and challenging. It disturbs the limits and conventions shaping the political vision of mainstream liberals, communitarians and Marxists. Above all, Lyotard attests to profound but reasonable and energizing incommensurabilities between standpoints that undermine the credibility of Rawls's notion of *reasonable* individuals arriving at principled, benign agreement. Lyotard takes rationality to be reasonable 'only if it admits that reason is multiple'.[30] For example, the standpoint of a radical ecologist, who is against economic growth and the subordination of animals to the interests of man, and the perspective of a neo-liberal, dedicated to maximizing self-interest within the context of perfect competition between capitalist enterprises, are sufficiently opposed to preclude easy compromise. It is also by no means clear that it would be reasonable for either party to compromise their beliefs, for to do so might derogate from their commitment to achieving the good and their own personal integrity. In a late essay specifically taking issue with Rawls's notion of justice, Lyotard urges, 'it is not demonstrated nor can it be demonstrated that distributive equality is what is just'.[31]

Lyotard's evocation of deep-seated difference and his radical valorization of difference and inventiveness are valuable contributions to political theory. They function most effectively, however, as critical reminders that politics and political theory are inclined to override difference in the interest of maintaining or constructing viable, unified polities. Lyotard's political standpoint in itself is incomplete, partial and unsustainable. It neither recognizes sufficiently nor promotes the values of community, trust and compromise, while pressing difference so far as to undermine the prospects for stable, co-operative social behaviour. For instance, Lyotard's specification of a *différend* as a logical feature of discourse is debatable. Interlocutors in dispute always share things in common, but there is no way of specifying either the significance or the limits of what is shared with logical precision. Hence it is as wrong for Lyotard to insist on dissensus on logical grounds as it is for Rawls to anticipate the logic of reasonable agreement.[32]

In *The Postmodern Condition* and *Just Gaming*, Lyotard denigrates unificatory political structures so as to promote the heterogeneity of language games. Plurality, the multiplicity of standpoints, an inventive commitment to creative innovation are counterposed to the hegemony of consensus and enduring unity. This valorization of difference, however, leaves questions unanswered, notably the compatibility of different games, and the possibility of unjust, unequal practices within and between practices. In *Just Gaming*, Lyotard gestures at resolving some of these questions by invoking the paralogical qualities of what he takes to be a Kantian notion of reflective judgement, whereby unfounded prescriptions are to be made. The invocation of judgements lacking supporting criteria, however, would seem to state, without resolving, the problems facing Lyotard's politics. Lyotard is remiss in eschewing considered reflection on criteria that may allow individuals, differently situated and entertaining different goals, to co-operate and unite in terms of a respect for shared practices and principles. Haber, in criticizing Lyotard, observes, 'What is needed is a theory which respects difference while also allowing an open-minded examination of sameness ... Consensus cannot simply be ruled out of court.'[33]

Lyotard's *The Differend* highlights the injustice that arises out of an insensitivity to profound incommensurabilities. Justice, in contrast, is said to consist in the evocation of the feeling of a *différend* that signals awareness of discursive exclusion. Lyotard emphasizes that there is no meta-discourse into which *différends* can be translated, reworked and remedied. The upshot of this valorization of a non-discursive sublime feeling is that difference is taken to constitute a universal limit, precluding the possibilities involved in individuals making and experiencing an inter-subjective world in which their different interests can be satisfied along with their common interests in participating in public deliberations over the pursuit and distribution of goods. Drolet remarks: 'With no apparent basis for a shared discourse, Lyotard's post-modern politics fails to respond adequately to the critique launched against deconstructivism and post-modernism; a critique that contends that deconstructivism and post-modernism can offer no *corpus praescriptum* for human life.'[34]

Lyotard's divesting the human community of resources that are required for delivering a moral and political order engenders in his later writings an express concern for the inhuman that is only to be glimpsed on the edges of socialized humanity's homogeneous perspective. At the end of a late essay included in *Lectures d'enfance*, Lyotard allows full vent to his melancholic sense of the evaporation of the possibilities for redeeming contemporary neo-totalitarian instrumentalist conformity. He observes:

> With the destruction of totalitarian systems and their replacement by 'permissive' neototalitarianism (or, rather, possibilist neototalitarianism, which Arendt picks up from David Rousset and which is essential to these organizations, underscores this side of the question now more than ever), the very idea of an alternative is extinguished, and with it, that of a revolution . . . Birth or infancy, beginning, and finally the ability to judge, surely remain, but in loneliness.[35]

Lyotard's melancholic commemoration of an inhuman otherness, glimpsed beyond the vision of socialized humanity, that resists the projected complete dehumanization of man in the frenzied technological response to the threat of extinction, is a process of imagining that serves as a warning or reproach. At times the reproach is muted in that Lyotard balefully recognizes that contemporary liberal capitalism assures rights and open critique, but the sense of the system's limits and insidious foreclosing of imaginative possibilities is a constant theme of the late essays. Lyotard's late political theorizing, however, follows his earlier work in eschewing the constructive engagement of dealing with the assortment of hopes, concerns and possibilities that men and women bear towards the actual concrete circumstances of living together.

Marx, Lyotard and Hegel

Lyotard's philosophy and politics are shaped decisively by his confrontation with Marx. The force of his commitment to difference is expressed through his rejection of the totalizing character of Marxist theory. His essays on Algeria disclose a sensitive and hard-fought recognition of the folly involved in viewing complex events through the prism of a perspective that forecloses on the differences in actual experience. Likewise, his involvement in and reflection on the events of 1968 express a revolutionary perspective that takes its staging of inherently disruptive events to represent a direct counterpoint to the centralized takeover of power associated with orthodox Marxism. Lyotard's notion of the *différend*, which highlights deep incommensurabilities, resonates with his own sublime breaking of the Marxist faith and testifies to an appreciation of deep-rooted perspectival differences that is ignored in the Marxist image of unificatory communism.

Lyotard's sensitivity to difference and his advocacy of pluralism are justifiable counters to the confines of Marxist theory. His opposition to the overly general and absolutist formulation of Marxist theory is salutary. Marxism postulates an overall directionality to history. Marx's projected image of an unalienated communist society tends to serve as a fixed, normative standard determining the depiction of contemporary society and its predecessors as harbouring alienation and division. Nonetheless, Lyotard abstracts from the variety of possible and actual interpretations of Marxism that postmodern pluralism, ironically promoted by Lyotard, legitimates.[36] There are plausible interpretations of Marx, and theories deriving from Marxism, that take Marxism in directions that do not conform to an absolutist theory grandly dictating the course of past and future events. A non-determinist Marxism, which is relaxed about allowing a plurality of factors into explanations of social phenomena, runs counter to Lyotard's assumption of an absolutist Marxism committed to maintaining a rigid general theory of history and an equally fixed notion of the determination of political and social behaviour by class. Rational-choice Marxism, empirically-minded Marxist historians, analytical Marxists and Hegelian Marxists in distinct ways all open up Marxism to engage with empirical investigation and rival schools of philosophy and social science.[37]

Lyotard's absolutist reading of Marx, ignoring the diversity of interpretive possibilities offered by Marxism, is matched by the absolutism of his rejection of Marxism. Lyotard's schematic reading of Marx lends itself to overplaying the sharpness of his break with Marxism. Certainly his depiction of a *différend* between himself and a former colleague as necessarily precluding meaningful dialogue is questionable.[38] Just when, if at all, dialogue becomes impossible is a contingent question of social dynamics, rather than an event to be analysed in logical terms. What interlocutors share precludes precise specification, and it is equally impossible to specify what they may or may not come to share after dialogue.[39] It is therefore inadvisable to designate a *différend* in terms of the logic of language rather than as a psychological and social occurrence.

Throughout his career Lyotard is sensitive to the development of society along one-dimensional lines. This focus upon the systemic force of social conformity shows an affinity with the Frankfurt School of Marxist theory and thereby exhibits the continuing impact of Marxism on Lyotard's thinking. Even in essays revealing his drift from Marx, Lyotard articulates a continuing sense of the alienation experienced in society. His involvement in the pressure for educational reform in 1968 reflects the significance he attaches to resistance to developing cultural conformity. In *The Postmodern Condition*, he depicts the systemic development of a culture of performativity in contrast to which he elaborates a postmodern pluralism. In *The Differend*, he identifies the genre of economic discourse as tending to override all other discourses in its intrusive imposition of a demand to save time in all activities. In later essays, Lyotard refers to the neo-totalitarian character of social development that is dedicated to complexifying the system so as to heighten its effectivity. His persistent critique of a system that constricts differential developments and the powers of the imagination is an unexamined but persisting legacy of his early commitment to a Marxist notion of alienation.

Lyotard's identification of the systemic neo-totalitarian tendencies of the prevailing system, driven by the economic imperatives of maximizing economic efficiency, is the counterpart of his increasingly melancholy appeal to an otherness that is the fount of human creativity and energy. His sense of the conformism engendered within apparently benign liberal democracies owes much to his reading of the self-reproducing powers of capital. This reading of capital, in turn, is closely aligned to Marx's political economy, particularly

Marx's specification of the self-reproducing infinity of capital in the *Grundrisse*.[40] Lyotard's account of the contemporary system and social development, however, is highly general. It is allusive rather than specific in the claims it makes about the directionality and instrumentalist logic of contemporary society. It certainly neither emulates the depth of Marx's study of capital nor matches the breadth of Marx's projections of the impact of capital on culture, social relations, political behaviour, the formation of nation states and the operations of globalism.

Lyotard, in insisting upon an absolute, radical break between himself and Marx, is abrogating the standpoint that he embraces in his *Phenomenology*, where he accepts that 'Marx's theory is not a dogma but a guide for action.'[41] In the same text, Lyotard also strikes an uncharacteristically subverting coda to his critique of Hegel. In *Phenomenology*, Hegel is contrasted unfavourably with Husserl because Hegel is construed as effecting a rationalist closure of meaning by effacing the originary immediacy of reality in the transparent self-consciousness of a closing absoluteness. Lyotard, however, suggests a contrary reading of Hegel in remarking:

> At the same time, if we admit that 'the *Phenomenology of Spirit* is militant philosophy, not yet triumphant' (Merleau-Ponty), if we view Hegelian rationalism as open, the system as a step, then perhaps Husserl and Hegel finally converge on the position, 'We wish to see the true in the form of result' of the *Philosophy of Right* – but on condition that this result also be a moment.[42]

The possibility of interpreting Hegel as maintaining an *open* system is not pursued elsewhere in Lyotard's writings. It is a reminder, though, that Hegel may be interpreted in a different spirit than is generally undertaken by Lyotard. The closure involved in Lyotard's interpretation of Hegel as an absolutist, bent upon construing all reality as so many expressions of an identical formulaic subject, is at the very least debatable. There are many interpretations of Hegel, but to fix on his claims to absolutism so as to dismiss his project is to deny access to a subtle and imaginative rereading of the human condition that interprets the patterns of complex, cross-cutting meaning that socially situated conscious and self-conscious human beings trace in their activities. The absolute dismissal of Hegel is to refigure an absolutism that undermines the positive possibilities of realigning a postmodern philosophy of difference with a Hegelian conception of the complexity of modernity.

Gillian Rose, in an astute article on postmodernism entitled 'The postmodern complicity', signals the dangers of such a postmodern closure of the past. She concludes:

> Paradoxically, the claim advanced formerly by modern and now by postmodern architecture and philosophy, that each alone offers a genuine 'opening' disowns previous openings – attempts to renegotiate potentiality and actuality – by characterising the other position without differentiation as 'total', 'closed', 'functionalist', 'rationalistic', 'dominatory', instead of comprehending illusion: the relation between the limit of the meaning at stake and its configuration or form. I conclude that the use of architecture in philosophy bolsters a tendency to replace the concept by the sublimity of the sign, which is, equally, to employ an unexamined conceptuality without the labour of the concept.[43]

An openness to Hegel would serve as an antidote to Lyotard's exaggerated promotion of difference and inventiveness and to his antipathy to all forms of social and political organization that aim to achieve consensus and unity. Hegel's reading of the modern world is subtle and complex. He perceives the modern world as exhibiting complex, contradictory features. He observes the advent of difference in the form of individualism and in the endless pursuit of particular needs processed by market transactions. A section of society, however, is taken by Hegel to be alienated from the instrumentalist and self-interested culture of civil society and all members of society are seen to be affected deeply by the market's valorization of particular interests. To counterbalance the particularity engendered in modern society, Hegel observes and aims to foster the development of political organizations and civil associations capable of dealing with these contrary elements so as to maintain a complex and differentiated sense of community.[44]

Hegel's reading of the development of the modern world underrates the contingency of events and the possibilities of democracy. It also misrecognizes patriarchy as being compatible with individual freedom and contrives to interpret monarchy as symbolizing man's free spirituality. It is a reading of the modern world, however, that recognizes significant features of modern life, namely the dual aspirations for community and individual difference. Hegel is right to see that modes of individuality are engendered in social practices of the modern world and that individualism is a powerful force that demands recognition. Lyotard is remiss in ignoring its force and its promotion by contemporary social forces, such as the market and associational groups. Likewise, he underrates the need to consider ways in which to foster countervailing forms of community and social solidarity.

O'Neill is perceptive in suggesting that Hegel's insights into the necessary and complex constitutive relations between the individual and social practices should not be abandoned lightly. He is also right to signal the one-sidedness of Lyotard's countervailing image of a repressed subjectivity aiming to stand apart from mass conformity. O'Neill remarks:

> Lyotard misconceives the grand narrative of reason and freedom by dislocating the formal contradiction between reason and freedom, or between society and the individual. But contradiction is constitutive of the master narrative of modernity ... One does not 'post' modernity by dissolving the dialectical transformation of contradiction in the grand narrative into the mini-narrative of unlimited individuation versus total conformity.[45]

A persisting weakness of Lyotard's philosophical perspective is its omission of a convincing account of subjectivity, that is exacerbated by a related omission of a detailed review of social practices. Lyotard is inclined to deprecate the force of subjectivity and to see all social practices as obeying a common logic in social development. Both of these standpoints are questionable, and at the least require considerable argument, given the manifest differences between social practices, the important role attributed to subjectivity in social and ideological practices, and the role of reflective agency as a conceptual condition of thought and action.

Grand narratives revisited

To read Lyotard is to enter an exciting and imaginative world in which theoretical ingenuity is dedicated to showing the limits of theory. Grand narratives serve as a metaphor for what Lyotard opposes throughout his career, namely the purported power of theory to explain and direct social and intellectual life. For Lyotard, grand narratives miss their mark: reality eludes the network of concepts. The failure of grand narratives, however, is also seen as an ethical and political failure insofar as general theories are invoked to order and repress members of society. Lyotard makes a strong case for denying the claims of general theory to provide an uncontestable absolutist explanation of social and ethical life, and his promotion of difference and inventiveness is a salutary rejoinder to the misguided universalism of general theories of politics.

Lyotard's case against grand narratives, however, is pressed too far. For one thing, he assumes that classic general theories purporting to explain reality and shape society, like Hegelianism and Marxism, must be held as uncontestable absolutist forms of explanation. Again, he tends to assume that all theories that aim to achieve a social consensus or sense of community share in the rationalist folly of grand narratives. In pressing his case against grand narratives, Lyotard also argues for the necessary failure of general forms of explanation and practical procedures to achieve unity and social consensus. In so doing, his argument assumes the absolutist guise that he denounces. Lyotard's absolutist commitment to an essential otherness within experience is particularly pronounced in his later essays. In 'On a hyphen', an essay that testifies to a *différend* that he sees as occluded by the hyphen in the designation Judaeo-Christian, Lyotard is sympathetic to the mystery and otherness that he takes to be recognized in Judaism. He remarks, 'The Torah is not the Voice but rather its deposited letter. The language of the Other is not dead but estranged or foreign.'[46]

Lyotard's own absolutism in interpreting Hegel and Marx and in insisting upon an otherness that repels theoretical explanation tends to undermine the force of his argument against grand narratives. While a notion of the uncontestability of general explanations and their absolutist rhetoric must be rejected as Lyotard commends, it is inadvisable to reject the impulse to develop general explanations of human thought and practice. Lyotard's vision of the role of politics, philosophy, art, science and the meaning of social development constitutes a connected set of explanations that makes grand claims that he never fully acknowledges. While there is no knock-down way of evaluating these claims, it can certainly be ventured that Lyotard's general framework of explanation is problematic. His perspective exhibits logical tensions, a lack of empirical and conceptual support for its account of social development and the significant omission of a developed analysis of the relations between subjectivity and inter-subjective forms of social practice that render its reading of the social world uncertain and speculative.

Above all, perhaps, Lyotard is too ready to dismiss the notion of self-consciously developing a grand narrative. Hegel's philosophy develops an account of the self and its implication in society and history as generating and explaining recourse to grand narratives. Hegel's dialectical explanation of the source of thought and practice in self-consciousness and freedom explains and justifies the impulse to provide grand self-conscious explanations as being the consummation of conscious and self-conscious reflections on the conditionality of freedom. Bernstein remarks,

> Self-consciousness in its full sense, which of course can never be complete, requires the self to traverse the conditions of its own comportment in and towards the world, which is just as Heidegger, Hegel and others have argued, to recollect and appropriate the traditions to which the self in question belongs ... Narrative repetition, grand narration, just is the collective form of human self-consciousness.[47]

Postmodernism is associated with the name of Lyotard. *The Postmodern Condition* popularized and provided a philosophical legitimation of a term that signalled a cultural turn away from systematic theorizing and assured notions of political and social progress. In the aftermath of his death, Lyotard's work as a whole can be seen as constituting a powerful challenge to holistic forms of reason and prevalent modern notions of consensual political and cultural progress. The contemporary world, however, cannot turn its back on its past. Hegel's identification of the particular and different in developing forms of social practice and Marx's notion of the one-dimensional self-reproducing and aggrandizing powers of capital are not to be abandoned lightly. Classic theorists of modernity such as Hegel and Marx can only be pigeon-holed as outmoded theorists by a self-subverting closed reading of their works that is thereby unable to recognize continuing *modern* aspects of social and cultural practice.

Notes

1 Introduction

1. See for instance the influential role assigned to Lyotard and *The Postmodern Condition* in popularizing the notion of postmodernity in D. Lyon, *Postmodernity* (Buckingham: Open University Press, 1994).
2. See, amongst other recent and informed commentaries that look beyond *The Postmodern Condition* in assessing Lyotard's thought, J. Williams, *Lyotard: Towards a Postmodern Philosophy* (Cambridge: Polity Press, 1998) and S. Sim, *Jean-François Lyotard* (London: Prentice Hall and Harvester Wheatsheaf, 1996).
3. See J.-F. Lyotard, 'Answer to the question: what is the postmodern?', in J.-F.Lyotard, *The Postmodern Explained to Children: Correspondence 1982–1985* (London: Turnaround, 1992).
4. N. Fraser and L. Nicholson, 'Social criticism without philosophy: an encounter between feminism and postmodernism', in *Theory, Culture and Society*, 5/2–3 (June 1968), 376.
5. For Lyotard's reservations about narratives, see his 'Apostil on narratives', in *The Postmodern Explained to Children*, p. 29.
6. Lyotard's thought is essentially critical, and directed against antagonists who valorize the theoretical. His most notable opponent is Hegelian rationalism, but structuralism in its various guises and systems theory also figure amongst his opponents.
7. See J.-F. Lyotard, 'Rewriting modernity', in Lyotard, *The Inhuman: Reflections on Time* (Cambridge: Polity Press, 1991).
8. For an analysis of the circumspection evident in contemporary liberal political theory, for instance in the post-liberalism of John Gray and the specifically political conception of justice envisaged in Rawls's *Political Liberalism*, see G. Browning, 'Contemporary liberalism', in G. Browning, A. Halcli and F. Webster (eds.), *Understanding Contemporary Society: Theories of the Present* (London: Sage, 2000).
9. For a clear statement of Habermas's post-metaphysical standpoint, see J. Habermas, 'Reconciliation through the use of public reason: remarks on John Rawls's *Political Liberalism*', *Journal of Philosophy*, 92 (March 1995), 109–31.
10. See J. Butler and J. W. Scott (eds.), *Feminists Theorize the Political* (New York and London: Routledge, 1992) for an interesting collection

of articles that bear upon a feminist politics of recognition and post-modernism.
11. See J.-F. Lyotard, *The Differend: Phrases in Dispute*, trans. G. Van Den Abbeele (Manchester: Manchester University Press, 1988).
12. Williams, *Lyotard: Towards a Postmodern Philosophy*, chap. 2.
13. J.-F. Lyotard, *Peregrinations*, ed. D. Carroll (New York: Columbia University, Press, 1988), pp. 1–15.
14. J.-F. Lyotard, 'Mainmise', in Lyotard and E. Gruber, *The Hyphen*, trans. P.-A. Brault and M. Naas (New York: Humanity Books, 1999), p. 1.
15. See Lyotard, *The Differend*, for a clear recognition of his advancement of a distinct perspective.
16. J.-F. Lyotard, *The Postmodern Condition: A Report on Knowledge*, trans. G. Bennington and B. Massumi (Manchester: Manchester University Press, 1983).
17. C. Rojek, 'Lyotard and the decline of "society"', in C. Rojek and B. Turner, *The Politics of Jean-François Lyotard: Justice and Political Theory* (London: Routledge, 1998), p. 20.
18. See, for instance, S. Sim, *Jean-François Lyotard*; J. Williams, *Lyotard: Towards a Postmodern Philosophy*; B. Readings, *Introducing Lyotard: Art and Politics* (London: Routledge, 1991); G. Bennington, *Lyotard: Writing the Event* (Manchester: Manchester University Press, 1988).
19. Bennington, *Lyotard: Writing the Event*, p. 9.
20. For the latter reading of politics, see the essays in Lyotard, *The Inhuman*, and J.-F. Lyotard, *Postmodern Fables*, trans. G. Van Den Abbeele (Minneapolis: University of Minnesota Press, 1997).
21. J. Habermas, *Between Facts and Norms* (Cambridge: Polity Press, 1996), p. 9.
22. For useful surveys of contemporary post-metaphysical liberalism, see M. Evans, 'Liberalism and inoffensiveness', *Politics*, 15/3 (Sept. 1995), 191–6; S. Chen, 'Liberal justification: a typology', *Politics*, 18/3 (Sept. 1998), 189–96.
23. J. Martin, 'The social and the political', in F. Ashe, A. Finlayson, M. Lloyd, I. Mackenzie, J. Martin and S. O'Neill, *Contemporary Social and Political Theory* (Buckingham: Open University Press, 1999), p. 175.
24. I. M. Young, *Justice and the Politics of Difference* (Princeton, Princeton, NJ: University Press, 1990), p. 4.
25. A. Phillips, *Democracy and Difference* (Cambridge: Polity Press, 1993).
26. For a critical considered focus upon *The Differend* see the section on Lyotard in D. Furrow, *Against Theory: Continental and Analytic Challenges in Moral Philosophy* (London and New York: Routledge, 1995).

27 For a lively article that highlights how the term 'political correctness' functions in a pejorative way due to the deprecation of political activity in mainstream political ideologies, see E. Frazer, 'Politics and correctness', *Politics*, 14/1 (1994) 3, 9–14.

28 J. Keane, 'The modern democratic revolution: reflections on Lyotard's *The Postmodern Condition*', in A. Benjamin (ed.), *Judging Lyotard* (London and New York: Routledge, 1992).

29 J.-F. Lyotard, 'Futility in revolution', in Lyotard, *Toward the Postmodern*, ed. R. Harvey and M. Roberts (Atlantic Highlands, NJ: Humanities Press, 1993), pp. 87–115. This piece was published in J.-F. Lyotard, *Rudiments païens: genre dissertatif* (Paris: Union Générale d'Éditions, 1977).

30 R. Boyne, 'Postmodernism, the sublime and ethics', in J. Good and I. Velody (eds.), *The Politics of Postmodernity* (Cambridge: Cambridge University Press, 1998), p. 214.

31 J.-F. Lyotard, *Phenomenology*, trans. B. Bleakley (Albany, NY: State University of New York Press, 1991). See also D. Carroll, *Paraesthetics: Foucault, Lyotard, Derrida* (London and New York: Methuen, 1987), p. 32.

32 J.-F. Lyotard, 'Apostil on narratives', in Lyotard, *The Postmodern Explained to Children*, p. 29.

33 J.-F. Lyotard, 'Memorial to Marxism', in Lyotard, *Driftworks*.

34 J.-F. Lyotard, 'Judicieux dans le *Différend*', in J. Derrida, V. Descombes, G. Kortian, P. Lacoue-Labarthe, J.-F. Lyotard and J.-L. Nancy, *La Faculté de juger* (Paris: Les Éditions de Minuit, 1985), pp. 234–5.

35 J.-F. Lyotard, *Signed Malraux*, trans. R. Harvey (Minneapolis: University of Minnesota Press, 1999), p. 270.

36 J.-F. Lyotard, *Postmodern Fables*; see for instance the opening fable, 'Marie goes to Japan', in which the eponymous heroine is expected to discuss a number of culturally acceptable topics such as difference, alterity and multiculturalism.

2 Postmodernity and the Delegitimation of Modernity

1 See D. Lyon, *Postmodernity* (Buckingham: Open University Press, 1994). For a retrospective assessment of its reception, see P. Anderson, *The Origins of Postmodernity* (London and New York: Verso, 1998).

2 F. Fukuyama, *The End of History and the Last Man* (London: Hamish Hamilton, 1992).

3 See, for instance, the essays in part 1 of B. Turner (ed.), *Theories of Modernity and Postmodernity* (London: Sage, 1990).

4 For a highly critical account of the nature of modern liberalism, which is particularly severe on its support for procedural neutrality, see R. Beiner, *What's the Matter with Liberalism* (Berkeley, CA, and London: University of California Press, 1992). See also the affiliated criticisms offered in the opening chapter of J. Gray, *Enlightenment's Wake: Politics and Culture at the Close of the Modern Age* (London and New York: Routledge, 1995).
5 J.-F. Lyotard, interview in *Lotta Poetica*, 3rd ser. 1/1 (1987), 82.
6 See J.-F. Lyotard, interview, *Culture and Society*, 5/2–3 (1988); and 'Apostil on narratives', in Lyotard, *The Postmodern Explained to Children: Correspondence 1982–1985*, trans. ed. J. Pefanis and M. Thomas (London: Turnaround, 1992), p. 29.
7 See the critique of Lyotard undertaken by Honneth in which Lyotard's disavowal of general principles is seen as undermining the promotion of conditions allowing for agonistics. A. Honneth, 'An aversion against the universal: a commentary on Lyotard's *Postmodern Condition*', *Theory, Culture and Society*, 2/3 (June 1988), 9.
8 B. Readings, *Introducing Lyotard: Art and Politics* (London: Routledge, 1991), p. 85.
9 Ibid., p. 85.
10 J. M. Bernstein, 'Grand narratives', in D. Wood (ed.), *On Paul Ricoeur: Narrative and Interpretation* (London and New York: Routledge, 1991), p. 110.
11 D. Coole, 'Master narratives and feminist subversions', in J. Good and I. Velody (eds.), *The Politics of Postmodernity* (Cambridge: Cambridge University Press, 1998), p. 123.
12 Lyon, *Postmodernity*, p. 12.
13 For evidence of the dissemination of managerialism into the public sector, see O. Hughes, *Public Management and Administration* (London and New York: Macmillan, 1994).
14 For an authoritative account of the intensification of processes of commodification see D. Harvey, *The Condition of Postmodernity* (Oxford and Cambridge, MA: Blackwell, 1990).
15 For Lyotard's sense of the actual production of alienation in social conditions, see J.-F. Lyotard, 'On theory: an interview', in Lyotard, *Driftworks*, ed. R. Mckeon (New York: Columbia University Press, 1984).
16 J.-F. Lyotard, *The Postmodern Condition: A Report on Knowledge* trans. G. Bennington and B. Massumi (Manchester: Manchester University Press, 1984), p. 13.
17 B. Smart, *Modern Conditions, Postmodern Controversies* (London and New York: Routledge, 1992), p. 175.
18 Lyotard, *The Postmodern Condition*, p. 21.

19 Ibid., p. 9.
20 Ibid., p. 14.
21 Ibid., p. 63.
22 See once again the questions raised in Readings, *Introducing Lyotard*, p. 85.
23 Lyotard, *The Postmodern Condition*, pp. 18–23.
24 S. Connor, *Postmodernist Culture: An Introduction to Theories of the Contemporary* (Oxford: Blackwell, 1997), p. 27.
25 The link between the modern state and science is taken as being a standard argument explaining modernity in Pierson's review of the role of the state in debates about modernity and postmodernity. C. Pierson, *The Modern State* (London and New York: Routledge, 1996), p. 38.
26 For the complexity within the notion of modernity see C. Taylor, *Sources of the Self: The Making of the Modern Identity* (Cambridge: Cambridge University Press, 1989).
27 Lyotard's references to Plato and his separation of the justification of science from science itself do not acknowledge that Plato held a negative view of science and empirical investigation in general. The sciences for which he showed respect were deductive in character. See Plato, *The Republic of Plato*, trans. with an introduction and notes by F. M. Cornford (London: Oxford University Press, 1941), 6. 502c–509c, pp. 211–56.
28 Connor, *Postmodernist Culture*, p. 28.
29 P. Scott, 'The postmodern university', in A. Smith and F. Webster (eds.), *The Postmodern University: Contested Visions of Higher Education in Society* (Buckingham: Open University Press, 1996), p. 41.
30 Lyotard, *The Postmodern Condition*, pp. 53–60.
31 Ibid., p. 54.
32 See the chapter on the nature of normal science in T. Kuhn, *The Structure of Scientific Revolutions* (Chicago: University of Chicago Press, 1962), pp. 23–35.
33 Lyotard, *The Postmodern Condition*, p. xxiii.
34 Ibid., p. 31–7.
35 Ibid., p. 33–4.
36 Ibid., p. 36–7.
37 Ibid., pp. 11–14.
38 Ibid., p. 40.
39 J. Habermas, *The Philosophical Discourse of Modernity* (Cambridge: Polity Press, 1987), p. 7.
40 Lyotard,'Apostil on narratives', p. 30.
41 See J.-F. Lyotard, 'A postmodern fable', in J.-F. Lyotard, *Postmodern Fables*, trans. G. Van Den Abbeele (Minneapolis: University of Minnesota Press, 1997), p. 97.

42 J.-F. Lyotard, 'Anima minima', in Lyotard, *Postmodern Fables*, p. 235.
43 J.-F. Lyotard, 'A bizarre partner', in Lyotard, *Postmodern Fables*, p. 127.
44 See C. Norris, 'Postmodernism', in G. Browning, A. Halcli and F. Webster (eds.), *Understanding Contemporary Society: Theories of the Present* (London: Sage, 2000) and M. Luntley, *Reason, Truth and Self: The Postmodern Reconditioned* (London and New York: Routledge, 1995).
45 Lyotard, *The Postmodern Condition*, p. 10.
46 Lyotard, 'A postmodern fable', p. 99.
47 Ibid., pp. 83–103.
48 See, for instance, C. Turner, 'Lyotard and Weber: postmodern rules and Neo-Kantian values', and L. van Vucht Tijssen, 'Women between modernity and postmodernity', in B. Turner (ed.), *Theories of Modernity and Postmodernity* (London: Sage, 1990). They concentrate exclusively upon *The Postmodern Condition*.

3 The Development of Lyotard's Thought

1 R. Rorty, 'Cosmopolitanism without emancipation: a response to Jean-François Lyotard', in Rorty, *Objectivity, Relativism and Truth: Philosophical Papers*, vol. 1 (Cambridge: Cambridge University Press, 1991), p. 218.
2 Recognizing differences can pose very awkward questions to common arrangements. The styles of education thought appropriate are liable to vary from cultural group to cultural group. See B. Parekh, 'The cultural particularity of liberal democracy', in D. Held (ed.), *The Prospects for Democracy: North, South, East, West* (Cambridge: Polity Press, 1993).
3 J.-F. Lyotard, 'A bizarre partner', in Lyotard, *Postmodern Fables*, trans. G. Van Den Abbeele (Minneapolis: University of Minnesota Press, 1997), p. 127.
4 Rorty, 'Cosmopolitanism without emancipation', p. 221.
5 There are contrasting views on Lyotard's estimate of phenomenology. See A. Kroker, *The Possessed Individual* (London: Macmillan, 1992), who takes Lyotard to be sympathetic to phenomenology. See also M. Gane, 'Lyotard's Early Writings: 1954–1963', in C. Rojek and B. Turner (eds.), *Lyotard and the Political: Justice and Political Theory* (London: Routledge, 1998), for a viewpoint that takes Lyotard to be negative towards phenomenology.
6 J.-F. Lyotard, *Phenomenology* (New York: State University Press of New York, 1991), p. 45.
7 Ibid., p. 89.

8. Ibid., p. 101.
9. Ibid., p. 66.
10. Ibid., p. 123.
11. Gane, 'Lyotard's early writings'.
12. Lyotard, *Phenomenology*, pp. 65–9.
13. D. Carroll, *Paraesthetics: Foucault, Lyotard, Derrida* (London: Methuen, 1987), p. 32.
14. C. Rojek, 'Lyotard and the decline of "society"', in C. Rojek and B. Turner (eds.), *Lyotard and the Political*, p.15.
15. B. Readings, *Introducing Lyotard* (London: Routledge, 1991), p. xxxi.
16. J.-F. Lyotard, 'The dream-work does not think', in J.-F. Lyotard, *The Lyotard Reader*, ed. A. Benjamin (Oxford: Blackwell, 1989), p. 37. This chapter is a translation of part of J.-F. Lyotard, *Discours, figure* (Paris: Klinckstock, 1971), pp. 239–70.
17. G. Bennington, *Lyotard: Writing the Event* (Manchester: Manchester University Press, 1988). The title of this text signals the significance it attaches to writing as an event.
18. See Lyotard, *Discours, figure*.
19. J.-F. Lyotard, 'The connivances of desire with the figural', in Lyotard, *Driftworks*, ed. R. Mckeon (New York: Columbia University Press, 1984), p. 57. This is a translation of pp. 271–9 of Lyotard, *Discours, figure*.
20. Ibid.
21. Lyotard, 'The dream-work does not think'.
22. J.-F. Lyotard, 'On theory: an interview', in Lyotard, *Driftworks*, p. 29.
23. J.-F. Lyotard, *Libidinal Economy*, trans. I. Hamilton Grant (London: Athlone, 1993), pp. 43–94.
24. Ibid., p. 261.
25. Ibid., p. 248.
26. Ibid., p. 1.
27. Ibid., p. 142.
28. Ibid., p. 102.
29. P. Dews, *Logics of Disintegration* (London: Verso, 1987), p. 138.
30. Lyotard, *Libidinal Economy*, pp. 261–2.
31. Ibid., p. 262.
32. K. Hutchings, *Kant, Critique and Politics* (London and New York: Routledge, 1996), p. 128.
33. J.-F. Lyotard, *Duchamp's Trans/Formers*, trans. I. Mcleod (Venice, CA: Lapis Press, 1990), p. 49.
34. J.-F. Lyotard, 'One of the things at stake in women's struggles', in Lyotard, *The Lyotard Reader*, p. 120. This essay appeared in J.-F. Lyotard, *Rudiments païens: genre dissertatif* (Paris: Union Général d'Éditions, 1977).

35 J.-F. Lyotard, 'Futility in revolution', trans. K. Berri, in J.-F. Lyotard, *Toward the Postmodern*, ed. R. Harvey and Mark Roberts (Atlantic Highlands, NJ: Humanities Press, 1993), p. 114. This essay appeared in Lyotard, *Rudiments païens: genre dissertatif*.
36 J.-F. Lyotard, *Just Gaming*, trans. W. Godzlich (Manchester: Manchester University Press, 1985), p. 14.
37 Ibid., p. 21.
38 Ibid., p. 30.
39 Ibid., p. 36.
40 Ibid., p. 100.
41 H. Haber, *Beyond Postmodern Politics: Lyotard, Rorty, Foucault* (London and New York: Routledge, 1994), pp. 35–6.

4 Beyond the Postmodern Condition

1 J.-F. Lyotard, *The Postmodern Condition: A Report on Knowledge*, trans. G. Bennington and B. Massumi (Manchester: Manchester University Press, 1984).
2 For Lyotard's reservations about narratives, see 'Apostil on narratives', in Lyotard, *The Postmodern Explained to Children: Correspondence 1982–1985* (London: Turnaround, 1992), p. 29.
3 See J.-F. Lyotard, 'Answer to the question: what is the postmodern?', in Lyotard, *The Postmodern Explained to Children*.
4 Modernity is certainly a concept that is more complex than is often acknowledged. Reflection on the critical aspects of Hegel's and Rousseau's reflections on their contemporary worlds highlights the problems of labelling figures as being either promoters or critics of modernity. For a sense of the variegated pathways of modernity, see C. Taylor, *Sources of the Self: The Making of the Modern Identity* (Cambridge: Cambridge University Press, 1989).
5 See C. Norris, 'Postmodernism: a guide for the perplexed', in G. Browning, A. Halcli and F. Webster (eds.), *Understanding Contemporary Society: Theories of the Present* (London: Sage, 2000).
6 J.-F. Lyotard, *The Differend: Phrases in Dispute*, trans. G. Van Den Abbeele (Manchester: Manchester University Press, 1988).
7 Lyotard is more explicit about this criticism, which I think is debatable, in 'Wittgenstein "After"', in Lyotard, *Political Writings*, trans. B. Readings and K. Geiman (London: UCL Press, 1993), pp. 19–23.
8 Lyotard, *The Differend*, p. 11.
9 Ibid., p. 46.
10 Ibid., p. xiii.
11 Ibid., p. x.

12 Ibid.
13 Ibid., p. 10.
14 Ibid., p. 13.
15 J. Heller, *Catch-22* (London and New York: Jonathan Cape Ltd, 1962).
16 Lyotard, *The Differend*, p. 4.
17 Ibid., p. 18.
18 Ibid., p. 19.
19 Norris, 'Postmodernism: a guide for the perplexed', p. 37.
20 Lyotard, *The Differend*, p. 55.
21 Ibid., p. 57.
22 Ibid., pp. 92–3.
23 Ibid., p. 91.
24 For a related and more focused account of Hegel and Auschwitz, see J.-F. Lyotard, 'Discussions or phrasing "after Auschwitz"', in *The Lyotard Reader*, ed. A. Benjamin (Oxford: Blackwell, 1989).
25 Lyotard, *The Differend*, p. 147.
26 Ibid., p. 150.
27 Ibid., p. 171.
28 Ibid., p. 181.
29 Ibid., p. 179.
30 Ibid., p. 180.
31 Ibid., p. 181.
32 Ibid., p. 135.
33 Ibid., p. 129.
34 P. Sedgwick and A. Tanesini, 'Lyotard and Kripke: essentialisms in dispute', *American Philosophical Quarterly*, 32/3 (July 1995), 277.
35 J. Williams, *Lyotard: Towards a Postmodern Philosophy* (Cambridge: Polity Press, 1998), pp. 74–9.
36 Lyotard, 'Answer to the question: what is the postmodern?'.
37 Ibid., p. 24.
38 J.-F. Lyotard, '*Sensus Communis*', in A. Benjamin (ed.), *Judging Lyotard* (London and New York: Routledge, 1992), p. 11.
39 Ibid., p. 24.
40 J.-F. Lyotard, 'The sign of history', in *The Lyotard Reader*, p. 393.
41 J.-F. Lyotard, *Lessons on the Analytic of the Sublime*, trans. E. Rottenberg (Stanford, CA: Stanford University Press, 1994), p. ix.
42 Ibid., p. 8.
43 E. Schaper, 'Taste, sublimity, and genius: the aesthetics of nature and art', in P. Guyer (ed.), *The Cambridge Companion to Kant* (Cambridge, Cambridge University Press, 1992), p. 384.
44 Lyotard, *Lessons on the Analytic of the Sublime*, pp. 54–5.
45 Ibid., p. 55.
46 Ibid., p. 123.

47 J.-F. Lyotard, 'Introduction: about the human', in Lyotard, *The Inhuman: Reflections on Time*, trans. G. Bennington and R. Bowlby (Cambridge: Polity Press, 1991), p. 2.
48 S. Sim, *Jean-François Lyotard* (Hemel Hempstead: Prentice Hall and Harvester Wheatsheaf, 1996), p. 130.
49 Lyotard, 'Introduction: about the human', in *The Inhuman*, p. 1.
50 J.-F. Lyotard, 'Can thought go on without a body', in *The Inhuman*, p. 15.
51 Ibid., p. 23.
52 J.-F. Lyotard, 'Newman: the instant', in *The Inhuman*, p. 82.
53 J.-F. Lyotard, 'Re-writing modernity', in *The Inhuman*, p. 34.
54 See J.-F. Lyotard, 'Unbeknownst', in *Postmodern Fables*, trans. G. Van Den Abbeele (Minneapolis: University of Minnestoa, 1997).
55 J.-F. Lyotard, *Lectures d'enfance* (Paris: Éditions Galilée, 1991).
56 Lyotard, 'A postmodern fable', in *Postmodern Fables*, p. 93.
57 Lyotard, 'The intimacy of terror', in *Postmodern Fables*, p. 206.
58 M. Frank, 'Dissension et consensus selon Jean-François Lyotard et Jürgen Habermas', *Les Cahiers de philosophie* (special issue on Lyotard), 5 (1988), 163–84.
59 Lyotard, 'Introduction: about the human', in *The Inhuman*, p. 3.
60 P. Anderson, *The Origins of Postmodernity* (New York and London: Verso, 1998).
61 See J.-F. Lyotard, *Signed Malraux*, trans. R. Harvey (Minneapolis: University of Minnesota Press, 1999), pp. 289–301. For a condensed but perceptive review of Malraux's notion of the imaginary museum see also Lyotard, 'A monument of possibles', in *Postmodern Fables*.
62 Lyotard, *Signed Malraux*, p. 289.
63 Ibid., p. 289.
64 Ibid., p. 301.
65 Ibid.

5 Lyotard and the Political

1 See, for instance, the comments by Sim in his recent book, *Jean-François Lyotard* (Hemel Hempstead: Prentice Hall and Harvester Wheatsheaf, 1996), pp. 1–16.
2 See J.-F. Lyotard, *The Differend*, trans. G. Van Den Abbeele (Manchester: Manchester University Press, 1988).
3 Ibid. The notion of linking is presented as contingent and open in this book.
4 J.-F. Lyotard, *Political Writings*, trans. B. Readings and K. Geiman, foreword and notes by B. Readings (London: UCL Press, 1993).

5 See B. Readings, *Introducing Lyotard: Art and Politics* (London and New York: Routledge, 1991).
6 J. Williams, *Lyotard: Towards a Postmodern Philosophy* (Cambridge: Polity Press, 1998), p. 3.
7 J.-F. Lyotard, *The Postmodern Condition: A Report on Knowledge*, trans. G. Bennington and B. Massumi (Manchester: Manchester University Press, 1983), pp. 31–7.
8 For a classic critique of the distributive paradigm in politics that was in part inspired by Lyotard, see I. M. Young, *Justice and the Politics of Difference* (Princeton, NJ: Princeton University Press, 1990), chap. 1.
9 J.-F. Lyotard, 'The situation in North Africa', in Lyotard, *Political Writings*, p. 178.
10 J.-F. Lyotard, 'The North African bourgeoisie', in Lyotard, *Political Writings*, p. 186.
11 J.-F. Lyotard, 'Algerian contradictions exposed', in Lyotard, *Political Writings*, p. 198.
12 Ibid.
13 Ibid., p. 207.
14 Ibid.
15 M. Gane, 'Lyotard's early writings 1954–1963', in C. Rojek and B. Turner (eds.), *The Politics of Lyotard: Justice and Political Theory* (London: Routledge, 1998), p. 155.
16 J.-F. Lyotard, 'The state and politics in the France of 1960', in Lyotard, *Political Writings*, p. 268.
17 Ibid., p. 269.
18 Ibid.
19 Ibid., p. 276.
20 J.-F. Lyotard, 'The name of Algeria', in Lyotard, *Political Writings*, p. 168.
21 Ibid., p. 169.
22 See J.-F. Lyotard, 'Rewriting modernity', in Lyotard, *The Inhuman: Reflection on Time* (Cambridge: Polity Press, 1991), pp. 24–36.
23 J.-F. Lyotard, *Dérive à partir de Marx et Freud* (Paris: Union Générale d'Éditions, 1973).
24 J.-F. Lyotard, 'Preamble to a charter', in Lyotard, *Political Writings*, p. 41.
25 Ibid.
26 Ibid.
27 Ibid., p. 44.
28 Ibid., p. 42.
29 J.-F. Lyotard, 'Nanterre, here, now', in Lyotard, *Political Writings*, p. 59.
30 Ibid., p. 61.

31 J.-F. Lyotard, 'Adrift', in Lyotard, *Driftworks*, ed. R. Mckeon (New York: Columbia University Press, 1984), p. 16.
32 J.-F. Lyotard, 'On theory: an interview', in Lyotard, *Driftworks*, p. 31.
33 J.-F. Lyotard, 'One of the things at stake in women's struggles', in *The Lyotard Reader*, ed. A. Benjamin (Oxford and Cambridge: Blackwell, 1989), p. 120.
34 J.-F. Lyotard, *Just Gaming*, trans. W. Godzich (Manchester: Manchester University Press, 1985), p. 100.
35 J.-F. Lyotard, 'The tomb of the intellectual', in Lyotard, *Political Writings*, p. 7.
36 J.-F. Lyotard, 'A svelte appendix to the postmodern question', in Lyotard, *Political Writings*, p. 27.
37 M. Drolet, 'The wild and the sublime: Lyotard's post-modern politics', *Political Studies*, 42/2 (June 1994), 271.
38 J.-F. Lyotard, *Heidegger and 'the Jews'*, trans. A. Michel and M. Roberts (Minneapolis: University of Minnesota Press, 1990), p. 22.
39 W. van Reijen and D. Veerman, 'An interview with Jean-François Lyotard', *Theory, Culture and Society* (special issue on postmodernism), 5/2–3 (June 1988), 302–3.
40 J.-F. Lyotard, 'Gloss on resistance', in Lyotard, *The Postmodern Explained to Children: Correspondence 1982–1985*, trans. ed. J. Pefanis and M. Thomas (London: Turnaround, 1992), 106.
41 Ibid., p. 110.
42 J.-F. Lyotard, 'The survivor', in Lyotard, *Toward the Postmodern*, ed. R. Harvey and M. Roberts (Atlantic Highlands, NJ: Humanities Press, 1993), 163.
43 J.-F. Lyotard, 'The wall, the gulf and the sun: a fable', in Lyotard, *Political Writings*. It is presented in longer form as two essays, 'The wall, the gulf and the system' and 'A postmodern fable', in Lyotard, *Postmodern Fables*, trans. G. Van Den Abbeele (Minneapolis: University of Minnesota Press, 1996).
44 Lyotard, 'The wall, the gulf and the sun', in Lyotard, *Political Writings*, p. 113.
45 Ibid., p. 123.
46 J.-F. Lyotard, 'Unbeknownst', in Lyotard, *Postmodern Fables*, p. 187.
47 Ibid., p. 194.
48 Ibid., pp. 195–6.
49 J.-F. Lyotard, 'The other's rights', in S. Shute and S. Hurley (eds.), *On Human Rights: The Oxford Amnesty Lectures 1993* (New York: Basic Books, 1993), 143.
50 Ibid., pp. 145–6.

51 Ibid., p. 146.
52 G. Bennington, *Lyotard: Writing the Event* (Manchester: Manchester University Press, 1988), p. 175.
53 R. Blaug, 'Deliberative democracy', *Politics*, 16/2 (May 1996), 74.
54 J.-F. Lyotard, 'A bizarre partner' and 'The intimacy of terror', in Lyotard, *Postmodern Fables*.

6 Hegel and the Critique of Closure

1 See G. W. F. Hegel, *Hegel's Science of Logic*, trans. A. Miller (London: George Allen & Unwin, 1969).
2 Ibid., pp. 824–44.
3 G. W. F. Hegel, *Lectures on the History of Philosophy*, vol. 1, trans. E. S. Haldane and F. H. Simpson (London and New York, 1892).
4 For a recent, interesting account of scholarship on the *Parmenides*, see C. Meinwald, 'Goodbye to the third man', in R. Kraut (ed.), *The Cambridge Companion to Plato* (Cambridge: Cambridge University Press, 1992).
5 Hegel, *Lectures on the History of Philosophy*, vol. 2, trans. E. S. Haldane and F. H. Simpson (London and New York, 1892), p. 1.
6 Plato, *Parmenides*, 166 B, trans. F. M. Cornford in *The Collected Dialogues of Plato*, ed. E. Hamilton and H. Cairns (Princeton, NJ: Princeton University Press, 1963), p. 956.
7 See J.-F. Lyotard, 'After the sublime: the state of aesthetics', in Lyotard, *The Inhuman: Reflections on Time*, trans. G. Bennington and R. Bowlby (Cambridge: Polity Press, 1991).
8 G. W. F. Hegel, *The Phenomenology of Mind*, trans. J. Baillie (London and New York: George Allen & Unwin, 1961), pp. 81–2.
9 J.-F. Lyotard, 'Apostil on narratives', in Lyotard, *The Postmodern Explained to Children: Correspondence 1982–1985*, trans. J. Pefanis and M. Thomas (London: Turnaround, 1992), p. 29.
10 J. Williams, *Lyotard: Towards a Postmodern Philosophy* (Cambridge: Polity Press, 1998), p. 119.
11 J.-F. Lyotard, *The Differend*, trans. G. Van Den Abbeele (Manchester: Manchester University Press, 1988), pp. 19–25.
12 A brilliant if idiosyncratic interpreter of the dialogue form of Plato's philosophy is Strauss. See his classic, L. Strauss, *The City and Man* (Chicago: University of Chicago Press, 1964).
13 S. Connor, *Postmodernist Culture: An Introduction to Theories of the Contemporary* (Oxford: Blackwell, 1997), p. 31.
14 See C. Jencks, *Culture* (London: Routledge, 1993), p. 145. See also J. Bernstein, 'Grand narratives', in D. Wood (ed.), *On Paul Ricoeur:*

NOTES

Narrative and Interpretation (London and New York: Routledge, 1991), p. 107.

[15] P. Anderson, *The Origins of Postmodernity* (London and New York, Verso: 1998), p. 34.

[16] See F. Jameson, Foreword, in J.-F. Lyotard, *The Postmodern Condition: A Report on Knowledge*, trans. G. Bennington and B. Massumi (Manchester: Manchester University Press, 1984), p. xx; Williams, *Lyotard*, pp. 118–21; and B. Readings, 'Foreword', J.-F. Lyotard, *Political Writings*, trans. B. Readings and K. Geiman (London: UCL Press, 1993), p. xv.

[17] For a classic statement of the non-metaphysical interpretation of Hegel, see K. Hartmann, 'Hegel: a non-metaphysical view', in A. Macintyre (ed.), *Hegel: A Collection of Essays* (Garden City, NJ: Doubleday, 1971).

[18] See Hegel, *Hegel's Science of Logic*, trans. A. Miller (London: George Allen & Unwin, 1969), p. 139.

[19] This sketch of the *Philosophy of Right* necessarily appears rather speculative (in the pejorative sense). For a more developed reading of the *Philosophy of Right* see G. K. Browning, *Hegel and the History of Political Philosophy* (London and New York: Macmillan, 1999).

[20] See R. Plant, *Hegel* (London: George Allen & Unwin, 1973); R. Hardimon, *Hegel's Social Philosophy: The Project of Reconciliation* (Cambridge: Cambridge University Press, 1994).

[21] J.-F. Lyotard, *Phenomenology* trans. B. Bleakley (Albany, NY: State University of New York Press, 1991), pp. 65–9.

[22] Ibid., p. 65.

[23] J. M. Bernstein, 'Conscience and transgression: the exemplarity of tragic action', in G. K. Browning (ed.), *Hegel's Phenomenology of Spirit: A Reappraisal* (Dordrecht: Kluwer Academic Publishers, 1997), p. 79.

[24] See J. Flay, 'Rupture, closure and dialectic', and J. Burbidge, 'Comment: on rupture, closure and dialectic', in Browning (ed.), *Hegel's Phenomenology of Spirit*.

[25] A. White, *Absolute Knowledge: Hegel and the Problem of Metaphysics* (Athens, Ohio: Ohio University Press, 1983).

[26] For Rosen's views on Hegel see M. Rosen, *Hegel's Dialectic and its Criticism* (Cambridge: Cambridge University Press, 1982). For Hegel's account of identity and difference see Hegel, *Hegel's Science of Logic*, pp. 408–39.

[27] Lyotard, *The Postmodern Condition*, p. xxiv.

[28] Ibid., p. 34.

[29] Ibid., p. 15.

[30] F. Dallmayr, *G. W. F. Hegel: Modernity and Politics* (London: Sage, 1993), p. 8.

31 See Browning, *Hegel and the History of Political Philosophy*.
32 J.-F. Lyotard, 'Analysing speculative discourse as language game', in *The Lyotard Reader*, ed. A. Benjamin (Oxford and Cambridge: Blackwell, 1989), pp. 267–74.
33 Hegel, *Science of Logic*, pp. 137–57.
34 Ibid., p. 149.
35 Lyotard, 'Analysing speculative discourse as language game', p. 274.
36 Jean-François Lyotard, 'Discussions, or phrasing "after Auschwitz"', in *The Lyotard Reader*, p. 354.
37 Ibid., p. 386.
38 Lyotard, *The Differend*, p. 14.
39 Ibid., p. 96.
40 Hegel, *Phenomenology of Mind*, pp. 149–60.
41 Lyotard, *The Differend*, p. 50.
42 Ibid., p. 60.
43 J.-F. Lyotard, *Lessons on the Analytic of the Sublime*, trans. E. Rottenberg (Stanford, CA: Stanford University Press, 1994), p. 128.
44 Ibid., p. 130.
45 Ibid., p. 131.
46 J.-F. Lyotard, 'Something like communication . . . without communication', in Lyotard, *The Inhuman*, p. 115.
47 R. Abbinnett, *Truth and Social Science: From Hegel to Deconstruction* (London: Sage, 1998), p. 37.
48 G. W. F. Hegel, *Hegel's Philosophy of Right*, trans. T. M. Knox (Oxford: Oxford University Press, 1967), p. 17.
49 G. Bennington, *Lyotard: Writing the Event* (Manchester: Manchester University Press, 1988), p. 136.
50 J.-F. Lyotard, 'A postmodern fable', *Postmodern Fables*, trans. G. Van Den Abbeele (Minneapolis: University of Minnesota Press, 1997), p. 97.
51 J. O'Neill, 'Lost in the post: (post)modernity explained to youth', in C. Rojek and B. Turner (eds.), *The Politics of Jean-François Lyotard: Justice and Political Theory* (London: Routledge, 1998), p. 134.

7 Marx and the End of Emancipation

1 J.-F. Lyotard, 'Afterword – a memorial of Marxism: for Pierre Souryi', in Lyotard, *Peregrinations: Law, Form, Event* (New York: Columbia University Press, 1988).
2 J.-F. Lyotard, *Phenomenology* (Albany, NY: State University of New York Press, 1991).
3 Ibid., p. 49.

4   Ibid.
5   Ibid.
6. Ibid., p. 50.
7   Ibid., p. 60.
8   Ibid., p. 46.
9   J.-F. Lyotard, *Libidinal Economy*, trans. I. H. Grant (London: Athlone Press, 1993).
10 See J.-F. Lyotard, *The Differend: Phrases in Dispute*, trans. G. Van Den Abbeele (Manchester: Manchester University Press, 1988), p. 176.
11 For Marx's clearest account of the infinite self-aggrandizement of capital, see K. Marx, *Grundrisse* (Harmondsworth, Penguin, 1974).
12 M. Gane, 'Lyotard's early writings 1954–1963', in C. Rojek and B. Turner (eds.), *The Politics of Jean-François Lyotard: Justice and Political Theory* (London: Routledge, 1998), p. 142.
13 Lyotard, *Phenomenology*, p. 129.
14 Ibid., p. 131.
15 Ibid., p. 123.
16 Ibid., p. 127.
17 Ibid., p. 123.
18 See my article on *The German Ideology*, G. K. Browning, '*The German Ideology*: the theory of history and the history of theory', *History of Political Thought*, 14/3 (1993), 455–73.
19 Marx, *Grundrisse*, p. 164. For an account of Marx's methodological assumptions, see my article, 'Infinity in Hegel and Marx: from the notion to the notion of capital', *Studies in Marxism*, 5 (1998), 1–16.
20 Lyotard, *Peregrinations*, p. 17.
21 J.-F. Lyotard, 'The name of Algeria', in Lyotard, *Political Writings*, trans. B. Readings and K. Geiman (London: UCL Press, 1993), p. 170.
22 J.-F. Lyotard, 'On theory: an interview', in Lyotard, *Driftworks*, ed. R. Mckeon, trans. R. McKeon, S. Hanson, A. Knab, R Lockwood and J. Maier (New York: Columbia University, 1984), p. 19. This piece was published in French in J.-F. Lyotard, *Dérive à partir de Marx et Freud* (Paris: Union Générale d'Éditions, 1973).
23 J.-F. Lyotard, 'March 23: unpublished introduction to an unfinished book on the movement of March 22', in Lyotard, *Political Writings*, p. 60. This is included in French in Lyotard, *Dérive à partir de Marx et Freud*.
24 J.-F. Lyotard, 'Adrift', in Lyotard, *Driftworks*, p. 14. This piece was originally published in Lyotard, *Dérive à partir de Marx et Freud*.
25 Ibid., pp. 14–15.
26 Lyotard, *Libidinal Economy*, p. 121.
27 Ibid., pp. 128–9.
28 Ibid., p. 106.

29 Ibid., p. 111.
30 Ibid., p. 103.
31 Ibid., p. 136.
32 Ibid., p. 137.
33 Ibid., p. 138.
34 Ibid., p. 140.
35 J.-F. Lyotard, *The Postmodern Condition: A Report on Knowledge*, trans. G. Bennington and B. Massumi (Manchester: Manchester University Press, 1984), p. 12.
36 Ibid., p. 40.
37 Ibid., p. 13.
38 Lyotard, *The Differend*, p. 179.
39 Ibid., p. 171.
40 Ibid.
41 Ibid., p. 176.
42 Ibid., p. 174.
43 J.-F. Lyotard, 'A svelte appendix to the postmodern question', in Lyotard, *Political Writings*, p. 26.
44 Marx, *Grundrisse*, p. 261. See my chapter entitled, 'Good and bad infinites in Hegel and Marx', in G. Browning, *Hegel and the History of Political Philosophy* (London: Macmillan, 1999).
45 Lyotard, 'A svelte appendix to the postmodern question', p. 27.
46 Ibid.
47 Ibid., p. 28.
48 J.-F. Lyotard, 'The wall, the gulf and the sun: a fable', in Lyotard, *Political Writings*, p. 115.
49 J.-F. Lyotard, 'The survivor', in Lyotard, *Toward the Postmodern*, ed. R. Harvey and M. Roberts (Atlantic Highlands, NJ: Humanities Press, 1993), pp. 162–3. This piece is published in French as 'Survivant: Arendt', in J.-F. Lyotard, *Lectures d'enfance* (Paris: Galilée, 1991).
50 T. Carver, *The Postmodern Marx* (Manchester: Manchester University Press, 1999). See also T. Carver, 'Post-Marxism', in G. Browning, A. Halcli and F. Webster (eds.), *Understanding Contemporary Society: Theories of the Present* (London: Sage, 2000).

8 Conclusion

1 The trails of discovery can be traced in the following texts: Lyotard, *Phenomenology*, trans. B. Bleakley (Albany, NY: State University of New York, 1991); Lyotard, *Libidinal Economy*, trans. I. Grant (London: Athlone Press, 1993); Lyotard, *The Postmodern Condition: A Report on Knowledge*, trans. G. Bennington and B. Massumi

(Manchester: Manchester University Press, 1984); Lyotard, *Lessons on the Analytic of the Sublime*, trans. E. Rottenberg (Stanford, CA: Stanford University Press, 1994); Lyotard, *Duchamp's Trans/Formers*, trans. I. Mcleod (Venice, CA: The Lapis Press, 1990). For Lyotard's critiques of Hegel and Marx, see respectively, 'Analysing Speculative Discourse as Language Game', in *The Lyotard Reader*, ed. A. Benjamin (Oxford: Blackwell, 1989) and *Driftworks*, trans. R. Mckeon, S. Hanson, A. Knab, R. Lockwood and J. Maier (New York: Columbia University Press, 1984). Open systems and liberal democracies are deprecated in Lyotard, 'The wall, the gulf and the sun: a fable', in Lyotard, *Political Writings*, trans. B. Readings and K. Geiman (London: UCL Press, 1993).

2 J.-F. Lyotard, *Peregrinations: Law, Event, Form* (New York: Columbia University Press, 1988).

3 K. Marx, *Grundrisse* (Harmondsworth: Penguin, 1974).

4 J.-F. Lyotard, *The Differend: Phrases in Dispute*, trans. G. Van Den Abbeele (Manchester: Manchester University Press, 1988).

5 J.-F. Lyotard, *The Inhuman: Reflections on Time*, trans. G. Bennington and R. Bowlby (Cambridge: Polity Press, 1991).

6 Lyotard, *Libidinal Economy*, p. 3.

7 J.-F. Lyotard, 'The other's rights', in S. Shute and S. Hurley (eds.), *On Human Rights: The Oxford Amnesty Lectures 1993* (New York: Basic Books, 1993), p. 143.

8 Lyotard, *The Differend*, pp. 129–50.

9 J.-F. Lyotard, 'The sublime and the avant-garde', in Lyotard, *The Inhuman*, chap. 7.

10 See J.-F. Lyotard, '*Logos* and *techne*, or telegraphy', in Lyotard, *The Inhuman*.

11 Lyotard, *The Postmodern Condition*, pp. 31–7.

12 See M. Luntley, *Reason, Truth and Self: The Postmodern Reconditioned* (London and New York: Routledge, 1995); and C. Norris, 'Postmodernism: a guide for the perplexed', in G. Browning, A. Halcli and F. Webster (eds.), *Understanding Contemporary Society: Theories of the Present* (London: Sage, 2000). See also Lyotard's comments on science in his essay, 'A bizarre partner', in Lyotard, *Postmodern Fables* (Minneapolis: University of Minnesota Press, 1997).

13 Lyotard, 'A bizarre partner', in *Postmodern Fables*, p. 134.

14 Lyotard provides a close reading of Aron's work on the philosophy of history in Lyotard, *Phenomenology*. Collingwood's classic account of history is given in R. G. Collingwood, *The Idea of History*, revised edn., ed. J. Van Der Dussen (Oxford: Oxford University Press, 1993), but it should be noted that additional materials are included with this revised edn., and important new materials relating to Collingwood's

philosophy of history have become available in recent years. For a short essay elaborating Oakeshott's philosophy of history, see M. Oakeshott, 'The activity of being an historian', in Oakeshott, *Rationalism in Politics and Other Essays* (London and New York: Methuen and Co., 1962).
15 These terms are used in Lyotard, *The Differend*.
16 See Lyotard's astringent remarks against consensus in Lyotard, *The Postmodern Condition*, pp. 67–9.
17 P. Dews, *Logics of Disintegration: Post-Structuralist Thought and the Claims of Critical Theory* (London and New York: Verso, 1987), p. 214.
18 M. Drolet, 'The wild and the sublime: Lyotard's post-modern politics', *Political Studies*, 42/2 (June 1994), 271.
19 P. Anderson, *The Origins of Postmodernity* (London and New York: Verso, 1998), p. 34.
20 J.-F. Lyotard, 'A postmodern fable', in Lyotard, *Postmodern Fables*, p. 100. Lyotard urges that his fable of development is distinct from great narratives of modernity because it does not claim to be explanatory; it charts the complexification of energy itself rather than being humanistic and its narrative is neither emancipatory nor reconciliatory. Lyotard's brief discussion of why his fable is not a grand narrative is not persuasive because his focus on development in his late work does function as an explanatory organizing theme and its tone of melancholia plays the same role that emancipation plays in a classic grand narrative such as Marxism, namely providing an overall framework in which to fit events and attitudes.
21 See J.-F. Lyotard, 'On theory: an interview', in Lyotard, *Driftworks*.
22 W. Connolly, *Identity/Difference: Democratic Negotiations of Political Paradox* (Ithaca, NY, and London: Cornell University Press, 1991), p. 74.
23 N. Rennger, *Political Theory, Modernity and Postmodernity* (Oxford: Blackwell, 1995), p. 8.
24 For an analysis of the circumspection involved in contemporary liberal political theory, evidenced for instance in the post-liberalism of John Gray and the more recent work of Rawls, see G. Browning, 'Contemporary liberalism', in G. Browning, A. Halcli and F. Webster (eds.), *Understanding Contemporary Society: Theories of the Present* (London: Sage, 2000).
25 See above. For a strong, hard-hitting critique of contemporary liberalism see R. Beiner, *What's the Matter with Liberalism* (Berkeley, CA: University of California Press, 1992).
26 For a perceptive critical account of communitarianism, see E. Frazer and N. Lacey, *The Politics of Community: A Feminist Critique of the*

Liberal-Communitarian Debate (Hemel Hempstead: Harvester-Wheatsheaf, 1993).
27 J. Rawls, *Political Liberalism* (New York: Columbia University Press, 1993).
28 Ibid., pp. 48–54.
29 See Lyotard, 'The other's rights'.
30 See Lyotard, *The Differend*, pp. 3–32.
31 Lyotard, 'A bizarre partner', in Lyotard, *Postmodern Fables*, p. 134.
32 Ibid., p. 131.
33 H. Haber, *Beyond Postmodern Politics: Lyotard, Rorty, Foucault* (London and New York: Routledge, 1994), p. 38.
34 Drolet, 'The wild and the sublime: Lyotard's post-modern politics', p. 271.
35 J.-F. Lyotard, 'The survivor', in Lyotard, *Toward The Postmodern*, ed. R. Harvey and M. Roberts (Atlantic Highlands, NJ: Humanities Press, 1993), pp. 162–3.
36 For a postmodern approach to Marx that accepts the possibilities of a variety of interpretations of Marx, see T. Carver, *The Postmodern Marx* (Manchester: Manchester University Press, 1998).
37 For a sense of this variety see the following, T. Carver and P. Thomas (eds.), *Rational Choice Marxism* (London: Macmillan, 1995); J. Roemer (ed.), *Analytical Marxism* (Cambridge: Cambridge University Press, 1985); T. Smith, *Dialectical Social Theory and its Critics: From Hegel to Analytical Marxism and Postmodernism* (Albany, NY: State University of New York Press, 1993).
38 J.-F. Lyotard, 'A memorial of Marxism: for Pierre Souyri', in Lyotard, *Peregrinations*.
39 For there to be communication at all there must be some things that are shared between interlocutors; this is a logical condition of discourse. There will also be differences. Philosophical debate on consensus/dissensus must be about discussing the range and limits of this identity/difference which are not logical conditions.
40 K. Marx, *Grundrisse* (Harmondsworth: Penguin, 1974), p. 270.
41 Lyotard, *Phenomenology*, pp. 127–32.
42 Ibid., pp. 65–9.
43 G. Rose, 'Architecture to philosophy: the postmodern complicity', *Theory, Culture and Society* (special issue on postmodernism), 5/2–3 (June 1988), 368.
44 See G. W. F. Hegel, *Hegel's Philosophy of Right*, trans. T. Knox (Oxford: Oxford University Press, 1967).
45 J. O'Neill, 'Lost in the post: (post)modernity explained to youth' in C. Rojek and B. Turner (eds.), *The Politics of Jean-François Lyotard: Justice and Political Theory* (London: Routledge, 1998), p. 131.

46 J.-F. Lyotard, 'On a hyphen', in J.-F. Lyotard and E. Gruber, *The Hyphen: Between Judaism and Christianity*, trans. P.-A. Brault and M. Naas (New York: Humanity Books, 1999), p. 24.
47 J. M. Bernstein, 'Grand narratives', in D. Wood (ed.), *On Paul Ricoeur: Narrative and Interpretation* (London and New York: Routledge, 1991), p. 120.

Select Bibliography

Works of Jean-François Lyotard in French

L'Assinat de l'experience par la peinture: Monoroy, Paris: Castor Astral, 1984.
Au Juste (with Jean-Loup Thébaud), Paris: Christian Bourgeois, 1979.
La Condition postmoderne, Paris: Minuit, 1979.
Dérive à partir de Marx et Freud, Paris: Union Générale d'Éditions, 1973.
Des dispositifs pulsionnels, Paris: Union Générale d'Éditions, 1973.
Le Différend, Paris: Minuit, 1983.
Discours, figure, Paris: Klinckstock, 1971.
D'un trait d'union, Paris: PUG, 1994.
Economie libidinale, Paris: Les Éditions de Minuit, 1974.
Instructions païennes, Paris: Galilée, 1977.
L'Enthousiasme: la critique kantienne de l'histoire, Paris: Galilée, 1986.
Heidegger et les 'juifs', Paris: Galilée, 1988.
'Judicieux dans le Différend', in J. Derrida, V. Descombes, G. Kortian, P. Lacoue-Labarthe, J.-F. Lyotard, J.-L. Nancy, *La Faculté de juger*, Paris: Les Éditions de Minuit, 1985.
La Guerre des Algériens, Paris: Galilée, 1989.
La Phénoménologie, Paris: Presses Universitaires de France, 1954.
Leçons sur l'anaytique du sublime, Paris: Galilée, 1991.
Lectures d'enfance, Paris: Galilée, 1991.
L'Inhumain: causeries sur le temps, Paris: Galilée, 1988.
Moralités postmodernes, Paris: Galilée, 1993.
Le Mur du pacifique, Paris: Galilée, 1979.
La Partie de peinture, Cannes: Maryse Canada, 1990.
Le Postmoderne expliqué aux enfants: Correspondance 1982–1985, Paris: Galilée, 1986.
Récits tremblants, Paris: Galilée, 1977.
Rudiments païens: genre dissertatif, Paris: Union Générale d'Éditions, 1977.
Signé Malraux, Paris: Bernard Grasset, 1996.
Sur la constitution du temps par la couleur dans les œuvres récentes d'Albert Ayme, Paris: Éditions Traversière, 1980.
Tombeau de l'intellectuel et autres papiers, Paris: Galilée, 1984.

English Translations of Works by Jean-François Lyotard

The Differend: Phrases in Dispute, trans. G. Van Den Abbeele, Manchester: Manchester University Press, 1988.
Driftworks, trans. R. Mckeon, S. Hanson, A. Knab, R. Lockwood, and J. Maier, New York: Columbia University Press, 1984.
Duchamp's Trans/Formers, trans. I. Mcleod, Venice, CA: The Lapis Press, 1990.
Heidegger and 'the Jews', trans. A. Michel and M. Roberts, Minneapolis: University of Minnesota Press, 1990.
The Hyphen: Between Judaism and Christianity (with E. Gruber), trans. P.-A. Brault and M. Naas, New York: Humanity Books, 1999.
The Inhuman: Reflections on Time, trans. G. Bennington and R. Bowlby, Cambridge: Polity Press, 1991.
Just Gaming, trans. W. Godzich, Manchester: Manchester University Press, 1985.
'An interview with Jean-François Lyotard', W. van Reijen and D. Veerman, *Theory, Culture and Society* (special issue on postmodernism), 5/2–3 (June 1988).
Lessons on the Analytic of the Sublime, trans. E. Rottenberg, Stanford, CA: Stanford University Press, 1994.
Libidinal Economy, trans. I. Hamilton Grant, London: Athlone, 1993.
The Lyotard Reader, ed. A. Benjamin, Oxford and Cambridge: Blackwell, 1989.
'The other's rights', in S. Shute and S. Hurley (eds.), *On Human Rights: The Oxford Amnesty Lectures 1993*, New York: Basic Books, 1993.
Peregrinations: Law, Form, Event, New York: Columbia University Press, 1988.
Phenomenology, trans. B. Bleakley, Albany, NY: State University of New York Press, 1991.
Political Writings, trans. B. Readings and K. Geiman, London: UCL Press, 1993.
The Postmodern Condition: A Report on Knowledge, trans. G. Bennington and B. Massumi, Manchester: Manchester University Press, 1984.
The Postmodern Explained to Children: Correspondence 1982–1985, trans. D. Barry, B. Maher, J. Pefanis, V. Spate and M. Thomas, ed. J. Pefanis and M. Thomas, London: Turnaround, 1992.
Postmodern Fables, trans. G. Van Den Abbeele, Minneapolis: University of Minnesota Press, 1997.
'Sensus Communis', in A. Benjamin (ed.), *Judging Lyotard*, London and New York: Routledge, 1992.
Signed Malraux, trans. Robert Harvey, Minneapolis: University of Minnesota Press, 1999.

Toward the Postmodern, ed. R. Harvey and Mark Roberts, Atlantic Highlands, NJ, and London: Humanities Press, 1993.

Studies on Lyotard and/or relating to Themes of his Work

Abbinnett, R., *Truth and Social Science*, London: Sage, 1998.
Anderson, P., *The Origins of Postmodernity*, London and New York: Verso, 1998.
Benhabib, S., 'Feminism and the question of postmodernism', in S. Benhabib, *Situating the Self*, Cambridge: Polity Press, 1992.
Benjamin, A. (ed.), *Judging Lyotard*, London and New York: Routledge, 1992.
Bennington, G., *Lyotard: Writing the Event*, Manchester: Manchester University Press, 1988.
Bernstein, J. M., 'Grand narratives', in D. Wood (ed.), *On Paul Ricoeur: Narrative and Interpretation*, London and New York: Routledge, 1991.
Bertens, H., *The Idea of the Postmodern*, London: Routledge, 1995.
Blaug, R., 'Deliberative democracy', *Politics*, 16/2 (May 1996), 71–7.
Browning, G. K., 'Lyotard's Hegel and the Dialectic of Modernity', in G. K. Browning, *Hegel and the History of Political Philosophy*, London and New York: Macmillan, 1999.
——, Halcli, A. and Webster, F. (eds.), *Understanding Contemporary Society: Theories of the Present*, London: Sage, 2000.
Brugger, N., Frandsen, F. and Pirotte, D. (eds.), *Lyotard, les deplacements philosophiques*, Brussels: De Boek Wesmael, 1995.
Callinicos, A., *Against Postmodernism: A Marxist Perspective*, Cambridge: Polity Press, 1989.
——, *Social Theory*, Cambridge: Polity, 1999.
Carroll, D., *Paraesthetics: Foucault, Lyotard, Derrida*, London: Methuen, 1987.
Carver, T., *The Postmodern Marx*, Manchester: Manchester University Press, 1999.
Connolly, W., *Identity/Difference: Democratic Negotiations of Political Paradox*, Ithaca, NY: Cornell University Press, 1991.
Connor, S., *Postmodernist Culture: An Introduction to Theories of the Contemporary*, Oxford: Blackwell Publishers, 1997.
Cornell, D., *The Philosophy of the Limit*, London and New York: Routledge, 1992.
Descombes, V., *Modern French Philosophy*, Cambridge: Cambridge University Press, 1981.
Dews, P., *Logics of Disintegration: Post-Structuralist Thought and the Claims of Critical Theory*, London and New York: Verso, 1987.

Drolet, M., 'The wild and the sublime: Lyotard's post-modern politics', *Political Studies*, 42/2 (June 1994), 259–73.

Frank, M., 'Dissension et consensus selon Jean-François Lyotard et Jürgen Habermas', *Les Cahiers de philosophie*, 5 (1988), 163–84.

Fraser, N., and Nicholson, L., 'Social criticism without philosophy: an encounter between feminism and postmodernism', *Theory Culture and Society* (special issue on postmodernism), 5/2–3 (June 1988), 373–94.

Furrow, D., *Against Theory: Continental and Analytic Challenges in Moral Philosophy*, London and New York: Routledge, 1995.

Good, J., and Velody, I. (eds.), *The Politics of Postmodernity*, Cambridge: Cambridge University Press, 1998.

Haber, H., *Beyond Postmodern Politics: Lyotard, Rorty, Foucault*, London and New York: Routledge, 1994.

Habermas, J., *The Philosophical Discourse of Modernity*, trans. F. Lawrence, Cambridge: Polity Press, 1987.

——, *Between Facts and Norms: Contributions to a Discourse Theory of Law and Democracy*, trans. W. Rehg, Cambridge: Polity Press, 1996.

Hegel, G. W. F., *The Philosophy of History*, trans. J. Sibree, New York: Dover Press, 1956.

——, *Hegel's Philosophy of Right*, trans. T. M. Knox, Oxford: Oxford University Press, 1967.

——, *Hegel's Science of Logic*, trans. A. Miller, London: George Allen & Unwin, 1969.

Hutchings, K., *Kant, Critique and Politics*, London, Routledge, 1996.

Hurley, R., 'Introduction to Lyotard', *Telos*, 19 (1974), 124–6.

Lacoue-Labarthe, P. (ed.), *L'Imitation des modernes*, Paris: Galilée, 1986.

Lent, A., (ed.), *New Political Thought*, London: Lawrence & Wishart, 1998.

Luntley, M., *Reason, Truth and Self: The Postmodern Reconditioned*, London and New York: Routledge, 1995.

Lyon, D., *Postmodernity*, Buckingham: Open University Press, 1994.

Macey, D., 'Obituary: Jean-François Lyotard, 1924–1998', *Radical Philosophy*, 91 (Sept./Oct. 1998), 53.

Marx, K., *Grundrisse*, Harmondsworth: Penguin, 1974.

——, and Engels, F., *Selected Works*, Moscow: Progress Publishers, 1970.

Matthews, E., *Twentieth Century French Philosophy*, Oxford and New York: Oxford University Press, 1996.

Norris, C. *What's Wrong With Postmodernism*, Hemel Hempstead: Harvester Wheatsheaf, 1990.

——, 'Postmodernism: a guide for the perplexed', in G. K. Browning, A. Halcli and F. Webster (eds.), *Understanding Contemporary Society: Theories of the Present*, London: Sage, 1999.

Pefanis, J., *Heterology and the Postmodern: Bataille, Baudrillard and*

Lyotard, Durham, NC, and London: Duke University Press, 1991.
Pierson, C., *The Modern State*, London and New York: Routledge, 1996.
Phillips, A., *Which Equalities Matter*, Cambridge: Polity Press, 1999.
Readings, B., *Introducing Lyotard: Art and Politics*, London and New York: Routledge, 1991.
Rennger, N., *Political Theory, Modernity and Postmodernity*, Oxford: Blackwell, 1995.
Rose, G., 'Architecture to philosophy: the postmodern complicity', *Theory Culture and Society* (special issue on postmodernism), 5/2–3 (June 1988), 357–72.
Schaper, E., 'Taste, sublimity and genius: the aesthetics of nature and art', in P. Guyer (ed.), *The Cambridge Companion to Kant*, Cambridge: Cambridge University Press, 1992.
Sim, S., *Jean-François Lyotard*, Hemel Hempstead: Prentice Hall and Harvester Wheatsheaf, 1996.
Smart, B., *Modern Conditions, Postmodern Controversies*, London and New York: Routledge, 1992.
Taylor, C., *Sources of the Self: The Making of the Modern Identity*, Cambridge: Cambridge University Press, 1989.
Turner, B. (ed.), *Theories of Modernity and Postmodernity*, London: Sage, 1990.
Williams, J., *Lyotard: Towards a Postmodern Philosophy*, Cambridge: Polity Press, 1998.
Wittgenstein, L., *Philosophical Investigations*, Oxford: Blackwell, 1953.
Young, I. M., *Justice and the Politics of Difference*, Princeton, NJ: Princeton University Press, 1990.

Index

Abbinnett, Ross 125
absolutism 3, 5, 6, 17, 19, 27, 32, 33, 34, 35, 38, 47, 108, 114, 115, 116, 120, 121, 125, 132, 148, 151, 152, 155, 157, 165, 167, 170
Adorno, Theodor 143
aestheticism 20, 21, 88
aesthetic(s) 13, 14, 31, 74, 75, 76, 77, 79, 82, 125, 126, 143, 145
agonism 9, 11, 22, 23, 26, 31, 37, 38, 39, 121, 126
Algeria 15, 16, 18, 87, 88, 91, 92, 93, 94, 95, 96, 98, 128, 131, 135, 145, 158, 159
Algerian War 87, 94, 96
alienation 24, 46, 53, 95, 100, 120, 135, 137, 139, 143, 159, 165, 166, 168
alterity 48, 130
Althusser, Louis 135
Althusserians 132, 139
Amnesty International 104
analytical Marxists 165
analytical philosophy 3
Ancient Greece 116
Anderson, Perry 84, 115, 158
Anglo-American political philosophy 160, 161
anthropomorphism 64
Apel, Karl-Otto 80
Arendt, Hannah 102, 145, 164
Aristotle 57
Aron, Raymond 153
art(istic) 48, 50, 51, 63, 75, 82, 116, 120, 121, 124, 150, 152
Auschwitz 65, 66, 68, 70, 73, 76, 101, 113, 122, 123
autonomy 46, 59, 83, 86, 154
avant-garde 3, 74, 81, 150

Bataille, Georges 139
  Madame Edwarda 139
Baudrillard, Jean 137
Bennington, Geoff 9, 49, 105, 126
Berlin (1953) 70, 142
Bernstein, Jay 23, 115, 118, 171
Blairite 133
Blaug, Ricardo 106
body 80, 103, 145
Boyne, Roy 17
Budapest (1956) 70, 76, 142
Burbidge, John 118
bureaucracy 29, 95, 96, 98

capital 19, 29, 30, 31, 53, 69, 70, 71, 131, 133, 135, 137, 138, 139, 140, 142, 143, 149, 166, 167, 170
capitalism 3, 22, 24, 33, 53, 54, 70, 75, 79, 82, 95, 96, 98, 106, 100, 103, 104, 131, 137, 143, 144, 146, 149, 162, 164
Carroll, David 17, 48
Cartesianism 64
Carver, Terrell 145, 146
  The Postmodern Marx 145
Cashinahua Indians 27
Castoriadis, Cornelius 130
catastrophe theory 30
Catch-22 66
civil society 38, 168
class 92, 93, 131, 134, 140, 142, 144, 165
collectivism 16
Collingwood, R. G. 153
commodification 24, 29, 33, 75, 101, 125, 143
communism 3, 15, 21, 22, 53, 93, 137, 139, 141, 165
communitarian(ism) 160, 161, 162

community 116, 120, 16, 148, 161, 163, 168, 169, 170
complexification 8, 15, 80, 158
conformity 20, 58, 89, 106, 126, 139, 158, 166, 169
Connolly, William 159
Connor, Steven 27, 29, 114
consciousness 17, 44, 46, 52, 54, 117, 118, 134, 141
consensus 3, 4, 7, 10, 17, 23, 36, 37, 40, 41, 82, 88, 89, 90, 106, 148, 150, 154, 156, 158, 163, 168, 171
contingency 4, 7, 12, 13, 17, 18, 25, 26, 46, 47, 67, 71, 72, 86, 113, 115, 121, 122, 132, 134, 141, 142, 145, 153, 156, 168
Coole, Diana 23
cosmopolitanism 40, 41
critical theory 3, 24
Czechoslovakia (1968) 70

Dallmayr, Fred 120
Davidson, Donald 80
deconstruction 4, 9, 10, 16, 23, 25, 48, 50, 51, 56, 61, 90, 96
Deleuze, Gilles 55
democracy 16, 61, 69, 98, 99, 103, 106, 125, 126, 148, 164
  deliberative democracy 69, 106
  liberal democracy 70, 86, 103, 145, 150, 161, 162, 166
  social democracy 40, 41,
Derrida, Jacques 42
Descartes, René 64
desire 12, 18, 43, 48, 50, 51, 52, 54, 55, 98, 99, 100, 118, 119, 140, 155
Deutsche-Französsische Jahrbücher 137
development 8, 14, 15, 23, 31, 39, 63, 71, 75, 82, 83, 84, 88, 90, 92, 103, 106, 124, 129, 132, 141, 144, 145, 146, 148, 149, 154, 157, 158, 170
Dewey, John 40
Dews, Peter 54, 155
dialectic(s) 31, 33, 48, 109, 111, 121, 122, 124, 126, 129, 130, 134, 141, 169
dialogue 65, 83
difference 3, 4, 5, 7, 8, 9, 10, 11, 12, 14, 16, 20, 21, 25, 32, 35, 36, 37, 41, 43, 47, 50, 51, 56, 61, 62, 63, 83, 86, 98, 105, 106, 113, 118, 122, 126, 142, 144, 148, 152, 156, 158, 159, 160, 162, 163, 164, 165, 168, 169, 170
différend 4, 6, 13, 14, 18, 63, 65, 66, 67, 68, 69, 70, 72, 73, 74, 76, 78, 79, 83, 84, 85, 89, 91, 95, 100, 101, 104, 106, 115, 123, 124, 129, 130, 131, 135, 141, 142, 144, 156, 157, 162, 163, 165, 166, 170
discourse 2, 9, 12, 13, 15, 18, 20, 23, 27, 29, 30, 31, 34, 36, 37, 40, 41, 47, 48, 49, 50, 51, 52, 53, 58, 61, 64, 72, 73, 74, 78, 79, 83, 90, 99, 101, 111, 115, 122, 123, 124, 126, 128, 133, 142, 143, 152, 153, 156, 158, 159
dissensus 17, 37
distributive justice 148
double bind 66, 71, 72
dream(s) 48, 50, 51
dreamwork 50, 51
Dreyfus, Alfred 80
Drolet, Michael 101, 157, 164
Duchamp, Marcel 56

Eastern Europe 145
ecologism 38
education 29, 30, 31, 32, 33, 37, 96, 97, 100, 166
emancipation 24, 32, 33, 34, 35, 36, 37, 39, 40, 41, 88, 95, 103, 128, 132, 140, 144, 146, 147
empirical sciences 33
Enlightenment 34, 36, 102
epistemology 22, 29, 32, 33, 59, 73, 90, 118
equality 90, 148
Eros 53

essentialism 3, 5, 12, 16, 25, 45, 46, 51, 53, 56, 57, 72, 113, 140, 142, 144, 145, 156
ethics 56, 57, 58, 59, 83, 113, 121, 125, 140, 156
event(s) 2, 3, 40, 41, 43, 49, 63, 85, 87, 89, 98, 102
existentialism 61
exploitation 140

family 38, 120, 126
fascism 55, 83, 94
Faurisson, Robert 67
feminism 4, 10, 16, 21, 23, 38, 56, 57, 99
Feuerbach, Ludwig 137
  On the Essence of Faith in Luther's Sense 137
Fifth Republic 94
figural 6, 12, 47, 48, 49, 50, 51, 54, 60, 112, 118, 130, 139, 146, 151
FLN 93, 95
Flay, Joseph 118
Fordism 95
Foucault, Michel 102, 155
France 42, 87, 91, 92, 93, 94, 98, 100, 135, 158
Frank, Manfred 83
Frankfurt School 142, 166
Fraser, Nancy 2
freedom 75, 76, 171
French Communist Party 91, 92, 93, 94
French Revolution 32, 75
Freud, Sigmund 50, 51, 53, 82, 136
Fukuyama, Francis 21
  The End of History and the Last Man 21
functionalism 24, 25, 80, 168

Gallo, Max 100
Gane, Mike 46, 94, 134
Gaullism 94
Geist 68, 69
gender 4, 23
genre of discourse 13, 65, 66, 68, 69, 70, 71, 73, 79, 133, 142, 143, 149, 156
global(ism) 18, 19, 29, 30, 31, 38, 53, 106, 167
grand narratives 1–5, 7, 9, 11, 12, 16, 17, 19, 21, 23, 28–9, 31–9, 40, 41, 43, 47, 56, 58, 61, 62, 63, 71, 84, 88, 90, 95, 96, 99, 106, 112, 113, 114, 115, 126, 128, 132, 133, 142, 144, 148, 149, 150, 151, 152, 153, 154, 155, 156, 158, 169, 170, 171
Guattari, Felix 55
Gulf War 16, 103

Haber, Honi 60, 163
Habermas, Jürgen 3, 9, 10, 36, 69, 80
  Between Facts and Norms 9
  The Philosophical Discourse of Modernity 36
Hardimon, Michael 116
Hegel, Georg Friedrich Wilhelm 1, 17, 18, 19, 35, 38, 44, 45, 47, 48, 61, 68, 70, 108–27, 148, 149, 152, 153, 165, 167, 168, 170, 171
  Encyclopedia of the Philosophical Sciences 32,
  Lectures on the History of Philosophy 109
  Lectures on the Philosophy of History 109
  Logic 109, 121
  Phenomenology of Spirit 112, 117, 118, 121, 123, 167
  Philosophy of Right 109, 116, 125, 167
Hegelian(ism) 2, 5, 33, 34, 35, 42, 46, 48, 68, 109, 111, 117, 118, 119, 120, 122, 124, 125, 150, 154, 170
Hegelian Marxists 165
Heidegger, Martin 101, 171
hermeneutics 32
heterogeneity 2, 3, 7, 13, 34, 35, 41, 48, 49, 65, 68, 69, 70, 76, 77, 78, 79, 99, 119, 143, 156, 163

INDEX

history 8, 23, 26, 32, 33, 38, 44, 46, 47, 56, 68, 70, 73, 75, 76, 79, 91, 109, 112, 114, 116, 122, 125, 128, 130, 132, 134, 141, 142, 148, 153, 165
holism 48, 112, 113, 151
Holocaust 67, 73
homogeneity 4, 18, 31, 41, 49, 71, 124, 164
humanism 15, 64, 65, 79, 80, 145
Hungary 145
Hussein, Saddam 103
Husserl, Edmund 11, 44, 45, 167
  Cartesian Meditations 44
  The Crisis of European Sciences and Transcendental Phenomenology 44
Hutchings, Kimberly 55

idealism 12, 33, 46, 47, 108, 131
identity 3, 4, 5, 7, 11, 26, 46, 47, 64, 84, 118, 119, 120, 152, 154, 159, 160
ideology 15, 16, 21, 83, 85, 91, 93, 169
imagination 14, 74, 75, 77, 78, 85, 100, 101, 124, 145, 160, 161
imperialism 59, 88, 92, 93, 117, 128, 132, 142, 158, 166
(in)commensurability 3, 4, 7, 8, 9, 11, 13, 14, 16, 17, 22, 32, 34, 36, 37, 56, 60, 63, 64, 66, 69, 71, 74, 77, 83, 86, 91, 116, 141, 142, 157, 165
indeterminacy 13, 22, 23, 25, 34, 36, 57, 60, 71, 75, 76, 81, 89, 99, 100, 114, 123, 145, 153, 154, 156
individual(s) 20, 26, 44, 45, 57, 83, 89, 90, 104, 106, 120, 159, 161, 162
individualism 26, 28, 116, 120, 126, 168, 169
individuality 4, 7, 41, 15
industrial revolution 138, 156
infinity 100, 115, 122, 124, 129, 133, 143
information society 24

inhuman 8, 63, 74, 80, 81, 82, 85, 88, 101, 104, 113, 122, 124, 145, 162
instrumentalism 24, 25, 29, 38, 86, 88, 106, 121, 124, 144, 145, 149, 164, 168
intellectual 100, 102, 129
intractability 9, 41, 86, 117
inventiveness 5, 7, 8, 17, 26, 31, 35, 37, 59, 63, 86, 89, 123, 156, 159, 162, 170
Ireland 83
Islam 103

Jameson, Frederic 115
Jencks, Charles 115
Jews 101
Judaism 170
justice 4, 9, 10, 12, 14, 17, 40, 57, 58, 59, 60, 90, 101, 104, 113, 141, 161, 162

Kafka, Franz 82
Kant, Immanuel 13, 14, 41, 57, 59, 63, 70, 74, 75, 76, 77, 78, 81, 111, 124, 125
  Critique of Judgement 76
Kantian 59, 60, 74, 78, 99, 113, 123, 124, 142, 150, 163
Keane, John 16
Kripke, Saul 72
Kuhn, Thomas 31

Lacan, Jacques 51
Lacanian 49
language game(s) 2, 5, 6, 7, 13, 22, 23, 25, 26, 27, 29, 34, 36, 37, 41, 59, 64, 99, 119, 121, 122, 123, 141, 150, 154, 163
Lenin 97
Levinas, Emmanuel 42
liberal(ism) 3, 15, 16, 40, 41, 79, 83, 104, 106, 160, 161, 162, 164
libidinal 11, 12, 18, 52, 53, 54, 55, 56, 60, 61, 78, 128, 136, 137, 138, 139, 140, 155, 156
linguistic(s) 48, 49, 50, 51, 54, 64, 65, 67, 117, 123, 153

Luntley, Michael 153
Lyotard, Jean-François
  'Analysing speculative discourse as language game' in *The Lyotard Reader* 121–3
  'Answer to the question what is the postmodern?' in *The Postmodern Explained to Children: Correspondence 1982–1985* 74
  Dérive à partir de Marx et Freud 51, 96, 98, 135, 136
  The Differend 7, 9, 13, 14, 62, 63, 64, 65, 66, 68, 69, 70, 71, 72, 73, 74, 75, 83, 99, 101, 113, 114, 121, 123, 132, 142, 151, 156, 163, 166
  Discours, figure 11, 12, 43, 47, 48, 49, 50, 51, 52, 54, 78, 112
  'Discussions or phrasing "after Auschwitz"' 113, 121, 122, 123
  Des dispositifs pulsionnels 51
  Duchamp's Trans/Formers 56
  L'Enthousiasme: la critique kantienne de l'histoire 75,
  Heidegger and 'the Jews' 101
  The Inhuman 14, 62, 63, 74, 79, 80, 81, 84, 96, 146, 151
  Instructions païennes 56
  Just Gaming 11, 12, 43, 56, 57, 58, 60, 76, 88, 99, 113, 154, 156, 159, 163
  Lectures d'enfance 63, 79, 82, 102, 164
  Lessons on the Analytic of the Sublime 14, 62, 63, 74, 76, 78, 84, 124, 157
  Libidinal Economy 11, 12, 18, 43, 51, 52, 53, 54, 55, 56, 57, 63, 78, 88, 99, 119, 128, 132, 136, 137, 138, 140, 141, 146, 151, 155, 156
  Mainmise in Lyotard, *The Hyphen: Between Judaism and Christianity* 6
  'On a hyphen' in Lyotard, *The Hyphen: Between Judaism and Christianity* 170
  'One of the things at stake in women's struggles' in *The Lyotard Reader* 56
  'The other's rights' in S. Shute and S. Hurley (eds.), *On Human Rights: The Oxford Amnesty Lectures 1993* 104
  Peregrinations: Law, Form, Event 6, 135, 151
  Phenomenology 11, 17, 42, 43, 44, 45, 46, 47, 48, 54, 56, 61, 112, 117, 131, 133, 134, 135, 146, 151, 155
  Political Writings 87, 144
  The Postmodern Condition: A Report on Knowledge 1, 2, 5, 6, 7, 8, 11, 13, 14, 17, 21–39, 42, 43, 51, 58, 60, 61, 62, 69, 71, 83, 88, 90, 99, 119, 121, 128, 132, 140, 141, 142, 144, 154, 156, 159, 163, 166, 171
  The Postmodern Explained to Children: Correspondence 1982–1985 36, 62, 101, 112
  Postmodern Fables 20, 37, 39, 41, 63, 79, 82, 103
  Rudiments païens: genre dissertatif 56, 99
  'Sensus Communis' in Benjamin (ed.), *Judging Lyotard* 75
  'The sign of history' in *The Lyotard Reader* 76
  Signed Malraux 63, 84, 85
  Tombeau de l'intellectuel et autres papiers 100, 143

Machiavelli, Niccolò 104
Mallarmé, Stéphane 50
Malraux, André 19, 20, 63, 84, 85
  Antimemoirs 84
managerialism 24, 25, 74, 81, 106
Mao Tse Tung 97
Martin, James 10
Marx, Karl 1, 17, 18, 19, 25, 32,

35, 38, 51, 53, 54, 61, 70, 97, 99, 128–47, 148, 149, 151, 153, 165, 166
Economic and Philosophical Manuscripts 139
The German Ideology 134
Grundrisse 143
Manifesto of the Communist Party 143
Marxism 2, 5, 7, 9, 12, 15, 16, 18, 24, 33, 34, 35, 42, 45, 46, 47, 52, 53, 56, 58, 69, 71, 86, 87, 88, 91, 92, 94, 96, 97, 98, 128, 129, 130, 131, 132, 133, 134, 135, 136, 140, 141, 142, 144, 145, 146, 150, 151, 152, 154, 158, 165, 166
materialism 12, 33, 45, 46, 47, 112, 117, 128, 131, 133, 134, 135, 146, 151
material(ity) 5, 40, 41, 43, 44, 134, 152
May 1968 9, 16, 18, 70, 87, 88, 96, 97, 104, 128, 131, 136
Merleau-Ponty, Maurice 12, 44, 45, 48, 50, 167
metalanguage 23, 57, 59, 71, 113, 121
metanarrative 2, 23, 39, 119
metaphor 12, 43, 48, 49, 150, 169
metaphysical 10, 13, 35, 36, 40, 54, 58, 111, 115, 116, 123, 125
metasubject 3
modern(ity) 1, 2, 3, 10, 17, 19, 21, 22, 23, 27, 28, 29, 31, 33, 34, 36, 37, 38, 39, 43, 57, 58, 59, 62, 74, 81, 82, 99, 108, 112, 114, 115, 116, 119, 120, 121, 126, 128, 132, 141, 149, 150, 158, 168, 169, 171
monarchy 168
Morocco 91, 92

Nanterre 96, 97, 98
narrative 2, 3, 17, 22, 23, 27, 31, 32, 34, 36, 37, 59, 62, 65, 70, 92, 96, 132, 158
nation 27, 28, 29, 167

nationalism 4, 18, 38, 59, 92, 93, 95, 98, 128, 135, 158
Nazi Germany 102
neo-liberal 162
neo-totalitarian(ism) 8, 9, 86, 87, 106, 111, 145, 164, 166
neutrality 21
Newman, Barnett 81
Nicholson, Linda 2
Nietzsche, Friedrich 55
nihilism 37, 84, 85, 136
North Africa 91, 92
normativity 36
Norris, Christopher 37, 63, 67, 153

Oakeshott, Michael 153
October Revolution 97
O'Neil, John 126, 169
ontology 59
Orwell, George 101, 102
1984 101, 102

pagan(ism) 9, 13, 56, 57, 58, 59, 60, 61, 159
Parmenides 109, 110
Parsons, Talcott 25
Pascal, Blaise 17
perception 12, 45, 48, 50
performativity 8, 14, 18, 19, 24, 29, 30, 31, 121, 140, 159, 162, 166
perspectival(ism) 33, 34, 35, 119, 155, 165
Petronius 62
phenomenology 11, 12, 40, 42, 43, 44, 45, 46, 47, 50, 54, 61, 117, 128, 131, 133, 134, 151
Phillips, Anne 10
philosophy 2, 4, 6, 10, 11, 13, 14, 15, 17, 18, 19, 33, 35, 38, 41, 42, 43, 48, 51, 56, 58, 59, 60, 61, 63, 65, 74, 76, 80, 88, 89, 100, 108, 109, 111, 112, 114, 116, 117, 121, 123, 150, 152, 166, 168
phrase(s) 13, 14, 64, 65, 68, 71, 72, 73, 83, 122, 123, 142, 143, 156

phrase regimen 13, 65, 68, 69, 70, 71, 72, 73, 122, 142
Plant, Raymond 116
Plato 13, 28, 56, 58, 59, 61, 65, 109, 110, 111, 112, 114
  Parmenides 108, 109, 110, 111, 112, 114
  Republic 110
  Timaeus 110
  Sophist 110
Platonist 55
pluralism 13, 25, 26, 37, 39, 140, 150, 165, 166
plurality 21, 24, 34, 41, 59, 60, 64, 90, 150, 153
poetry 12, 48, 50
political economy 19, 52, 53, 137, 140, 144, 166
post-industrial 30, 31, 100
post-Marxist 94
postmodern(ism) 21, 22, 23, 32, 34, 35, 37, 39, 40, 57, 58, 62, 63, 75, 99, 100, 103, 105, 113, 120, 121, 132, 140, 143, 145, 148, 150, 164, 165, 166, 167, 168
postmodernity 1, 2, 3, 11, 18, 19, 28, 29, 30, 31, 36, 38, 43, 62, 81, 112, 114, 115, 119
post-structural(ism) 54, 155
Pouvoir Ouvrier 12
pragmatism 40, 41
Prague Spring 70, 142
premodernity 22, 32
progress 37, 41, 152
proletariat 33, 53, 128, 135, 136, 141, 142, 144
Protestant 116

radical(ism) 8, 9, 16, 21, 23, 25, 26, 36, 39, 40, 42, 43, 49, 96, 97, 122, 128, 150, 154, 158, 160, 162
rational-choice Marxism 165
rationalism 3, 4, 5, 12, 16, 37, 40, 42, 46, 47, 53, 56, 61, 109, 118, 119, 152, 167, 168
Rawls, John 80, 161, 162, 163
  Political Liberalism 161
Rawlsian 153
Readings, Bill 22, 23, 49, 87, 115
realism 46, 74
reason 5, 6, 11, 12, 15, 36, 39, 41, 48, 51, 52, 53, 55, 56, 57, 60, 77, 78, 114, 116, 118, 121, 124, 142, 148, 150, 151, 152, 155
reductionism 12, 34, 51, 134
relativism 21
religion 116, 120
Rennger, N. J. 160
representation(alism) 40, 43, 48, 49, 50, 51, 52, 53, 67, 118, 137, 138, 155
republican 83
revolution(ary) 31, 33, 41, 51, 55, 57, 93, 95, 96, 97, 98, 103, 104, 131, 136, 144, 145, 159
rhetoric(al) 21, 23, 49, 55, 130, 139, 150, 155
right(s) 16, 32, 104, 105, 152
Rogozinski, David 101
Rojek, Chris 8, 48
Rorty, Richard 40, 41, 42, 80
Rose, Gillian 168
Rosen, Michael 118
Rousset, David 164
Russia 97, 102

Sartre, Jean-Paul 44, 45, 47, 102
Saussure, Ferdinand de 48, 49
scepticism 4, 5, 6, 21, 39, 51, 62, 69, 92, 150, 156
Schaper, Eva 77
science(s) 3, 8, 22, 23, 26, 27, 28, 29, 30, 31, 32, 33, 34, 35, 37, 44, 45, 46, 64, 80, 82, 88, 89, 141, 157
Searle, John 80
Sedgwick, Peter 72, 73
self 22, 25, 37, 38, 44, 46, 52, 119, 122
self-consciousness 33, 52, 59, 117, 118, 137, 167, 171
semiology 54
sex(uality) 41, 139, 151
Scott, Peter 30

Sim, Stuart 79, 80
Smart, Barry 25
social science 48
socialism 3, 33, 153
Socialisme ou barbarie 10, 16, 18,
    47, 87, 91, 128, 131, 142, 146
sociology 44, 58, 73, 74, 79, 84,
    90, 116, 147, 149
Socrates 110
Sophists 56
Souyri, Pierre 128, 129, 130
Spirit 32, 119
Stalin, Joseph 68
Stalinism 33, 93, 102, 135
state 27, 28, 29, 97, 167
Sterne, Lawrence 53
    Tristam Shandy 53
structuralism 2, 25, 42, 48, 49, 153
subjectivity 45, 108, 115, 116, 119,
    121, 127, 169, 170
sublime 4, 14, 63, 73, 74, 75, 76,
    77, 78, 79, 82, 84, 85, 88, 101,
    111, 113, 124, 125, 126, 145,
    150, 157, 164
system 25, 29, 38, 48, 49, 52, 80,
    86, 90, 97, 98, 99, 103, 104,
    109, 112, 113, 129, 141, 144,
    145, 146, 149, 150, 166, 167
systems theory 24

Tanesini, Alessandra 72, 73
Taylorism 95
technology 28, 33, 74, 79, 80, 81,
    82, 124, 157, 164

teleology 76, 77, 92, 116, 121
tensor(s) 52, 55
Thao, Tran Duc 133
Thébaud, Jean-Loup 57, 58
Torah 170
totalitarianism 9, 102, 141, 145,
    154, 164
Trotskyism 91, 93
trust 26, 90
Tunisia 91, 92

unity 17, 24, 36, 37, 110, 153, 156,
    163
universal(ity) 10, 13, 15, 19, 25, 27,
    29, 35, 36, 40, 41, 46, 48, 56,
    68, 69, 100, 123, 132, 141, 152
university 30, 33, 96, 97
utilitarian 153

verification 67

White, Alan 118
Williams, James 5, 72, 73, 88, 114,
    115
Wittgenstein, Ludwig 5, 25
Wittgensteinian 64, 150
working class 24, 33, 94, 95
wrong 65, 66

Young, Iris Marion 10
Young Hegelians 134

Zeno 109